AN INTRODUCTION TO TEACHING

ENGLISH AS AN ADDITIONAL LANGUAGE TO ADULTS

Jane Jordan

The
Basic Skills
Agency

Acknowledgements

Much of the content of the book has grown out of my work at the Stockport English Language Service teaching students and training teachers and volunteer tutors. I am grateful to the students and colleagues both in Stockport and elsewhere who have made this possible. In particular I should like to thank Rizwana Choudry, Carole Crompton, Eamonn Graal, Christina Healy and Hilary Montrose for their support, comments or contributions. In addition I have gained inspiration and knowledge from many of the resources listed at the end of each chapter, too numerous to mention individually.

©The Basic Skills Agency,
Commonwealth House, 1-19 New Oxford Street, London WC1A INU.

ISBN 1 85990 082 8

Design: Studio 21

First edition published September 1992

Reprinted October 1993

Revised November 1995

3rd Edition September 1998

Contents

Preface   5

Introduction   6

What is EAL? · A brief history of EAL · The need for EAL · Who are the students?
Where does EAL provision take place?

1. Adults as Learners   10

Student profiles · Needs and aspirations · Existing skills · Barriers to learning
Further reading

2. Planning a Learning Programme – 1   17

The processes involved · Finding out about a student · Analysing the goals
Assessing a student's competence in English · Negotiating a programme · Further reading

3. Language Awareness   26

The four language skills · Functions · Grammar · The first language and English
The place of grammar in teaching English · Vocabulary · Pronunciation
Spelling and punctuation · Further reading

4. Planning a Learning Programme – 2   40

Planning an individual programme · Identifying spoken language needs
Incorporating the needs into the learning programme · Planning a programme for a group
Further reading

5. Developing Listening Skills   49

The importance of listening · Listening in everyday life · Teacher language
What materials can you use? · How to present listening exercises · Checking understanding
Examples of listening materials · Further reading

6. Developing Speaking Skills 57

Methods for presenting and practising spoken language · Presentation of new language
Visuals · Vocabulary development · Practice: Drills, Dialogues · Using the language:
Role-play, Communication activities, Monologue, Games, Examples of materials ·
Pronunciation · How to teach pronunciation · Correcting · Further reading

7. Developing Reading and Writing Skills – 1 78

Planning: Needs, Skills, Prior learning, Assessing, Materials · Teaching reading to beginners:
Whole word, Context, Phonics, Reading aloud, Using a dictionary · Teaching basic writing
skills: Handwriting, Writing for communication, Guided writing activities · Further reading

8. Developing Reading and Writing Skills – 2 92

Reading skills: Silent reading, Understanding · Writing skills: Handwriting, Free writing
Identifying writing needs: Follow up work, Causes of errors, Correcting, Spelling, Dictation
Note-taking, Creative writing, Word processors and computers · Further reading

9. Lesson Planning, Record Keeping and Evaluation 103

Managing learning: Role of teacher, Independent learning, Working with groups
Planning a lesson: Aims and objectives, Content and methodology · Assessing and evaluating ·
Sample lesson plans · Keeping a record · Reviewing progress · Accreditation · Further reading

10. Resources 117

The range of materials · Selecting materials · Adapting materials: Simplifying a text
Making worksheets · Using equipment · Further reading

Glossary 128

Index 131

Preface to the Third Edition

This is an introduction to the teaching of English as an Additional Language (EAL) to adults. It is for anyone who intends to teach or is teaching English to adults whose first language is not English and who are resident in Britain. It is for volunteer tutors, teachers and trainers who have no specialist qualification in EAL or ESOL and who may work in a range of settings: adult education centres, further education colleges, open learning centres, the home, community organisations, prisons, industry and vocational training schemes.

It is intended to support people who are working towards the City and Guilds (9281) Initial Certificate in Teaching Basic Skills (ESOL). This certificate is designed to enable participants to demonstrate competence in teaching EAL to individual students. However, much of the content will also be of interest to people undertaking other initial qualifications in ESOL and Basic Skills Certificates such as the City and Guilds (9285) Certificate in Teaching Basic Skills and the (7324/02) Certificate in Basic Skills Support in Further Education.

In the Second Edition the section on teaching pronunciation was extended and additions were made to the chapter on programme and lesson planning to include strategies for teaching groups. Although the Initial Certificate in Teaching Basic Skills focuses on teaching an individual student, it was felt important to include this aspect as most EAL provision is in the form of group learning.

In this edition a number of changes and additions have been made to bring the book up to date, in particular the case studies and the reading lists. We hope that the methods and approaches described reflect current practice and that the book will provide a good grounding in the skills required to teach EAL to adults.

Introduction

What is EAL?

English as an Additional Language (EAL) is a term currently used to describe English Language Teaching to people whose first language is not English and who live in Britain on a permanent or long term basis. In other words, they need to use English in addition to their first and other languages. EAL aims to enable people to participate fully in British society and to gain access to opportunities such as employment, education and training.

There have been a number of terms which have attempted to define this area of English Language Teaching. English as a Second Language (ESL) is felt not to recognise the fact that many people may speak more than one language before they start to learn English. English to Speakers of Other Languages (ESOL) does not really distinguish those who learn English as an Additional Language and those who learn it as a Foreign Language (EFL). However ESOL is and will continue to be used as an umbrella term to include English Language Teaching (ELT) to all groups of students who are non-native speakers. English as a Foreign Language (EFL), on the other hand, refers to teaching English to people who come to the UK for a short period with the specific purpose of learning English and then returning to their country and those who learn English in their country of origin where English is not a national language. They want to learn English for pleasure, travel, business or as a means of international communication. Most EFL provision takes place in private organisations and Further Education Colleges.

A brief history of EAL

EAL provision was developed initially to meet the needs of immigrants mainly from the New Commonwealth countries who came to Britain in the late 1950s. This provision was seen as short term and was largely funded by the Home Office, the Department responsible for immigration, through Section 11 of the Local Government Act of 1966. The main providers of EAL tuition were Local Education Authorities.

These early schemes concentrated on teaching 'Survival English', mainly to women, often in their own homes, using volunteers and some part-time teachers. A further development took place in the 1970s when Industrial Language Programmes were set up to teach English in the work-place, mainly to men.

Since then EAL provision has developed to differing extents depending on the settlement patterns of immigrants and refugees as well as other local factors. There are now more group teaching and open learning opportunities as well as language support for students on other courses. English language support for technical and vocational purposes is also available as part of specially funded programmes.

The need for EAL

In 1996, under the title *Lost Opportunities*, the Basic Skills Agency published the results of a research project which assessed the English language needs of adults from minority linguistic communities. The survey was carried out among representative samples of Bengalis, Gujeratis, Punjabis, Chinese and refugee groups including Bosnians, Tamils, Somalis and Kurds. The analysis of the results concentrated on those not born in Britain. The assessment process consisted of a brief interview conducted by first language interviewers, self assessment and 20 tasks to measure listening, reading and writing skills.

The results show that whilst many are fluent in more than one language, only a fifth said they understand English 'very well' and over a quarter cannot read English at all. More than a third of Bengali and Punjabi speakers scored zero on the written test (they were unable to fill in a simple form). Only 14% of Bengalis, 29% of Gujeratis, 26% of Punjabis, 41% of Chinese and 32% of the refugee groups reach a 'survival' or beginner level of competence and very small proportions reach the 'ceiling'. Many factors such as age, employment status and previous educational experience affected performance.

This research shows a substantial unmet need with nearly three quarters of the sample operating below a beginner level. It indicates that there are thousands of people who are functionally illiterate in English and who cannot participate fully in an English speaking society nor make the full contribution of which they are capable.

Who are the students?

Adults who want to learn or improve their English are not a homogeneous group.

- They have come to the UK to live on a permanent basis for a variety of reasons: to join their family, to get married, to find employment, for business or as refugees.

- They can range in age from 16 to 60 plus.

- They can have widely differing educational backgrounds: some have no formal education and are not literate in any language while some are graduates.

- They vary in their level of English from beginner to advanced and may have different levels of competence in their language skills; for example, advanced spoken skills but basic written skills.

- They come from a wide range of countries, not only the New Commonwealth, e.g. Vietnam, Iran, Iraq, Somalia, Thailand, Turkey, Spain, South American countries. Many have a non-European first language with a different script.

- They may have work and family commitments which prevent them attending regularly or for more than a few hours a week.

The Basic Skills Agency sponsored research into drop-out and progression in EAL(ESOL) published in 1996 under the title *Where Next?*

This shows the following characteristics of EAL students. 70% are women and 60% are aged between 20 and 40. 63% are from Asia, in particular South Asia, 23% are of African origin, 12% European and 2% of Latin American origin. The majority were unemployed or unwaged with only 14% in part-time or full-time employment and 3% in other than EAL provision. 70% had previously reached secondary education or higher while only 6% had had no previous education. 67% had attended English classes before either in the UK or in their country of origin. 48% needed English to help them with 'everyday life', 16% 'to study further', 7% 'for work' and 7% for all these reasons.

Where does EAL provision take place?

EAL tuition is provided in a wide range of venues: adult education centres, community centres, Further Education colleges, Employment Training schemes, in the home and in prisons.

In some centres EAL is located alongside basic skills provision in literacy and numeracy, while in others it is linked with English as a Foreign Language (EFL) provision.

Approaches and materials in EAL are influenced by both these related fields. EAL includes general English language teaching and language support work in colleges and on training programmes.

There is a range of learning styles in which both teachers and volunteer tutors may work.

- *1:1 in the home or at a centre:* a tutor works individually with one student.

- *In a group or class:* (i) a teacher works with a number of students where most activities are carried out as a group. (ii) Students work on individual programmes within the group under the supervision of the group teacher. Sometimes volunteer tutors may work within the group to support the group teacher, especially where the group is mixed level. Groups may be made up of students with different first languages (multi-lingual) or who share a single first language (mono-lingual).

The research in *Where Next?* (BSA) indicates that 93% of students were in graded classes. Most group provision continues throughout the academic year and is usually part-time. 50% of classes were held once a week usually for 2 hours while 20% of classes offered intensive provision (17-21 hours a week). There is a move towards more intensive provision as this is shown to be more effective in helping students achieve their goals. 38% on intensive courses reached their goals compared with 14% on non-intensive. Students indicated a preference for small group work while teachers favoured more 1:1 work.

- *Linked Skills:* these courses offer tuition in a particular skill, usually a practical skill such as first aid or computer literacy, together with the English needed to learn the skill. A language teacher may work alongside the subject teacher.

- *Family Literacy:* these programmes have been developed for both first language English speakers and for linguistic minorities. They aim to break the cycle of low achievement by developing both the parents' and the children's language and literacy skills and by raising parents' awareness of how to help their children. There are a variety of models for delivering these programmes but the one initially promoted by the Basic Skills Agency consists of a 12 week programme with 8 hours tuition a week for both parents and their children of which 2 hours is a joint session.

- *Open Learning:* the student and teacher plan a learning programme which the student can carry out independently at the centre or at home with occasional tutor support. The student has flexibility about when to attend and has access to a teacher when necessary. There is also access to computers and computer assisted learning materials. There may be some small group sessions.

- *Language Support:* students on main-stream college courses or vocational training programmes may need to develop language skills relevant to their course. A language teacher may work alongside the subject teacher or the student may get individual or small group language tuition.

In a Basic Skills Agency survey 59% of the students were in colleges and 41% in Local Education Authority managed programmes. 70% got help with English in groups or classes, 5% 1:1 in the home, 1% 1:1 in a centre, 13% in linked skills courses, 4% on short courses and 8% in Open Learning.

1 | Adults as Learners

In the introduction some factors about EAL were described which make it clear that there is no such thing as a typical student. When adults come to learn or improve their English they usually have specific present needs and future plans. They can also bring with them a range of skills and knowledge which can help their learning. Sometimes they may lack skills or have commitments which can hinder learning.

EAL aims to meet the needs of individual students so, whether you are teaching on a one-to-one basis or in a group it is important for you to work with the student to identify the factors necessary to accommodate the requirements of the student and help learning.

Below are the profiles of five students who are in EAL provision.

1. Nazia

'I want to talk to the doctor and my child's teacher and help my children to learn. I also want to improve my own speaking, reading and writing.'

Nazia came from Pakistan 5 years ago to join her husband. She had attended school up to Year Ten. She speaks Urdu/Punjabi and is literate in Urdu. She learnt English for five years and has basic to elementary speaking, reading and writing skills. However, when she first arrived she found understanding and speaking English difficult.

She has attended part-time EAL classes over the last few years and had a home tutor but she has had several breaks, for example when her children were born. She does not have a lot of contact with English speakers, so she has not developed her English as much as she would have liked. She now has two children and the elder one has just started nursery school. Nazia is interested in joining a family literacy programme based at her child's school.

2. Abubaka

'I would like to develop my computer skills and then, perhaps, go on to an accounting course. I want to get a job.'

Abubaka is in his forties and from Somalia. He came to Britain as a refugee with his

10

wife and 5 children in the early 1990's. He had left school at 11 after 4 years primary education and is literate in Somali which uses the Roman alphabet. He had worked in a small family retail business. When he arrived he knew some very basic social English but was not literate in English and had practically no study skills.

He has attended EAL classes during the last few years and has progressed from beginner to intermediate. He has also learned some computer skills and developed some study skills. His attendance has not always been continuous as he has had a variety of unskilled jobs and has suffered from depression. He has gained communicative fluency but needs to improve his accuracy in written English.

3. Yasmin

'I am a trained teacher but my qualifications are not recognised as equivalent in Britain. In any case, it is very different teaching in a secondary school in this country, so I am thinking of training for something else. First of all I want to improve my conversational English.'

Yasmin arrived from India a short time ago. She is in her twenties. Her mother tongue is Gujerati and she has a degree in history and a teaching qualification from Baroda University in Gujerat. She has a good formal knowledge of English but lacks confidence in her ability to understand different accents and speak English to people in Britain.

Her qualifications are not recognised as equivalent in the UK but they would satisfy the General Entrance Requirement for higher education, so she could apply to do a BEd or another degree course. She is daunted at the prospect and the cost involved. She is also aware of the differences in the educational systems and does not feel confident about teaching in schools.

She has decided she would prefer to work with young children so she has enrolled on a nursery nursing course at a further education college as a mature student. Her previous qualifications are acceptable for entry and she can also get English Language support while studying. While waiting to start she is attending an advanced EAL group to practise her listening and speaking skills.

4. Omer

'I am a journalist but it will be a long time before my English is good enough to work here as a journalist. I also need to get any job to live.'

Omer is from Turkish Kurdistan and he came to Britain as a refugee. He has settled in Hackney and is working as a presser in a clothing factory in Bethnal Green, where all his fellow workers are Turkish.

Omer was a journalist in Turkey and was persecuted for his beliefs. He speaks Kurdish and Turkish. He learnt French at secondary school and completed university education in Istanbul. Most of his family are still in Kurdistan and he is worried about them.

His original intention was to learn English as quickly as possible and take up his journalistic career again but he found it necessary to take any work he could. He attends an Open Learning Centre to learn English. He is very tired when he arrives for lessons and his progress in English is disappointingly slow.

5. Ladda

'It was very difficult when I first came because I could not understand much English and I couldn't read or write at all. Now I know quite à lot but I want to learn more so I can get a better job.'

Ladda came to Britain from Thailand in 1996 with her English fiancé. She spoke practically no English. She had attended primary school and is therefore literate in Thai. She worked as a cleaner and in a restaurant.

She is now married and obviously gets plenty of practice listening to and speaking English at home. She is very determined to acquire good English language skills. She has attended a beginners EAL class and has now come to an EAL workshop where she can work with a tutor on her individual needs. She works part-time as a school cleaner and in a Thai restaurant at the weekends.

What do these profiles say about the needs and aspirations of these students?

Nazia wants to develop her own spoken language skills so that she feels more confident when explaining something to the doctor or talking to the nursery teacher about her son's progress.

She also needs to improve her literacy skills so that she can understand information from the school and help her children with their education. Eventually she would like to attend a college course and get a qualification herself.

Abubaka needs the English to cope with a specialist course, job search and interviews. He also has to deal with official letters and communicate with his children's school. He needs to improve his literacy skills, especially for formal situations, and his study skills need further development.

Yasmin first needs to practise listening to a variety of accents and speaking in everyday contexts. When she starts her course she will need to concentrate on English for study purposes.

Omer's aim is to get a job commensurate with his experience and training. He would need fluent and accurate English for this. He needs to consider whether this is realistic in the short term. In the meantime training for alternative employment with language support may be possible. English for interviews and job search is an immediate need.

Ladda needs English for everyday purposes; shopping, health, travel, and for social conversation with her husband and his family and people at work. She also needs specific work related English as well as job search and interview skills.

What skills do the students already have?

Nazia has a good basic knowledge of English to build on. She also has transferable skills from her own language. She is good at running a home and family. She is an excellent cook and enjoys doing embroidery.

Abubaka has some first language literacy which helped him when learning English. He has acquired reasonably good language skills in English and is good at maths. He has gained some formal qualifications in these subjects and he has identified the kind of work he would like to do.

Yasmin has high academic qualifications and therefore has study skills in her first language. She has a good formal knowledge of English.

Omer is also well educated in his first language and has learnt two other languages so will feel competent to learn English to an advanced level. He has the skills required for journalism in Kurdish and Turkish.

Ladda has basic skills in her first language and has work experience as a cleaner and restaurant worker which she is already putting to good use in Britain.

What barriers do the students face and how can they be overcome?

Nazia has lacked continuity with her English lessons and she has had little opportunity to use and develop her English. She is also very busy looking after her family. A home tutor went some way to solving these problems but she would prefer to go to a class and meet other people. However, the lack of a crêche and the distance to travel makes this difficult.

13

Abubaka has found it difficult to come to terms with living in Britain. He gets homesick and has little contact with English speaking people. This hinders his language development. He also gets depressed at the difficulty of getting the kind of work he would like to do. In his community the level of unemployment is very high. There is still a considerable gap between his skills and those needed for a job. He has to support his family so financially he cannot attend a training scheme or course unless he continues to receive benefit. He has been offered the chance to go on a training course where he will continue to receive his Job Seeker's Allowance. He will be able to take a qualification in Computer Literacy, practise job applications and interview skills and will also have the chance to develop his English further. He will then have the opportunity of a work placement where he can develop his skills further and gain vocational qualifications.

Yasmin's formal experience of learning English means that she lacks confidence in using everyday spoken English. This can easily be overcome by giving her plenty of practice in an advanced level class. The fact that she cannot transfer her qualifications is harder to deal with. She could decide it was worth spending the time and money to qualify as a teacher in Britain. It is possible that she might be accepted on a two year accelerated BEd for Overseas Trained Teachers but there are few places that offer this option. Taking a suitable alternative qualification meets her desire to work with young children, gives her time to gain confidence in her language skills and recognises some of her prior learning.

While **Omer** has got excellent transferable skills, the level of English required to be a journalist in Britain is daunting. Financially he is unable to attend full-time English classes. He is often too tired to study and has no-one to practise with. His concern for his family makes it difficult for him to concentrate at times. He could look for alternative employment in which he would be with English speaking people and which might leave him less tired. He could continue his open learning lessons, learning new skills and have more opportunities to use his English.

Ladda has no formal qualifications and has had to learn a different writing system. Her work commitments restrict the times and the number of hours she can attend classes. However her work experience is more important than qualifications in getting a job and eventually she may be able to attend a training course to upgrade her skills. As she works in the afternoons she is able to attend four hours of English a week in the mornings.

14

Such an analysis can be shown on a chart like the one below.

Name: **Nazia**		
Needs and Aspirations	Language Skills	Other Skills
• English for health, talking to teachers • To develop fluency • To develop literacy	• Fluent Urdu/Punjabi • Urdu literacy • Some speaking skills and basic literacy in English	• Organising • Parenting • Cooking • Embroidery
Barriers to learning	Ways of overcoming barriers	What else?
• Family commitments • Lack of confidence • Few opportunities to practise	• Home tutor • Family Literacy group with crêche at child's school • Encouragement	• Local mother and toddler group • Joining in parent-teacher activities

Further reading

Basic Skills Agency, 1993, *A Survey of User's of ESOL Programmes in England and Wales.*

Basic Skills Agency, 1996, *Where Next? Drop out and Progression from ESOL.*

Brooks Greg at al, 1996, *Family Literacy Works*, Basic Skills Agency.

Carr-Hill Roy et al, 1996, *Lost Opportunities, The Language Skills of Linguistic Minorities in England and Wales*, Basic Skills Agency.

Illes Eva, *Equal Opportunities = Unequal Opportunities?* Language Issues, Autumn/Winter 1996/97, NATECLA.

Jordan Jane, *Family Literacy for Linguistic Minorities*, Basic Skills, January 1998.

National Foundation for Educational Research (NFER), 1997, *Family Literacy Lasts*, Basic Skills Agency.

There are a number of books and readers which give cultural background and describe the personal experiences of people who have come to live in Britain. For example:

Ahmed Eid Ali, *The Somali Community in Cardiff;* Language Issues Autumn/Winter 96/97, National Association of Teachers of English and Community Languages (NATECLA).

Fitzpatrick Stella, Ed, 1996, *Our Experience,* Gatehouse Books.

Monaf Naznin, 1994, *New Home, Hard Work,* Gatehouse Books.

Tagoe Rebecca,1995, *Trader,* Gatehouse Books.

Molteno Marion, 1987, *A Language in Common,* Women's Press.

Our Lives: a series of readers, Croydon Language Scheme Book Group, 1990.

Warner Rachel, Ed, 1995, *Voices from Angola/Sudan/Uganda/Zaire,* Minority Rights Group.

Individuals and institutions can obtain information about the equivalence of overseas qualifications from the National Academic Recognition Information Centre in the UK (NARIC). There is no charge for this service for individuals, but organisations must pay a subscription charge. The address is: UK NARIC, ECCTIS 2000 Ltd., Oriel House, Oriel Road, Cheltenham, GL50 IXP Tel: 01242 260010.

2 | Planning a Learning Programme – 1

EAL is about trying to meet the needs of individual students. In order to do this and to plan an appropriate programme, whether the student is to be taught individually or in a group, the processes of assessment and negotiation are essential. Initial assessment is about finding out what the student already knows and what needs to be taught. Negotiation is essential because you and the student will have your own ideas about what should go into the learning programme. It is important that you are both involved in this planning procedure and that the outcomes are agreed by both of you.

What are the processes involved in establishing learning priorities?

1. *Finding out* as much as possible about a student's previous learning and experience, present circumstances, long and short term goals, perceived needs.

2. *Analysing* the goals in order to identify the language elements and levels of competence needed to achieve them.

3. *Assessing* a student's current competence in the four language skills (listening, speaking, reading and writing).

4. *Negotiating and planning* a programme of work, setting short term objectives for a specified timescale.

These processes do not necessarily take place in a fixed order and often overlap. Your initial assessment may have to be modified as you find out more about the student's competence.

The diagram on page 18 shows the procedure described and also introduces the concept of ongoing assessment and evaluation which will be dealt with in more detail in Chapter 9.

How can these processes be carried out?

1. Finding out about a student

Informal interview

When a student first comes to seek provision s/he will usually have an informal interview with a tutor or organiser. Most of the necessary background information can be acquired at this interview and recorded on the form used by your EAL programme. As this may be the student's first contact with the programme it is important that the interview is private, friendly and non-threatening.

If a student is not a complete beginner the interview may be conducted in English. This has the advantage that the interview can also become part of the assessment of the student's level of competence in spoken English.

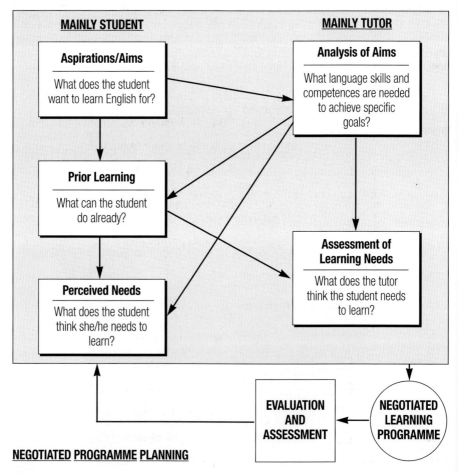

NEGOTIATED PROGRAMME PLANNING

Checklist A　　　　　　**PLANNING A PROGRAMME**　　　　　Date................................

Student's name ....　　Tutor's name ....

What do you want to use your English for?

	Tick Box		
		7. TV and radio	☐
1. With neighbours, friends, colleagues	☐	8. With my children's teachers/To help my children with their education	☐
2. In shops, banks, post office	☐	9. To read newspapers, books, magazines	☐
3. At the doctor's, dentist's, clinic	☐	10. To help me get a job	☐
4. With officials: at door, Town Hall, by post (letters, bills, forms)	☐	11. To help me in my job	☐
5. For travel: bus, train, car, plane	☐	12 To help me get a place at college or on a training scheme	☐
6. Using the telephone	☐	13. To help me in my studies	☐

Checklist A Urdu

Rizwana Choudry:
Stockport
English Language
Service

PLANNING A PROGRAMME

Checklist B

Break down the goals into smaller parts.
This checklist will help you identify the elements.

Listening
- Identify people's feelings, attitudes
- Understand telephone messages
- Understand the main points of a conversation, talk, lecture, news item
- Understand the details of a talk, conversation, etc.
- Understand questions
- Understand instructions
- Understand explanations
- Understand British accents

Speaking
- Give personal information
- Greet people and make social conversation
- Ask and answer questions
- Describe people, things, events
- Tell people what happened
- Talk about experiences
- Talk to people on the telephone
- Pass on a message
- Leave messages on an answerphone
- Ask when I don't understand
- Ask for or offer help
- Explain a problem, give reasons
- Give instructions
- Take part in a discussion
- Say what I think or feel
- Agree or disagree
- Express apologies, thanks, sympathy
- Invite people, accept and refuse invitations
- Tell people my future plans
- Read a story aloud

Reading
- Read signs and notices
- Read forms
- Read timetables, maps, diagrams
- Read messages
- Know alphabetical order
- Use a dictionary
- Use a telephone directory
- Understand newspaper headlines
- Understand the main points in an article or story
- Identify the important information in advertisements
- Understand abbreviations
- Understand instructions
- Read reports
- Understand formal, official language in letters and bills

Writing
- Fill in forms, timesheets
- Write cheques
- Write short messages
- Write a formal letter
- Write about my experiences and interests
- Write instructions
- Make notes when listening to someone
- Make notes about something I have read
- Write reports
- Write essays
- Write a list of information about myself for job applications (curriculum vitae)

20

Name: **Nazia**		
Goal: **To practise the English needed for contact with child's school**		
Skills and Knowledge	Can do	Needs to do
Listening: To information from teachers at formal/informal meetings To social conversation with teachers and other parents **Speaking:** Giving information about child's absence on the telephone and face-to-face Explaining a problem Asking questions about child's progress Taking part in conversations with teachers and other parents **Reading:** Letters from school about meetings, parents' evenings, visits, social events Children's books **Writing:** Filling in forms for class visits, attendance at parents' evenings, etc Writing letters about children's absence, holiday arrangements		

Name: **Abubaka**		
Goal: **To learn and practise the English needed for computer training**		
Skills and Knowledge	Can do	Needs to do
Specialist vocabulary **Listening:** To instructions To explanations of systems, software packages, etc **Speaking:** Asking questions to clarify understanding Explaining a problem Giving information about work done Asking for help **Reading:** Terminology handouts Instructions and explanations in a manual or on screen Understanding a diagram Tasks and assignments **Writing:** Copying accurately Knowledge of punctuation and spacing Paragraphing Taking notes Creating documents Writing assignments and reports Completing records such as logs, evaluation forms		

If a student is a beginner the interview should be conducted in the first language either directly by a bilingual tutor, or through an interpreter. It is preferable to use an independent interpreter but this is not always possible and students often bring along a friend or relative to interpret for them. The use of an interpreter with students who have limited skills in English can ensure an accurate exchange of information, avoid misunderstandings and enable a student to express desires and hopes with ease. It can also emphasise the abilities and skills of a student rather than her/his limitations and it is invaluable when negotiating a learning programme as this can involve difficult vocabulary and abstract concepts.

Checklists

These are useful as a guide to you and a student in selecting long-term goals and short-term objectives. Some examples of checklists are given on pages 19-20. Checklist A, for example, can help a student to identify the general areas s/he wants to work on. Such a checklist is not necessary for a student whose main goal is clear from the outset, such as **Abubaka** who needs language to help him with a training course and **Yasmin** who needs support for her studies.

Checklists can be in English and/or the first language and can be used for self assessment of prior learning as well as identification of needs.

2. Analysing the goals

Breaking down the goals

A long-term goal is usually very broad and achieving it may seem daunting. Therefore it needs to be broken down into the skills and knowledge required to achieve the goal. This may help a student to realise that s/he knows some things already and to clarify what still needs to be learnt.

Checklist B may help you do this breakdown. Some of the items can be subdivided even more into small manageable objectives. This kind of checklist requires considerable analysis and uses abstract concepts. The use of the first language is an asset with students up to intermediate level. At this stage it may be preferable for you to select the skills needed for the student's goal and then discuss them with the student giving examples like this.

Skill	Usage in health context	Example
Give description	Describe symptoms	I've got a headache and I feel sick.

If you are supporting a student on a training scheme or a college course you will need to consult the tutor on the course content and the communication skills needed in order to make an analysis.

On page 21 are some examples of analysing a goal.

Levels of competence

A checklist does not show the level of competence in a particular skill. You need to consider what level is required to carry out a task successfully and to be aware that many skills can be achieved at different levels. When a student says, *'Oh, I can do that'* you need to find out at what level of competence. It may be necessary to show the student that a higher level of competence is required in a particular context.

Compare:

'I was a journalist in Turkey. I speak Turkish, Kurdish and French. I can type.'

and

'I worked as a journalist for five years in Turkey writing for a regional newspaper. I speak fluent Turkish and Kurdish and am quite good at French. I have excellent typing skills and am learning word processing.'

There is a range of accreditation available in further education, much of which is competence based. Competences are about what people can do. Competence based accreditation schemes describe the performance criteria, the range of contexts and evidence required to demonstrate proficiency to a set standard.

Schemes such as Wordpower, accredited by City & Guilds and the London Chamber of Commerce, Open College certificates, and the RSA ESOL Profile, provide a framework of competence statements that can be useful in planning a programme, setting objectives and carrying out assessment, whether or not a student wishes to enter for a certificate. It is important to select competences and materials appropriate to the needs and interests of the student and not to follow the scheme as if it were a syllabus. Although Wordpower was originally designed for native speakers of English, and emphasises literacy, it can be suitable for EAL students especially those who are fairly fluent in English. However, it is important that individual learning programmes should provide a breakdown of language elements, including speaking and listening skills, that the student has to develop in order to demonstrate competence.

3. Assessing the student's current competence in the four language skills

The initial interview, if conducted in English, may be adequate in itself as a means of assessing listening and speaking skills. People can usually speak about themselves to some extent, feel confident about giving this kind of information and, of course, it is always appropriate.

The interview is a flexible method as it can be pitched at different levels. If a student has only given short answers and not shown whether she can speak more extensively, you can ask her/him to expand on some points. When assessing listening skills remember that a student may understand more than the level of the responses to the questions suggest. Reading and filling in a form together will give some information about a student's literacy skills.

In addition to the initial interview you will need to set tasks in each language skill in order to give more precise information about a student's language needs. These tasks should be carried out at a separate time from the initial interview. They should be chosen with care to suit the individual as far as possible. They should not take the form of formal tests and should be done in a collaborative, supportive way to give a student confidence. They should be accessible in format. In other words, they should not use exercise techniques which might be unfamiliar and would need practice to carry out successfully.

The kinds of task you might do are:

Speaking
- describing a picture or sequence of pictures
- describing a personal experience
- giving instructions, e.g. safety rules, how to cook something, how to use a machine
- talking about ideas, e.g. political, social, cultural, an aspect of a college course
- a simple role-play, e.g. asking for something in a shop, making an appointment, asking for a day off work

Listening
- listening to a story and sequencing pictures
- listening to and carrying out instructions

Reading
- self assessment on a range of texts
- reading one text at an appropriate level and answering oral or written questions

Writing
- writing or copying personal information in sentences
- writing about reasons for wanting English lessons
- writing the story or instructions listened to previously
- writing a note or a letter.

Subsequent chapters will focus on identifying a student's language needs from the assessment procedure.

4. Negotiating a programme

When all this information has been obtained you can then discuss with the student what the priority areas are and plan a programme with specific objectives for a specified period of time, such as five weeks or 20 hours, as appropriate. You should set a date to review progress and outcomes and plan the next stage of learning, if necessary. Some goals can be achieved in a short time while others may have to be worked towards in stages over a long period of time.

A beginner student is likely to rely on you to provide guidance and devise a structured programme which will give her/him the basic tools of the language.

Further reading

Basic Skills Agency, 1997, *Initial Assessment: an assessment test for reading, writing and maths.*

Basic Skills Agency, 1992, *Teaching ESOL,* A video for new tutors, focussing on listening and speaking skills.

Chanda Noyona, 1990, *Assessment of Prior Learning,* Basic Skills Agency Newsletter, No.37.

Hayward Annabel, Hardwick Richard, Tran Khai Hue, 1994, *Multilingual Negotiation Pack,* Language and Literacy Unit.

Moon Pauline, 1995, *Course Language Analysis,* Language and Literacy Unit.

Nankivell Claire, 1996, *Building the Framework,* Basic Skills Agency (report on Basic Skills Support in further education.)

Pill Liz, 1994, *Using the Basic Skills Standards for ESOL,* Basic Skills Agency. This provides guidance on developing learning programmes for EAL students working towards Wordpower.

Rees Shan, Sunderland Helen, Eds, 1995, *Working with the Criteria for the Assessment of English Language Skills: Examples of Current Practice,* Language and Literacy Unit.

Silk Sue, 1994, *Basic Skills Support – A guide for every teacher,* Basic Skills Agency.

Simpson Ann, 1990, *Assessing bilingual adults for training,* Basic Skills Agency Newsletter, No.39.

Stockport English Language Service, Davenport Centre, Stockport, Cheshire, 1990, *ESOL Initial Assessment Pack.*

Voss Liz, 1991, *Open Learning and ESOL,* Basic Skills Agency. This gives a more detailed description of planning, assessing and reviewing procedures.

Working Party, 1993, *Criteria for the Assessment of English Language Skills,* Language and Literacy Unit.

3 | Language Awareness

This chapter examines the important elements that need to be considered when teaching English and how they are used. These are:

1. **The four language skills**   3. **Grammar**   5. **Pronunciation**
2. **Functions**   4. **Vocabulary**   6. **Spelling and punctuation.**

If you plan to teach English it is essential that you are or become aware of how the language works. It is not enough that you can speak English yourself.

1. The four language skills

The four language skills are listening, speaking, reading and writing. They can be divided into oral and written skills or receptive (listening and reading) and productive skills (speaking and writing). The crucial factor in the receptive skills is understanding. The productive skills are more difficult and therefore often less advanced than their receptive equivalent.

In teaching, especially in the early stages, the skills are usually presented in the following order: listening, speaking, reading, writing. In reality the balance of the skills varies according to the context. When devising work for a particular context you need to analyse how the skills are used and how important each of them is in that context. In addition, a student may be mainly interested in practising oral skills or, on the other hand, may have good oral skills and want to concentrate on written skills.

Here is an example of an analysis made of the language skills used in a real situation.

Context: **Telephoning to order office supplies**	
Listening • Carefully to precise details, prices, sizes etc.,some technical details difficult to understand	*Speaking* • Asking to be put through to correct department • Saying what I wanted • Asking for information on prices and quantities • Asking for clarification of technical terms
Reading • Catalogue • Yellow Pages for numbers of suppliers	*Writing* • Noting the detail of prices, etc. • Completing a Purchase Order
Skills in order of importance: speaking, listening, writing, reading – but all almost equally important and essential to the task.	

2. Functions

What are functions?

Describing language in terms of functions is a way of classifying language according to meaning. A language function means the purpose for which the language is used. If you look at the analysis of the two contexts you will see that the descriptions of what was done under each skill are in terms of functions.

Asking for directions	*Can you tell me where . . .?*
Giving directions	*They're in the third aisle on the left.*
Requesting	*Can you put me through to office supplies, please?*
Asking for information	*How much are the . . .?*
Giving information	*They're £20 a dozen.*

There are a large number of language functions which can be grouped as follows.

Giving and asking for factual information:

- identifying – *'My name is...', 'He is a (student)', 'This is a...', 'Who is...?' 'What is...?'*

- describing (objects, people, places, feelings)

- describing routines, processes

- narrating (past events)

- describing recent events and experiences

- describing future plans and events

- instructing.

Social interaction:

- greeting and introducing people

- requesting

- inviting

- suggesting, etc.

Attitudes:

- apologising

- giving opinions

- agreeing

- expressing preferences, etc.

Functions and contexts

If you start thinking in this way about the language you use in different contexts you will find that the *same* functions are used in many *different* contexts. This has important implications for language teaching.

Function: **Narrating**	
Context	**Example**
Social	*We had a lovely weekend. We went to my cousin's wedding.*
Work	*I installed the new software this morning.*
Study	*I handed in my essay yesterday.*
At the doctor's	*I had back trouble a few years ago.*

This means that if you teach your student how to express a function in one context s/he can transfer that learning to another context.

Ways of expressing functions

It is also true that the same function can be expressed in different ways and to differing degrees of formality.

Function: **Suggesting**		
Informal ↓ Formal	*Let's have . . .* *What about having . . .* *Why don't we have . . .* *Shall we have . . .* *I suggest we have . . .* *If I might make a suggestion we could have . . .*	*a meeting about this(?)*

There can be so many ways of expressing a function it would be confusing to introduce a student to all of them! You can teach a beginner student the simplest and most generally useful way of expressing a function. Then at an intermediate level you can introduce a range of ways of expressing a function and an awareness of when to use a formal or informal style. You could also teach a student to use one or two ways but to recognise others.

You will need to identify the functions required for the contexts chosen by a student and select a way of expressing these functions appropriate to the level of the student.

Functions and grammar

Each function has particular grammatical features, vocabulary and expressions associated with it. This helps you to group teaching items in a meaningful way.

Function: **Describing**	
Language	**Example**
Statements often in Present Simple tense The verbs, BE, HAVE (GOT) IS MADE OF	*I **feel** sick* *She**'s got** a headache* *The container **is** round* *It **has** a lid* *It**'s made of** plastic*
Adjectives Frequency	*These toys are **colourful*** *He **usually** goes to work by train*
Prepositional phrases	***next** to the bank, the woman **with** glasses.*
Measurements There is (a) There are (some)	***6 feet** tall* ***There's** a pen in the drawer* ***There are** some spanners over here*

3. Grammar

What is grammar?

Grammar is the nuts and bolts of language. When people pick up a language informally they usually find it easy to learn essential vocabulary but much harder to put sentences together grammatically. They can get their meaning across and become quite fluent using their own 'system'. Incorrect usage becomes a habit and what are often called 'fossilised errors' develop. It is like having all the bits of self-assembly furniture but no instructions as to how to put it together. Some students come to EAL programmes because they are aware of this and want to learn to use the language correctly.

Some of the links between functions and grammar have already been described. Grammatical features are used to express other concepts such as:

- the timing of an action, e.g. *I work, I worked, I have worked*
- number, e.g. *book/books, glass/glasses, child/children, it/they, is/are*
- the subject, e.g. *I, we, he, she*
- the object, e.g. *me, them, us*
- possession: e.g. *my, our, his, their, John's*
- whether something is specific or not, i.e. **a** *student,* **the** *Prime Minister.*

As well as knowing grammatical forms a student needs to understand grammatical usage. It is a step in the right direction to be able to formulate the Present Simple tense correctly, but it is no good if the student does not know when and when not to use it.

Grammar is also about structure. It means knowing how to put the language together, what can go with what, the order of words.

Word order

Word order is very important in English. In the sentence, 'A man attacked two girls in the park,' English relies on the order of words to show who attacked whom. Word order is fairly rigid in English with few possible variations. Try adding 'brutally', 'teenage', 'last night' to the above sentence and think where you could or could not put them. The change of word order to indicate a question is an important structural feature: 'She has finished her assignment' becomes 'Has she finished her assignment?'

This fixed word order enables you to build up sentence patterns where different words can be slotted in to a particular framework.

Who?	did what?	where?	when?
I	walked	to the shops	this morning.
He	drove	to the airport	this afternoon.
They	arrived	at the station	this evening.

Practising sentence patterns helps a student to be aware of word order and to make up other sentences following the same pattern.

The first language and English

It is important to remember that EAL students have already learned at least one other language. The similarities and differences between the first language and English may, on the one hand, help learning by the transfer of knowledge and, on the other hand, may hinder learning because different habits have been formed.

Compare how this sentence is expressed in different languages.

	1	2	3	4	5
	I	work	in	an	office
Urdu:	1	5	3	2	
(transcription)	mai	daftar	me	kam karta (m) huĩ karti (f)	

30

	1	2	3	5	
Vietnamese:	*Tôi*	*làm việc*	*trong*	*ván*	*phòng*

	1	2	3	4	5
Spanish:	*Yo*	*trabajo*	*en*	*una*	*oficina*

Urdu – Different word order. Masculine and feminine forms of the verb. Three words to express *work*. No equivalent of *an*.

Vietnamese – Same word order. No equivalent of *an*. Two words for *work*. Two words for *office*.

Spanish – Word order the same. Equivalence for each word.

The place of grammar and functions for EAL teachers and students

It is essential to tackle these aspects of language teaching. In fact you cannot teach language without teaching grammar. The question is, rather, whether you teach grammar explicitly, by explaining the rules, or implicitly, by example. In either case plenty of practice is necessary for learning to take place. A student's level, educational background and whether you can use the first language will determine your approach to grammar. A beginner is usually taught through example and practice. A student like **Omer** (profiled in Chapter 1), who has already learned another language in a formal way may well find it useful to be given some rules and explanations.

All EAL teachers need a knowledge of grammar and functions to be able to select and organise the items to teach in a coherent and effective way. A knowledge of grammatical terms, while not essential, gives useful labels for reference. If you are unsure about grammar and usage it is essential that you develop your language awareness by referring to some of the grammar books listed at the end of this chapter. English language teaching course books often have useful contents pages which show the relationship between topic, grammar, functions and language skills. Teachers' books give guidance on how to present the items to students. Some knowledge of the similarities and differences between a student's first language and English can enable you to help a student transfer knowledge and alert you to possible difficulties.

A student needs to develop an understanding of English grammar and functions either implicitly or explicitly in order to transfer language learnt in one context to another.

For example, if a student learns a dialogue in a particular context without developing an understanding of the elements that make up the dialogue, s/he may know some phrases for that one situation but will be unable to transfer that learning to other situations. It is a 'phrase book' approach.

If students know some of the similarities and differences between their first language and English it can help their understanding of English and make them aware of aspects they need to learn.

4. Vocabulary

What is vocabulary?

Vocabulary means words. Words can initially be divided into two main groups.

1. The first is a small group consisting of little words that are used frequently in all contexts and which give structure to the sentence. They have little meaning in isolation. Such words are: *the, a, this, that, you, it, they, them, me, some, to, in, at, and, but,* etc.

It is very important to know these words and how they are used, as once learned they can be used in many different situations (these words are sometimes called *structural* words).

2. The second group is extremely large and consists of words that carry a lot of meaning in isolation, such as: *student, teacher, book, pen, learn, write, clever, carefully,* i.e. nouns, verbs, adjectives, adverbs. These words are the ones that can create a context. They present a big learning load for a student as each context has its own specific vocabulary, although, of course, many words have a wide general usage (these words are sometimes called *content* words).

Teaching vocabulary

When people talk about teaching vocabulary they usually mean words from the second group. It is useful to teach vocabulary on a thematic basis to link in with the context that has been selected. However, at times you may wish to group words according to:

- grammatical function –   *in, on, at, near,*
                              often, usually, sometimes, never
                              read, write, study, learn

- sound/spelling relationship –   *eat, heat, meat*

- how they are built up –   *beautiful, careful, wonderful*
                              economic, uneconomic, economist.

5. Pronunciation

What kind of pronunciation?

If a student says, *'I want to learn to speak English properly'* or *'People don't understand me'* there may be a need for the student to improve her/his pronunciation. However, first of all you need to identify what the difficulties are. There may not, in fact, be a significant problem with pronunciation. The student may simply be worried about having an accent and thinks it is necessary to aim at what is perceived as Standard English or Received Pronunciation. The student may need reassuring that having a different accent is perfectly acceptable as long as it is comprehensible to the listener.

English is an international language and there are many varieties of spoken English: Welsh, Scottish, Yorkshire, American, Caribbean, Indian, etc. No one of them is the 'correct' one. People who start learning another language as adults are very unlikely to achieve 'native speaker' pronunciation unless they have a very good ear for language. This does not matter. What does matter is that their pronunciation does not impede understanding. If this is the case they will lose confidence and be afraid to speak.

What is pronunciation?

When you listen to someone speaking you do not really hear the individual sounds. One sound merges with the next one and one word with the next. Some words have a lot of weight put on them and others hardly any. The voice rises and falls.

e.g.   *When'reyougoingout?*

When teaching pronunciation there are four aspects to consider:

(a) sounds   (c) intonation

(b) stress and rhythm   (d) fluency.

(a) Sounds

There are 44 sounds in English: 24 consonant sounds, 12 vowels and 8 diphthongs (2 vowel sounds together). We produce sounds by releasing air from the lungs and by using the vocal organs in various combinations and positions.

For example, we put our lips together and then open them to release the air to produce the sound 'p'. An important distinction between some sounds is whether the vocal cords are vibrated or not. When we produce the sound 'p' they are not vibrated, but the sound 'b' is produced in exactly the same way, except that the vocal cords are vibrated. Try making the two sounds and put your fingers on your neck near your larynx. You will feel the vibration when you say 'b'.

The tongue is very important in producing sounds as it has great flexibility of movement. The position of the tongue and the shape of the mouth are the main factors in producing vowel sounds. Detailed descriptions of how each sound is made can be found in standard books on pronunciation. Each sound can be represented by a phonetic symbol, or, more simply, by a 'key' word, i.e. a short commonly used word which contains the sound, such as 'ten' for 'e'. Be careful not to choose words that are subject to regional variation. The 'a' in the word 'bath', for example, would represent different sounds in the north and in the south of England. A student will have learnt another set of sounds for his/her first language. Where there are equivalent sounds there will be no problems. There is only likely to be difficulty where English sounds do not exist in the first language or where they are not used in the same combination. Sounds are produced differently at the beginning, middle and ends of words and some sounds can only be used in certain positions. For example the sound 'ng' cannot be used at the beginning of a word in English. Languages differ in the combinations possible and some consonant clusters such as *school, stream, film, crisps* can be difficult for some speakers so that they tend to put in an extra vowel, e.g. *sikool* or miss a sound out, e.g. *crips*.

Mispronunciation of a sound usually only becomes significant if it is confused with another sound. There are many words in English where only one sound distinguishes one word from another. These are called minimal pairs. Such pairs are: *fill/feel, nice/rice, tree/three.* Here an inability to produce these sounds differently may cause misunderstandings, although as they will be spoken in a context this will help the listener understand which word is intended. In Hindi 'p' is used for both 'f' and 'p' so *feel/peel, fill/pill* may be confused. Similarly 'e' and 'a' are not clearly distinguished as in *pet/pat.* Long vowels tend to be made short so a misunderstanding, if only momentarily, like the following can occur.

STUDENT: *I haven't got any pepper.*

TEACHER: *Pardon?* (Thinks – What does she want pepper for?)

STUDENT: *I haven't got any pepper to write on.*

TUTOR: *Oh! paper! Yes, here you are. Now, can you say, payper?*

Sounds omitted at the ends of words can also make a person difficult to understand. Cantonese speakers have problems with final consonant sounds. 'b', 'd', 'g' do not occur at the ends of words and are confused with 'p', 't', 'k' . These are also very lightly sounded and may not be heard by the listener. Even though consonant sounds are not sounded at the end of a word as they are at the beginning, the sound is nevertheless there. The way the 't' is sounded at the beginning and end of 'tent' illustrates this.

(b) Stress and rhythm

This is the beat of the language. There are two types of stress (i) word stress and (ii) sentence stress.

(i) *Word stress*

In words of two syllables or more, one syllable is stressed more than the other(s). This is invariable and is best learnt when the word is first taught. English tends to stress the first syllable but of course there are many variations, e.g. *training, college, trainee, computer, application, apply*. The stress on a word can change when an extra syllable is added as in '*photograph*', '*photographer*'. There are pairs like '*I refuse to do this*', and '*Leave your refuse here*', where the noun is stressed on the first syllable and the verb on the last syllable. The meanings can be quite different as in this example or connected as in '*Prices will increase*' and '*An increase in prices is likely*'. A few words have alternative stress patterns, e.g. *controversy* and *controversy*.

(ii) *Sentence stress*

Within a sentence some words are stressed and others are unstressed. The stressed words or syllables are timed fairly evenly giving English its characteristic rhythm. Small structural words, such as *and, but, to, of, the, a, is, are, he, her* tend to be unstressed and the words with more meaning stressed, e.g. '*She took her exam last week.*' When words and syllables are unstressed they are pronounced with a shorter or weak vowel sound. This is often the sound /ə/ known as 'schwa' as in 'ago'. Compare 'and' when it is stressed as in '*Not biscuits and cake!*' and when it is unstressed as in '*bread and butter*'. Here the 'a' is pronounced /ə/ and the 'd' almost disappears as well. The verb 'to be' and auxiliary verbs, when unstressed, are often contracted. For example: *I am → I'm, he will → he'll, 'I'm sure she'll pass.*'

We often give extra stress or prominence to the words in the sentence that are particularly important according to the meaning we want to convey. Prominent words can also be words that are not normally stressed. For example:

I don't live in Manchester. (but she does)

I don't live in Manchester. (but I work there)

When we give special stress or prominence to a word or syllable we usually say it louder and we also change the tone, making it higher or using a falling or rising tone.

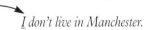

I don't live in Manchester.

Each language has its own stress patterns so a student may find it difficult to adapt to the stress patterns of English.

(c) Intonation

This is the tune of the language. Within the normal speaking range of our voices the tone or pitch can be at a low level or a high level and can rise or fall to convey meaning and feelings. Other languages use different intonation patterns; some are spoken almost on a level and in others, like Cantonese and Mandarin, the meaning of a word changes according to the tone. In English there are many possible intonation patterns to show different moods and attitudes but at a simple level it is best to concentrate on two main tones:

(i) the falling tone

(ii) the rising tone.

As we have already seen, stress and intonation are closely linked. Changes of tone usually take place towards the end of the sentence and the rise and fall starts on the, last stressed syllable, or, if one syllable is prominent, on the last prominent syllable.

The use of the two tones is often related to a combination of grammatical factors and attitude. Thus the falling tone is often associated with the idea of being definite. It is used for statements, 'wh' questions (questions beginning with a question word), strong commands and to correct information. For example:

What's the time?

It's half past three.

No, sorry, it's half past four.

Don't forget your appointment.

When you really want to thank someone you use a falling tone:

Thank you.

The rising tone is usually associated with uncertainty and politeness. It is used for Yes/No questions, 'echo' questions (when you repeat a question because you haven't heard or to query what has been said), statements as questions, greeting and polite comments. For example:

Are you going now?

Now? No, not just yet.

Well, could you turn the light off please?

All right.

Thank you (this is just a polite response, not heartfelt).

A rising and falling tone are used in alternative questions, lists and where a phrase or clause precedes the main clause. For example:

Does she come from India or Pakistan?

He comes to classes on Monday, Tuesday and Thursday.

After work

After I have finished work, } *I go swimming.*

Sharper rises and falls indicate stronger feelings and attitudes.

If students do not recognise English intonation patterns they will be unable to pick up the signals which say, *'I'm asking a question'* or *'I'm angry'*. Similarly they will be unable to convey these signals. Using the wrong stress and intonation patterns can often make a student harder to understand than making the sounds wrongly. It can also make someone sound abrupt and rude.

Another approach to intonation patterns developed by D. Brazil (1985) associates the falling tone with giving new information and the rising tone with referring to information known to or shared between the speaker and listener. This approach is used by Hewings (1993).

(d) Fluency

This means the smooth transition between one word and the next and the speaking in phrase groups rather than word-by-word. If a student does not blend one word with the next s/he sounds stilted. It is important to practise using contractions and linking one word with the next where appropriate; for example where one word ends with a consonant and the next begins with a vowel such as *'after all'*.

For example: *'I'm going for an interview tomorrow.'*

Instead of: | I | am | going | for | an | interview | tomorrow.

In conclusion, listen carefully to identify the problem areas and only deal with those that interfere with comprehension. An awareness of the differences between a student's first language and English will help.

6. Spelling and punctuation

Spelling

The written form of the language attempts to represent the sounds made in the spoken language. In some languages a letter or group of letters consistently represents the same sound, in other words they are written phonetically. In English, however, particularly in relation to vowel sounds there are various ways of spelling the same sound, e.g. *vain, vane, vein* and the same spelling can have different sounds, e.g. *meat, head*. Sometimes the spelling is more related to meaning than sound, e.g. words that sound the same like *sun* and *son* are distinguished by their spelling. An advantage of having a spelling system not always directly related to sound is that one spelling of a word can represent different pronunciations.

Pronunciation, of course, will affect spelling as a student is likely to spell words as s/he pronounces them. Students who use the same alphabet as English will also find that the different sound values given to the letters in the first language influence both spelling and pronunciation in English. A student who is used to a phonetically written language may feel frustrated at the vagaries of English spelling.

Punctuation

Punctuation makes a text easier to read by breaking it up. Some punctuation rules are to do with grammar and some with meaning. Some represent the information conveyed by pauses, falling and rising intonation, etc., in the spoken language. For example, at the end of a sentence you may drop your voice and take a breath. When you write you put a full stop and start again with a capital letter. The conventions in other languages may be different and the system in English may have to be learnt, e.g. in some languages where a different script is used there are no capital letters. Some EAL students find it difficult to identify the end of a sentence and where to put the full stop.

The diagram opposite illustrates the aspects of language described in this chapter.

Further reading

Abell Sue, 1994, *Helping Adults to Spell*, Basic Skills Agency.

Blisset Celia, Hallgarten Katherine, 1992, *First English Grammar*, Language Teaching Publications.

Bolitho R, Tomlinson B, 1995, *Discover English*, Heinemann.

Collins Cobuild Basic Grammar, 1995, Longman.

Crystal D, 1988, *Rediscover Grammar*, Longman.

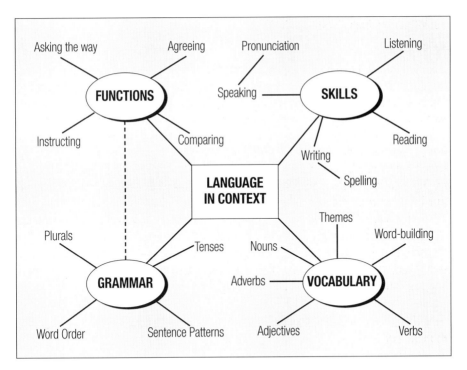

Greenbaum Sidney, 1991, *An Introduction to English Grammar,* Longman.(Includes sections on spelling and punctuation).

Hayward Lorna G, *A Practical Guide to Asian Languages in Britain,* FEEL Publications, 86 Henshaw Road, Small Heath, Birmingham B10 OSX

Leech G and Svartvik J, 1975, *A Communicative Grammar of English,* Longman.

Leech Geoffrey, 1990, *An A-Z of English Grammar and Usage,* Longman.

Swan Michael, 1980, *Practical English Usage,* Oxford University Press.

Thomson A J and Martinet A V, 1986, *Practical English Grammar,* (4th ed) Longman.

Brazil D, 1985, *The Communicative Value of Intonation in English,* University of Birmingham, English Language Research.

O'Connor J D, 1980 ed. *Better English Pronunciation,* Cambridge University Press.

O'Connor J D and Fletcher Clare, 1989, *Sounds English,* Longman.

Swan Michael and Smith Bernard, 1987, *Learner English,* Cambridge University Press.

Basic Skills Agency, 1994, *Spelling Pack.*

Payne J, 1995, *Spelling,* Collins Cobuild English Guides.

Pratley Rhiannedd, 1988, *Spelling It Out,* BBC.

4 | Planning a Learning Programme – 2

The last chapter examined the language elements you should be aware of when assessing and teaching a student. This chapter will look at ways of putting these elements together into a learning programme or syllabus and identifying spoken language needs and incorporating them into a learning programme by focusing on an individual student.

What approach is suitable for EAL students?

As EAL students need to use English in their everyday lives and for specific purposes it is not usually appropriate to follow a strictly sequenced grammatical or functional syllabus.

A beginner student certainly needs a syllabus that covers the basic structures within relevant contexts. However, there needs to be flexibility about the order in which structures are taught to account for individual needs. It is no good if the language a student wants to use at the shops or the parents' evening comes in Lesson 25 of a course s/he has just started.

Most EAL students have already learned some English, maybe formally in classes in their country of origin or informally by listening to and using the language in everyday life. Their knowledge of the language will be unpredictable according to their experience. In one context they may be able to use an advanced level of English, while in another they may not know quite basic vocabulary. They do not want to spend time on a course doing things they can do already.

Therefore a suitable approach for EAL students is a learning programme based on language competencies in terms of the skills, functions, grammar and vocabulary which a student needs to learn to achieve the goals already identified. It is also necessary to try and grade the language so that it is within reach of a student. A student who can already do some of the competences will have this prior learning credited and will practise the language and skills needed to achieve the competences they cannot do. Some intermediate level students who want to improve their accuracy may need a syllabus that practises basic grammatical structures but in a way which takes account of the level of vocabulary and fluency already acquired.

The aim of EAL is to develop the required competence at the right level as quickly as possible. Setting manageable targets helps towards this end and some goals can be achieved quickly. However, it must be said that some competences can take a long time to achieve; for example 'describing a past experience' involves a lot of work with tenses that can take months if not years to be able to use proficiently. You may also need to encourage a student not to aim for perfect English before s/he feels able to go and try something new.

Planning a programme for an individual student

Identifying spoken language needs

When you have identified the main learning goals with a student and analysed the skills and language required to achieve these goals the student's current level of competence needs to be assessed in order to identify what aspects of language have to be worked on.

First of all select some appropriate tasks for a student in order to assess listening and speaking skills. In Chapter 2 some activities were suggested for this more detailed stage of assessment. As the student is speaking note down how successful communication has been, as well as any problem areas, using these headings:

- **Functions**
- **Grammar**
- **Vocabulary**
- **Pronunciation.**

It can be helpful to record the student if s/he is happy about this so you can both listen and identify successful communication and errors.

Then agree on the priority items especially in relation to the goals and skills you have already discussed.

The following is an example of part of an oral assessment of **Ladda**, (one of the students profiled in Chapter 1) and a sample plan to show how the teaching items identified could be incorporated into the student's learning programme.

Assessment of needs

Since coming to Britain **Ladda** has already learned a considerable amount of English. When she joined the EAL workshop she had an initial interview and a broad assessment of her existing skills and her main learning goals were identified and entered on her planning chart. The tutor had already begun to identify some of **Ladda's** specific language needs. The tutor then asked her to carry out some oral tasks to find out more about her language competence. Here is a transcription of part of the assessment with tutor comments.

> **Describing her job**
>
> S.   I have a part-time job. I cleaning in Milltown School.
>
> T.   *How often do you do that? Every day?*
>
> S.   One week, five day, one day three hours.
>
> T.   *How do you like that?*
>
> S.   Yes, Yes, Yes I do.
>
> T.   *Can you tell me what you do at work?*
>
> S.   I have been to work every day. I start work at half past three. Half past three to six forty-five. When I start I sweeping the floor first, then I mopping. I'm cleaning carpet, clean the table, wash cups, a cup of tea, yes, I wash a cup. Then when I finish my time I talk to my friend. Then after talking I come back home.

Analysis

The communication was generally successful.

Functions

Giving information in answer to questions – successful, except she did not pick up the *'How do you like...?'*

Describing a routine – successful, good sequencing some correct verb forms.

Grammar

Not clear about usage of present simple *(I clean)* and present continuous *(I am cleaning)*. Needs to use the present simple for a routine. Incorrect form of present continuous – omission of *'am'*.

Wrong use of *'have been'*.

Omission of *'at'* with time.

Uncertain about singular and plural – *the table(s), a cup (the cups)*.

Word order – successful but *'5 days a week, 3 hours a day'*.

Vocabulary

Quite adequate for the task. Note: come/go.

Pronunciation

Clear. Easy to understand on the whole. *'v'* sound – *'five days'* sounded like *'Friday'*. *'th'* in *'them'* like *'d'*. *'six'* like *'sik'* *'f'* for *'p'* in *'cup'*. Rising intonation at end of every sentence makes her sound questioning and surprised.

Name: .... Lac ......   **PLANNING A PROGRAMME**   ....

Tutor's name: ....

Initial Assessment

Level of English:

Listening: .... Good understanding of interview questions ....

....

Speaking: .. Can give personal information without difficulty.
Quite fluent. Errors eg tenses ....
Reading: ... Can read words on farm. High frequency words .....
Can try unfamiliar words. Reads slowly word by word ....
Writing: .. Prints clearly. Can fill in farm with help in spelling
some words ....

Personal Goals:

   English for work as waitress ....
   Improve grammar ....
   Social talk with in-laws and people at work ....
   Making appointments and talking to the doctor ....

Priority goal: English for work as waitress ....

Skills/knowledge	Can do	Needs to do
Checking and taking bookings		✓
Snaring to table	✓	
offering drinks etc.	✓	
Taking orders	✓	move practice - polite.
Suggesting		✓ forms - intonation
Giving information about food		✓
Dealing with a complaint		
Reading menu	✓	✓ more difficult words
Writing orders (using numbers)	✓	

Assessed needs Polite forms for offering etc. ....
Pronunciation - of food items, number (five, six), days of week. -
Sounds: 'v' 'p' 'f' 'th' 'at" + time. Tenses: I work / am working.
I worked / have worked. I'll work Question forms. Plurals: - adding -s

43

Incorporating the needs into the learning programme

Below is a planning chart showing how **Ladda's** goals and language needs were recorded.

The tutor and **Ladda** then agreed on a learning programme which concentrated on the priority goal and included the assessed needs. This would also go some way to meeting the second goal as grammatical items would be dealt with. Remember this outline is for guidance and can be modified. Some items may prove easy for **Ladda** and be done more quickly than expected, others may take longer and need extra practice. Additional needs will be identified and added to the programme.

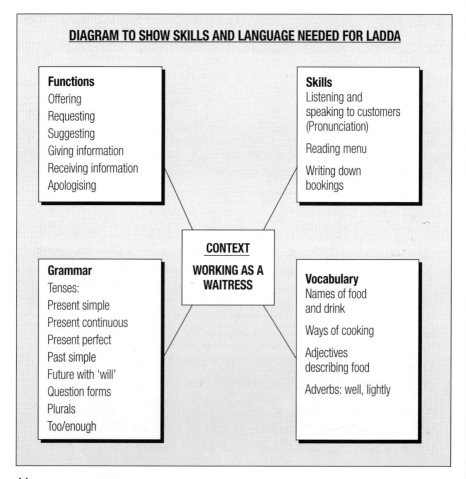

DIAGRAM TO SHOW SKILLS AND LANGUAGE NEEDED FOR LADDA

Functions
Offering
Requesting
Suggesting
Giving information
Receiving information
Apologising

Skills
Listening and speaking to customers (Pronunciation)

Reading menu

Writing down bookings

CONTEXT
WORKING AS A WAITRESS

Grammar
Tenses:
Present simple
Present continuous
Present perfect
Past simple
Future with 'will'
Question forms
Plurals
Too/enough

Vocabulary
Names of food and drink

Ways of cooking

Adjectives describing food

Adverbs: well, lightly

A LEARNING PROGRAMME

Aim: To practise English for work as a waitress

Objectives:

The student will be able to:

1) describe work routine using present simple and time phrases 2) ask questions for information 3) make polite requests 4) pronounce numbers and prices clearly 5) describe ingredients and how food is cooked 6) make offers and suggestions 7) understand complaints and apologise 8) state intentions

Session 1 Describe work routine - present simple, time phrases Greetings. Asking questions - Have you booked? What name? How many people? Polite requests - Please wait a moment. Please come this way.

Session 2 Revision. Listen to people ordering a meal, identify on menu, write numbers. Check vocabulary. Read and say items on menu. Practise numbers. Offering - Would you like a/some...? Dialogue. Describe food - rich, spicy, sweet, hot, sour. Grammar - a/an/some; plurals - glass/glasses, plate/plates

Session 3 Revision. Answer questions based on menu - What's in it? How is it/are they cooked? Describe ways of cooking - It's/they're fried/boiled etc. Suggesting - I suggest you have. This is very good. Grammar, present perfect - Have you booked/ordered/finished? Roleplay

Session 4 Revision. Listen to complaint - use of 'too', 'not enough', 'very', 'under/over-cooked'. Apologise. State intention - I'll change it, I'll get another, I'll call the manager. Dialogue/roleplay

Materials Menu, food pictures, taped dialogues, listening exercises, pronunciation exercises. Worksheets to back up activities and grammar

A GROUP PROFILE

Name	Country/First Language How long in Britain	Previous Education	Work Experience	Level of English	Goals	Language Needs
Naseem	Pakistan Urdu/Punjabi 6 years in Britain	School at 16 Learnt English for 3 years at school	Housewife Mother – 3 children	L. 3 S. 2-3 (confident but not structured) R. 2 W. 2	To talk to doctor, clinic. Watching TV. Talk on telephone. Talk to teachers. Read letters from school. Write notes.	Word order Tenses weak Articles
Vimla	India Hindi 2 months in Britain	College educated English as part of course	Housewife	L. 3 S. 3 but lacks confidence R. 4 W. 3	To get on a training course for a job – perhaps office skills. To develop confidence in speaking. To read newspapers.	Some errors in structure – more complex tenses, prepositions, spelling and punctuation
Fatimah	Saudi Arabia Arabic 1 year in Britain	Graduate in history Some English at school	Secretary Mother – 2 children	L. 3 S. 3 R. 3 W. 2-3	To talk to doctor, neighbours, school	Present Perfect, Conditionals, Modals Articles Handwriting Spelling
Alex	Hong Kong Cantonese 5 years in Britain	Completed Secondary Education English for 6 years at school	Waiter in Chinese restaurant	L. 4 S. 3 Fluent but errors R. 3 W. 3 Good handwriting	English for work To improve grammar To write business letters	Past tenses Plurals Pronunciation – final consonants
Kamsorn	Thailand Thai 1 year in Britain (English husband)	Primary education. Little English before coming to Britain	Working as Care Assistant	L. 3 S. 3 R. 2 W. 1-2	To improve English for work especially literacy skills To talk to doctor Travel To improve accuracy	Weak structure – tenses, articles, plurals Final consonant sounds
Adnan	Bosnia Bosnian 2 years in Britain	Graduate in Engineering Little English before coming to Britain as refugee	Engineer Unemployed in Britain	L. 3 S. 2 R. 3 W. 2-3	To deal with everyday needs. To get a job commensurate with skills. Willing to train in related field.	To improve accuracy in tenses, usage, etc. Extend vocabulary To develop writing skills

Key: **L** = Listening; **S** = Speaking; **R** = Reading; **W** = Writing. The levels are those used in the Stockport English Language Service but they are broadly equivalent to the English Speaking Union 9 – level scale.

Planning a programme for a group

If you are working with a group of students and want to draw up a programme which still meets individual needs, it is helpful to start by drawing up a group profile.

This should include the information obtained from Initial and Diagnostic Assessment such as background, prior learning and experience, level of English, goals and assessed language needs. An example of such a profile is on page 46.

From this you will be able to identify common goals and needs. You can see at a glance which students are at the same level in the different skills, and which goals and assessed language needs are shared. You can then draw up group objectives with the students for the programme. Next, individual needs not catered for in the programme can be identified and objectives agreed for each student.

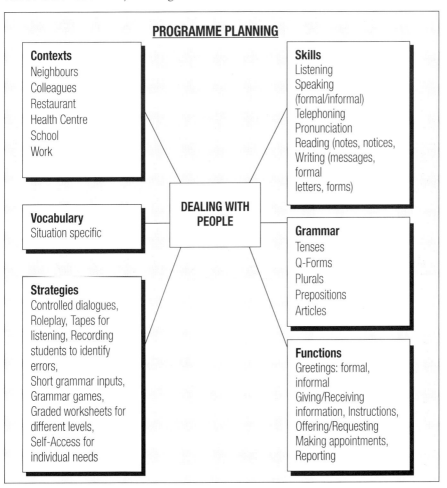

PROGRAMME PLANNING

Contexts
Neighbours
Colleagues
Restaurant
Health Centre
School
Work

Skills
Listening
Speaking
(formal/informal)
Telephoning
Pronunciation
Reading (notes, notices,
Writing (messages,
formal
letters, forms)

DEALING WITH PEOPLE

Vocabulary
Situation specific

Grammar
Tenses
Q-Forms
Plurals
Prepositions
Articles

Strategies
Controlled dialogues,
Roleplay, Tapes for
listening, Recording
students to identify
errors,
Short grammar inputs,
Grammar games,
Graded worksheets for
different levels,
Self-Access for
individual needs

Functions
Greetings: formal,
informal
Giving/Receiving
information, Instructions,
Offering/Requesting
Making appointments,
Reporting

The group profile shows that the students are roughly at similar levels in their listening and speaking skills, but there is a wider range when it comes to literacy. The contexts in which the students want to improve their English are various but several have an interest in work related English, while others would like to focus on health and school topics. All need to work on tenses and some other grammatical items such as articles would be useful for everyone. Formal and informal letters or notes could be a common theme at different levels.

One approach could be to use a range of contexts and include something for everyone in the programme. Another approach might be to work on the same functions and grammar but practise them in different contexts according to interest in sub-groups.

Strategies to cater for individual needs and different levels of literacy need to be identified. There is more on this in Chapter 9. The diagram on page 47 shows a possible theme and a breakdown of what might be included in a term's programme. From this specific objectives and an outline plan can be derived.

Further reading

Hemmingway Patty, 1994, *ESOL Syllabus Design*, Language & Literacy Unit, Southwark, (2nd Edition).

Nunan David, 1988, *Syllabus Design*, Oxford University Press.

Voss Liz, Basic Skills Agency 1991, *Open Learning and ESOL*.

5 | Developing Listening Skills

The previous chapters have been concerned with identifying needs and planning a learning programme. This chapter begins to look at teaching methods by examining ways of developing listening skills. It considers what is involved in listening, the teacher's use of language and how to practise listening with a student.

1. The importance of listening

You have to listen to a language before you can speak it. It is the basis upon which all the other language skills are built. Listening to English is the principal way learners of English get information both about the language and about the situations within which they will be using English. It is important at all levels from beginner to advanced. In any teaching situation, whether it is 1:1, in a group, in the workplace or in a college, a student must be able to listen effectively to learn. In some methods of teaching students spend a long time listening to the language before they are expected to speak. You can also encourage students to listen actively outside the classroom. When they are listening to the radio or TV, or to friends or colleagues talking they can extend their knowledge of English by mentally noting words, phrases, expressions and tone. They can practise the listening skills learnt in the classroom.

2. Listening in everyday life
To what and to whom do we listen?

In Chapters 2 and 3 some listening tasks students might have to do in 'real life' and some ways listening skills are used in different contexts were outlined.

As well as understanding you, students may need to understand other teachers, administrative staff, officials, public announcements, people on the telephone, television or radio programmes, supervisors, friends and workmates. Sometimes listening simply involves receiving the information (monologue, e.g. a broadcast, lecture, announcement) and sometimes it involves responding to it (conversation, dialogue, discussion).

Why do we listen?

We listen with different purposes and with differing levels of concentration according to what is being listened to and how interested we are in it. If we are listening to a set of instructions we listen carefully to every word because it is all important. Sometimes we just want to get specific factual information and listen only for that (e.g. the time of a train, the platform it leaves from), so we ignore the rest of the information. If we are listening to a friend telling a story we may listen to the gist of it because the details are not important to us. At other times picking up the mood of the other person is most important – s/he is angry, upset, frightened, happy.

How do we listen and understand?

Of course, we have to be able to understand most of the language, the vocabulary and the structure, but other things help as well. When people speak it is usually unscripted, not prepared in advance, so there is a lot of what is called redundant language. This means hesitations, repetition, going off the point. If we are listening for gist we try to select the main points or key words. Tone, stress and intonation give us more clues. Non-verbal communication, such as gestures and facial expression, can also be very helpful. Think how much more difficult it is understanding people on the telephone. Finally, context is a crucial element in understanding: the place you hear the language in, the person you are listening to, things around you, other visual clues such as maps, diagrams, notices.

3. Teacher language

In the teaching situation you have control over the language a student listens to. The main person s/he will listen to is you. As it is important that a student understands you, you need to think carefully about the language you use and how you say it. Make sure that when you give instructions to a student you use language at the right level. If you are bilingual think what is best said in the first language and what in English. Here are some guidelines to help you.

- Speak clearly and, for beginner and elementary students, slightly more slowly.

- Speak naturally without distorting rhythm and intonation.

- Use the normal contractions of colloquial speech, e.g. *I've, he's, it's, you've,* etc.

- Pause between sentences not words.

- Repeat your original sentence two or three times if the student does not understand at first. S/he may simply need time to process the information.

- Only paraphrase if you realise that you have used language which is too difficult.

- Teach the student useful phrases; *'I'm sorry I don't understand,' 'Please can you say it again?', 'What does that word mean?'*

- Do not speak for too long without checking understanding.

- Make a clear distinction between the language you use to instruct the student and the language items you are teaching.
- Use visual materials, real objects, gestures and actions to create context and illustrate meaning.

Using the first language

If you can speak a student's first language, even to a small extent, it can be very useful. You can use it to avoid long complicated explanations, to check for meaning or understanding and to explain an activity. However, presentation of new structures and vocabulary should be in English and it is also useful for a student to learn the language of instruction in English. As your lesson may be the student's only experience of learning English in a structured way it is essential to maximise her/his exposure to English.

Here is an example of a tutor giving instructions in English at two levels.

(i) Beginner

Teach simple instruction words. Use gestures to convey the meaning to start with.

T. Look at the picture *(point)*. There are two people. They're in a shop. What kind of shop is it?

S. Fruit and . . . and . . . What is potato?

T. Potatoes. They're vegetables.

S. Yes. Vegetables.

T. It's a greengrocer's. It sells fruit and vegetables. This is the shop assistant and this is Naseem. She buys some fruit and vegetables.

Listen *(point to ear)*. Tell me *(point to mouth)* what she buys. *(Point to pictures of items and name them)*. Apples, potatoes, peas, tomatoes. Listen *(play tape)*. What does she buy?

S. *(Points to picture)*. Tomato.

T. Good. Tomatoes. You say it. *(point to mouth)*. Tomatoes.

S. Tomatoes

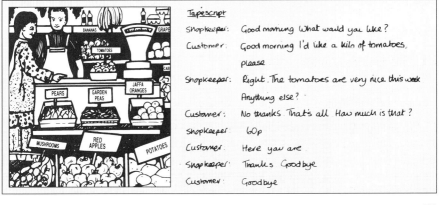

Tapescript

Shopkeeper: Good morning What would you like?

Customer: Good morning I'd like a kilo of tomatoes, please

Shopkeeper: Right. The tomatoes are very nice this week Anything else?

Customer: No thanks That's all. How much is that?

Shopkeeper: 60p

Customer: Here you are.

Shopkeeper: Thanks Goodbye

Customer: Goodbye

(ii) Elementary to intermediate

Keep the instructions clear and simple. You can rely more on the language but still point to the sections the student has to fill in or tick. At this level the tapescript would be longer with the shopper buying more items. Choose the appropriate weight system.

'Now I'm going to play you a tape. You'll hear two people talking. They're in a shop. One is the shopkeeper and the other is the customer. Listen and tick the things the customer buys. *(Point to worksheet). (Play tape).* Now listen again and check your answers. This time put a circle round how much she buys, like this. *(Point to example on worksheet).* Put a circle round how much she spends altogether. *(Point to list of prices on worksheet.)* Are you ready?, *(Play tape again).*

LISTENING SHOPPING ELEMENTARY

1) LISTEN
2) LISTEN

Tick what the shopper buys ☑
Circle how much or how many she buys (1lb)

apples ☐	½ kg/1lb	1kg/2lbs	1½ kg/3lbs
bananas ☐	3	4	6
oranges ☐	4	6	8
carrots ☐	½ kg/1lb	1kg/2lbs	2 kg/4lbs
mushrooms ☐	125 gms/¼lb	200 gms/6ozs	250 gms/½lb
lettuce ☐	1	2	3
tomatoes ☐	250 gms/½lb	½ kg/1lb	750 gms/1½lb

3) How much does she spend altogether?

£3.50 £3.15 £4.25 £4.50

52

4. What materials can you use?

Outside the classroom there is no way of controlling the English that a student has to listen to. Therefore you must train a student to listen effectively even when s/he does not understand everything. Students often need encouraging to believe that they do not, in fact, have to understand every word someone says to be able to get the main points. Nevertheless the listening material needs to be within the grasp of a student. It is no good if there is too much unknown language.

- You can tape short pieces of authentic spoken English of the type a student wants to be able to listen to. Authentic means it is 'real' language, not specially prepared for teaching; for example, an extract from the radio or TV news, some friends discussing a topic, an instructor demonstrating how to do something. You can use video too if you have the facilities.

- You can tape your own specially prepared materials; for example, a dialogue with a hairdresser, a job interview, a set of instructions, a story. This way you can make sure the material is the right level for a student but remember to include some repetition and hesitations and some unknown words as well.

- You can select appropriate material from commercially prepared books and cassettes. These are usually graded for different levels which can be helpful. They try to be as authentic as possible but sometimes can sound rather artificial.

By providing a range of listening materials you can give a student the chance not just to listen to you but to different voices and accents. If you want to make your own audio tapes there is more about this in Chapter 10.

5. How to present listening exercises to a student

- First of all prepare the student for what s/he is to hear. Prediction helps understanding. Set the scene. Teach any necessary vocabulary.

- As we usually listen with a purpose in mind tell the student in advance what you want her/him to listen for, either orally or in the form of pre-listening questions.

- Give the student a task that will check understanding. (See list overleaf).

- Play the tape once and ask for the student's self assessment. Could s/he understand it well, a bit, not at all?

- Play the tape several times until the student can pick out the required information or make the required responses.

- Play the tape in sections to focus on a little bit at a time.

- Encourage the student to work out or guess difficult bits.

- Encourage the student to make notes in English or in the first language or to give first language explanations if appropriate.

- Instil confidence by drawing attention to the language the student can understand relatively easily.

- When the student feels secure in understanding, play the whole tape through again.

6. Checking understanding

It is never enough to say, *'Do you understand?'* A student may say *'Yes'* out of politeness or because s/he thinks s/he does, while in fact s/he doesn't. If a student does not have good reading and writing skills it is best to use methods of checking that do not involve using these skills. Some methods for checking understanding are:

- carrying out an action;

- marking places on a map or diagram;

- drawing;

- identifying pictures;

- sequencing pictures;

- answering oral questions;

- retelling the story – if you have used video you can turn the sound down and ask the student to provide the commentary;

- identifying the mood and attitude of the speakers from tone and body language (if using a video);

- selecting from multiple choice answers.

If you speak a student's language some of these activities can be done in the first language as the main aim is to check understanding and not to practise speaking.

7. Examples of the types of listening materials you can use
(a) Listening for detail
This is one of the most intensive kinds of listening.
(i) Ask the student to carry out some instructions. See the illustration opposite for an example.

(ii) Give a set of directions and ask the student to draw the route on a map.

(b) Listening for specific information

(i) An airport announcement. The student writes down or ticks the times of arrival and departure.

(ii) A customer enquiring about prices. The student matches items and prices.

(iii) Descriptions of people or objects. The student identifies the corresponding pictures.

(iv) Making arrangements. The student notes down the day, time and place.

(c) Listening for gist/the main points

(i) People discussing an event. The student answers questions about their opinions or ticks true/false statements.

(ii) A story. The student sequences pictures or sentences.

(iii) A lecture/The news. The student identifies the main points from a list.

(iv) Social conversation. The student identifies the topics discussed.

Examples of these kinds of activities can be found in the resources listed on the next page.

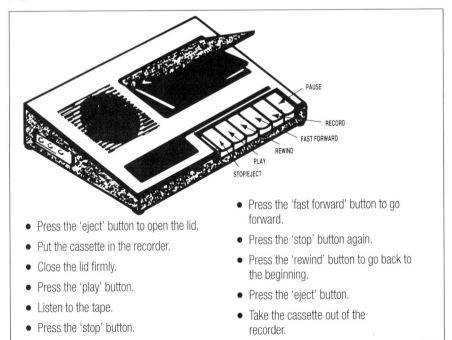

- Press the 'eject' button to open the lid.
- Put the cassette in the recorder.
- Close the lid firmly.
- Press the 'play' button.
- Listen to the tape.
- Press the 'stop' button.

- Press the 'fast forward' button to go forward.
- Press the 'stop' button again.
- Press the 'rewind' button to go back to the beginning.
- Press the 'eject' button.
- Take the cassette out of the recorder.

Further reading

There are comparatively few resources aimed specifically at EAL students. Most English Language Teaching materials are designed for the EFL market. As such, some of the situations and cultural contexts may not be relevant to EAL students but you can select the ones that are appropriate. The cassettes can provide good examples of authentic or near authentic language and the books give useful guidance on how to use the materials.

Blundell Lesley and Stokes Jackie, 1981, *Task Listening*, Cambridge University Press (Intermediate).

Doff A (Series Ed) 1991-93, *Cambridge Skills for Fluency*, Listening, Books 1-4. Cambridge University Press.

Longman Listening Skills, 1989, Elementary to Intermediate, Longman.

Lynch Tony, 1983, *Study Listening*, Cambridge University Press, (study skills – advanced).

Maley A (Ed), *Oxford Supplementary Skills*, Listening, Elementary (1981) to Advanced (1989) Oxford University Press.

Richards J, 1990, *Listen Carefully*, Oxford University Press.

Soars J & Soars L (Eds), *Making Headway, Everyday Listening and Speaking*, Intermediate (1992), Pre-Intermediate (1993), Oxford University Press.

St. Clair Stokes J, 1984, *Elementary Task Listening*, Cambridge University Press.

White G ,1998, *Listening*, Oxford University Press.

Wilkins Mary and Spiegel Marina, 1993, *Chart Your Course in English*, Wilkins & Spiegel Publications, (EAL – beginner and elementary).

6 | Developing Speaking Skills

This chapter looks at a variety of ways of teaching and giving practice in spoken English including the teaching of pronunciation. It is important to remember that receptive skills (listening and reading) are always in advance of productive skills (speaking and writing). The distance between them varies from one individual to another according to their language experience. If a person has practised both listening and speaking from the start then the gap might be quite small. If, on the other hand, a person has had plenty of opportunity to listen to the language but not much chance or not enough confidence to practise it, then the gap might be considerable. This can be the case with some EAL students who have lived for some time in Britain.

There are, therefore, three aims.

1. To teach new language and then give a student the opportunity to practise it. This obviously applies to beginners or near beginners but is necessary at all levels.

2. To draw out language that a student already knows but does not use very much and give her/him the confidence to use it.

3. To try and replace wrongly learnt forms with correct ones.

Methods for presenting and practising spoken language

The methods described here have been developed primarily for class teaching. However, they are equally suitable for one to one teaching with minor adaptations as necessary (e.g. only two people in a dialogue or role-play).

Presentation of new material and repetition

If you do not speak a student's language you must use a direct method presenting the English you want to teach clearly so that the student can understand. This method can be used at all levels, from beginner to advanced. With intermediate and advanced students it may also be combined with explanation and written examples.

If you can speak a student's first language you can translate the key words or give a brief explanation. However, it is still essential that you repeat the English enough times for the student to grasp the new language. Too much use of the first language is not helpful in the learning process. It has already been said that a student must listen before speaking. There would also be little point in speaking without understanding.

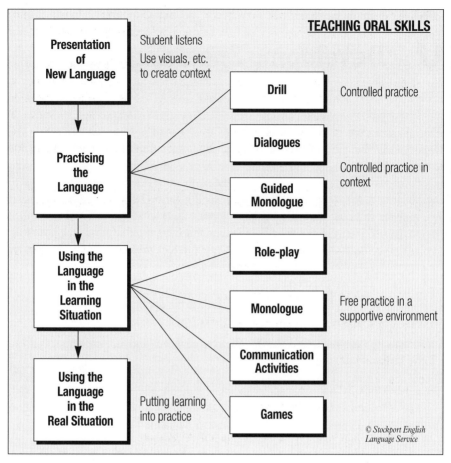

Presentation of New Language — Student listens / Use visuals, etc. to create context

Drill — Controlled practice

Practising the Language

Dialogues

Guided Monologue — Controlled practice in context

Using the Language in the Learning Situation

Role-play

Monologue — Free practice in a supportive environment

Communication Activities

Using the Language in the Real Situation — Putting learning into practice

Games

© Stockport English Language Service

Therefore you must present the new language to a student so that the meaning is clear. You are not just teaching the meaning of individual words but the meaning of words in a sentence. Remember, too, that meaning is not only conveyed by words but by gesture and facial expression.

A new teaching item can be a grammatical feature (e.g. a verb tense, adding –s to make plurals), a function (e.g. complaining, inviting) or vocabulary (e.g. words on a theme: tall, short, slim, fat, pretty, plain, handsome).

Demonstrate the meaning of what you are saying by using actions, pictures or real objects. These provide the context for the language and enable you to set the scene outside the teaching situation.

Do not teach words in isolation. This simply results in the student knowing lists of words but not being able to put them together meaningfully, e.g. NOT *'pen'?* but *'Have you got a pen?'*, NOT *'baby...sick...no come'* but *'My baby's sick. I can't come.'*

When you are introducing new vocabulary you can simply put it into a naming pattern, i.e. *'This is the library'. 'This is a spanner'*, before using the words in the sentence you want to practise.

When a student has listened sufficiently then s/he must have the chance to repeat the language several times to get it right and to help her/him remember it. Encourage a student to imitate your pronunciation as far as possible. It helps to develop good habits from the beginning but remember that comprehensibility is the aim, not perfection. Encourage a student to imitate some of the non-verbal language as well, such as gesture and expression, as this is used differently in different cultures.

Target – to teach how to ask and say where places are in an area. To teach *'near, next to, opposite'* e.g. *'Where's the bank?' 'It's near the post office.'*

Known vocabulary – supermarket, station, school, bank, post office, garage, park (whatever is appropriate to the area). Where? questions already known.

Materials – simple map of the area showing places with pictures and labels.

1. Check that the student knows the names of the places.
T.   Look at the map. What's this?
S.   (It's) the school, etc.

2. Demonstrate the new language
   Use objects in the room to show the meaning of 'near, next to, opposite'.

3. Present the new words in the context you want to practise
T.   Look at the map again. Listen.
   Where's the bank? It's next to the Post Office.
   Where's the supermarket? It's opposite the garage.
   Where's the park? It's near the school.

4. Repetition
T.   Now you answer after me.
   (Point to self) Where's the bank? *(Point to student)*
   (It's next to the Post Office).
S.   It's next to the Post Office, etc.

T.   Now you ask me. *(point to student)* Where's the garage?
S.   Where's the garage?
T.   It's opposite the supermarket, etc.

Note

(i) The dialogue can be recorded on tape using two people to show that one person is asking and another answering. Sometimes beginner students repeat everything and do not realise you are asking a question. If you cannot tape it you can use a picture of two faces to illustrate conversation or use your hands like puppets to make the same point.

(ii) Make sure the student answers the questions using *'it's'* and does not repeat the name of the place being asked about. *'The park is near the school'* is a statement giving information. *'It's near the school'* is an answer to a question.

(iii) Contractions are used like *'It's'* to teach natural spoken English but a student needs to know the full form as well as s/he will hear it elsewhere and needs to use it when, for example, asking questions *'Is it..?'* Show the student like this: *Where is..?* (Indicate with your hands the two words coming together) *Where's? It is... It's*, etc.

Visuals

It is important to use visual materials to create context. You may find the items listed below useful.

- Photographs
- Pictures from magazines, brochures, catalogues, text books, picture dictionaries
- Real objects
- A calendar
- Tape measure
- Samples of materials/substances
- Timetables
- Maps, A-Z
- Packets and labels
- Leaflets and manuals
- Forms
- Tickets
- Bills
- Newspapers/magazines/TV Times/Radio Times
- Advertisements
- Telephone book/Yellow Pages, a telephone

Some of these resources may be available in other languages so that you can make use of a student's first language. This gives value to a student's language and is useful for enhancing understanding.

Vocabulary development with intermediate and advanced students

Sometimes a particular goal of a student is to extend vocabulary. There is obviously no point in learning lists of words out of context but it can be useful to develop vocabulary on a theme or to show how related words are built up, e.g. *economics, economic, economy, economical, economist, uneconomical.*

At this level the meaning of new vocabulary can be shown by the language context not just a visual demonstration. Explanations and definitions can be used and the student should be encouraged to use a dictionary effectively.

Practice

1. Drills

Drills are to language learning what scales are to playing music. A drill is a set of sentences which follow the same pattern but with one or two words changed every time. Although the emphasis in language teaching is on communicative activities, drills are useful in that they give repetitive practice to establish habits and encourage fluency. They are good for practising grammatical and functional patterns. There is a place for such activities just as there is for learning some things by heart (e.g. irregular verb forms).

How they can be used

(i) To practise new language as in the extract from a lesson described on page 62. They help a student get the order of words right, to remember to put all the little words in, to get the pronunciation right, to say the sentence fluently. As a student progresses you build upon structures practised earlier, e.g. *'I'm looking for a shirt' – 'I'm looking for a blue/long-sleeved/striped shirt.' 'I liked science' – 'I liked science because it was interesting/because we had a good teacher'.*

(ii) To give a student practice in saying something correctly and overlaying incorrect forms. For example, an intermediate student consistently says, *'I not go'* for *'I didn't go'.* You could make a list of things s/he did the day before and another list of things s/he does on other days and practise like this.

'Yesterday was a holiday. I stayed at home. I got up late. I went shopping. I took the children to the park. I didn't go to work/get up early/wash the vegetables/cut up the meat/pack the dishwasher/clean the kitchen.'

(iii) Always demonstrate clearly what a student has to do. Make sure that a student is not repeating something s/he does not understand. Make the drills as realistic as possible. Put them in a context and use visuals if appropriate.

(iv) Use them sparingly for a short time only.

(v) You can record the drill on audio-tape together with correct responses for the student to practise independently.

Some examples

(i) Single word substitution

T. Would you like a biscuit?
S. *(Repeats)*
T. Would you like a cake?
S. *(Repeats)*
T. Would you like a chocolate?
S. *(Repeats)*

When you have demonstrated the drill you can simply 'cue' the word to be changed, 'biscuit/cake/chocolate'.

(ii) Progressive substitution

T. I had my car repaired last week.
S. (Repeats)
T. He
S. He had his car repaired last week.
T. washing machine
S. He had his washing machine repaired last week.
T. on Friday
S. He had his washing machine repaired on Friday.

This helps students understand word order and structural changes.

(iii) Incremental

T. I typed.
S. I typed.
T. a letter
S. I typed a letter.
T. to the manager
S. I typed a letter to the manager.
T. this morning
S. I typed a letter to the manager this morning.

This type of drill helps fluency.

(iv) Contextual

Here the cue is a sentence which sparks off an appropriate response. For example:

T. The car's dirty.
S. Yes, it needs cleaning.
T. The tyre's worn.
S. Yes, it needs replacing.
T. The brake is stiff.
S. Yes, It needs adjusting.

2. Dialogues

Writing and selecting dialogues

In language teaching dialogues are scripted conversations between two or more people. They can show a student how language is used in a situation. However, in a situational dialogue there can be a wide range of grammatical features, expressions and functions. A dialogue prepared for listening practice and a dialogue for speaking practice are different. The first can contain some unknown language, hesitations and repetitions, while the second should only contain language a student already knows and needs to produce, or the language that you plan to teach a student. Therefore it is important to keep your dialogues fairly short and purposeful.

Here is an example.

Asking for directions

A. Excuse me, could you tell me where the library is, please?

B. Yes, go straight along this corridor, through those doors, up the stairs on your left to the second floor. When you get there turn right and the library is straight in front of you.

A. Second floor, turn right. Thanks very much.

B. You're welcome.

Suitable dialogues can also be selected from published materials. Check the content is appropriate and what structures and vocabulary are included.

Uses of dialogues

- to show a new language item in a context

- to practise a new item in a context

- to practise making appropriate responses

- to improve pronunciation and fluency

- to give a student confidence by having a clear script to work to.

How to present a dialogue

- It is best to record the dialogue on tape. You can then play it several times and it always sounds the same. It also gives a student the opportunity to hear a different voice. This is important in a 1:1 situation. If this is not possible you will have to read both parts yourself.

- Play the tape two or three times and check comprehension.

- You can either play the tape before drilling the important structures to set them in a context or drill the structures first.

- When you are both happy about the language in the dialogue, ask the student to take one of the parts. It is usual for a student to play the part s/he would in real life. So in the example above s/he could play either part. S/he might equally be in a situation where she needs to ask for or give directions.

- Play the tape and stop it after each sentence the student is to speak. Ask her/him to repeat it.

- Then play the tape and stop it before each sentence and see if the student can say it. Alternatively you can each take your parts without using the tape at this stage.

- It is better if a student listens to and repeats the dialogue rather than reads it. Reading can impede pronunciation and fluency. However a written transcription of the dialogue is useful for a student to keep for reference.

- If a student cannot read the use of the tape is even more important. S/he could keep a copy of the tape to listen to and practise at home.

Using the language

1. Role-play

What is role-play?

Drills and dialogues are both ways of practising language that are guided and controlled by a tutor. They give valuable support to a student in the learning process. However, the language is chosen by the tutor. There is no opportunity for the student to decide on the language to use or to have to think for her/himself and respond to something unexpected. They may also suggest that there is only one correct form of English for a given situation.

Role-play is a step nearer being able to use the language in a real situation outside the learning context. It is more flexible than dialogue, allowing for a variety of responses. It encourages students to listen to the other person and to make their own responses. You can draw language out of a student as you discuss what the possibilities are in a particular situation. You can explore degrees of formality, gestures, and tone. You can introduce variables such as dealing with unhelpful or hostile people. All this helps to build a student's confidence.

Role-play can be used in the same kinds of situation as scripted dialogue. The possibilities are endless: inviting a friend for coffee, taking something to be repaired and explaining the problem, phoning a college to ask for a creche place, a job interview, asking the supervisor for a day off, etc.

Uses of role-play

- Role-play can be used at any level.

- It can be used as the culmination of controlled work such as drills and dialogues.

- It can be used to check learning.

- It can also be used as a starting point. In this case it is used diagnostically to find out how much a student knows and what aspects of language need further practice. For this reason it is a very useful technique with intermediate and advanced students.

How to conduct a role-play
Method A
The tutor sets up a functional framework for the role-play. This can give quite detailed guidance and in a sense is an intermediate stage between dialogue and free role-play.

For example:
Ladda has been practising taking orders in a restaurant. A role-play based on this situation could be structured as follows:

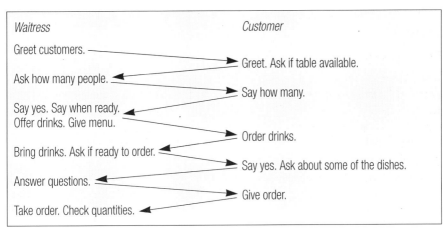

Note: This method requires a knowledge of functional terms. If you have used this language when teaching and the student understands the terms there is no problem. Sometimes, however, the functional description is harder than the language a student is expected to produce.

Go through the role-play step by step discussing with the student the best way of expressing the functions. Then act out the whole exchange. As with dialogues the student should play her/himself and the tutor the other part. If you record it on tape you can both listen and identify the strengths and weaknesses.

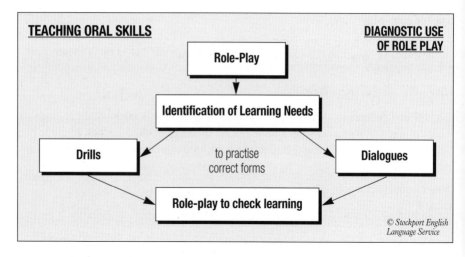

TEACHING ORAL SKILLS   DIAGNOSTIC USE OF ROLE PLAY

Role-Play → Identification of Learning Needs → Drills / Dialogues (to practise correct forms) → Role-play to check learning

© Stockport English Language Service

Method B

Set the scene in a more general way. For example:

'You are the waitress and I am the customer. I haven't booked but you are not very busy. You offer me drinks and take the order. I ask you some questions about the food and you try to answer them.'

You then act out the situation without much preparation, record it and then discuss how it went afterwards.

2. Communication activities

These are materials devised to give a student practice in asking for and giving information. Like role-play they give students the opportunity to formulate their own questions and responses in a given situation. Again the emphasis is on fluency rather than correctness of language.

These activities are usually used as pairwork exercises with a class but can be used effectively in a 1:1 situation with you and the student forming the pair.

The materials are based on the information-gap principle. Person A has some information which is not held by Person B. Person B must ask appropriate questions to obtain this information. Sometimes only one person lacks information and sometimes both people lack certain but different information which they must obtain from each other. The information can be pictorial, diagrammatic or written. When the missing information has been obtained it can be written or drawn on the worksheet.

Here is a simple example.

3. Monologue

Not all spoken language is interactive. Sometimes it is necessary to speak at greater length to somebody where little or no response is expected.

This often occurs in more formal situations such as on a college course, a training course or at work. A student may have to give instructions to a colleague, describe a process or present a talk to other students or trainees. If a student needs to be able to do any of these things, then choose a relevant topic and help the student plan the task.

This can be a guided activity with much of the content provided in the form of outline notes or information that the student reads or listens to and then retells.

It can be a free activity with the student providing the input. S/he can make notes on what she is going to say. However, it is better not to write out the whole thing as it then becomes more of a written exercise. The presentation can be recorded and discussed in the same way as a role-play.

4. Games

These add fun to a lesson, give lots of useful practice and can be used at all levels. There are many games which can fit in with particular types of language practice.

Kim's Game

Show a number of objects on a tray. Cover them and see how many the student can remember. Good for vocabulary.

Pelmanism

Place card sets face down. Pick up two cards at a time. If they match keep them, if not put them back. Good for matching words, pictures, words to pictures, opposites.

Snap

Similar to above but each player takes cards from a pack.

Adding items to a list

Each player has to remember all the items on a list and add a new item.
'I went shopping yesterday and I bought . . .'
'I'm going on holiday next week and I'm taking . . .'

Bingo

Use pictures and words instead of numbers. Past tenses can be practised by reading out the infinitives. The student has to find the past tense form on the card, e.g. *take/took, write/wrote.*

Guessing games

Twenty questions to discover an object or well-known person. Describe an object or person without naming them.

Pronunciation

Some general points that can be made are:

- it is usual to combine pronunciation work with general speaking practice. This way it is closely related to the context a student is working on;

- don't be a perfectionist. Only concentrate on the aspects that stop a student being understood;

- become aware of the likely pronunciation difficulties for speakers of particular languages;

- when you and the student have identified the problems you want to work on, choose one problem at a time and work on it for about five minutes;

Seeing a teacher
Practise

a) Cover the text. Practise the dialogue with another student.

b) Say your name and your child's name. Practise asking to see your child's teacher.

Gwen Lewis goes to her daughter's school. She wants to speak to her daughter's teacher. She goes to the school office.

Gwen	*Good morning*
School Secretary	*Morning*
Gwen	*My name is Gwen Lewis, I'm Amanda Lewis's mother. She is in Year 10, Mrs. Woodward's class.*
School Secretary	*. . . Oh yes . . .?*
Gwen	*I'd like to see Mrs. Woodward. Is she free?*
School Secretary	*Have you got an appointment?*
Gwen	*No, I haven't*
School Secretary	*. . . Well, I'm sorry, all the teachers are in a staff meeting at the moment. Can I help you?*
Gwen	*Well, I don't think so really. I'd like to discuss quite a lot of things with her about Amanda's GCSE subjects. When is she free?*
School Secretary	*Just hold on, I'll go and check.*

Practise in other situations
Seeing the bank manager
Role play

Work in pairs

1. **A** wants to see the bank manager.

A

You own a shop.
You go to your bank.
You have a business account.
You want to see the manager.
You would like to discuss a loan.
You do not have an appointment.

B

You are a bank clerk.
You are friendly.
The manager is busy.
The bank normally has an appointments system.

Tape it and listen to it.
Is it clear?
Did **A** get an appointment?
If not try again.

2. **A** wants to see the bank manager again.

A

You own a shop.
You go to your bank.
You have a business account.
You want to see the manager.
You would like to discuss a loan.
You do not have an appointment.

B

You are a bank clerk.
You are tired and bad-tempered.
The manager is busy.

Tape it and listen to it.
Is it clear?
Did **A** get an appointment?
If not try again.

From: *Chart your Course in English*, Wilkins and Spiegel (1993)

- be aware of how you produce individual sounds, where you put the stress on words and in sentences and how you use intonation to express different meanings;

- nobody can produce sounds they are unable to hear. The first step is listening and learning to discriminate similar sounds, to hear the stress and intonation.

How to teach pronunciation

1. Sounds

If a sound does not exist in a student's language the student will substitute another similar sound. Sounds are significant only when in contrast with another. Therefore, if a sound is mispronounced and becomes indistinguishable from another, meaning is affected. For example, if a student says *'It costs t(h)ree pounds'* the context makes it clear that *'three'* and not *'tree'* is intended. However, if the student asks, *'Have you got a pan?'* and means *'pen'* or a *'pin'* confusion could arise. It is useful, therefore, to practise sounds which give difficulty in minimal pairs such as *chip/cheap, day/they, shop/chop.* It is hard to contextualise this kind of practice but always choose words that are known to a student. There is no point in practising uncommon words the student is never likely to use. The student may be able to produce one of the sounds but not the other or may produce a sound somewhere between the two.

(i) First the student needs to learn to discriminate between them.

First of all demonstrate as far as possible how the two sounds you want the student to distinguish are made. Get her/him to touch the throat to feel the vibration if one of the sounds is voiced (i.e. the vocal cords are vibrated). Exaggerate slightly but do not distort the sounds. Watching someone make the sounds can help a student distinguish them at first. Write down the pairs of words. Say one word in each pair and ask the student to identify which one by pointing to it or circling it. If a student cannot read, select words that can be shown pictorially and ask her/him to identify the picture.

For example:

To discriminate *p/b*

pin/ (bin)   (tap) /tab   (pill) /bill   cap/ (cab)   (park) /bark   pack/ (back)

To discriminate *i/ee*

seat/sit   leave/live   feel/fill

To discriminate e/a

pen **pan** **man** **men**

To discriminate *'teen'* and *'ty'* in numbers.

16/60   15/50   13/30

To discriminate the sound of 'ed' in past
tense endings

	t	d	id
arrived		✔	
visited			✔
watched	✔		

Another way is to say pairs of words and ask the student to say whether they are the same or different, e.g. tin/tin – S thin/tin – D.

You can say some words beginning or ending with the sounds you are practising and ask the student to tick the sound being used. With this exercise you do not have to keep to minimal pairs, e.g.

	sh	ch		
1	✔		Say	1 shop
2		✔		2 cheque
3		✔		3 chip
4	✔			4 shoe
5		✔		5 change

When a student can hear the difference between individual words it can be useful to put the words into sentences to practise discrimination in context, but it is not always possible to think of pairs of realistic sentences. Usually, one or two examples are enough.

I often walk in the park.
I often work in the park.

I'd like some blue shorts, please.
I'd like some blue shirts, please.

(ii) Next the student has to try to produce the sounds.

Demonstrate the sounds again and ask the student to repeat the sound in isolation first. Then practise the sound in words and in sentences. There is no need to keep to minimal pairs at this stage. Use examples that are relevant and familiar to the students. Remember that some sounds need to be practised in the middle or at the end of words as well as, or instead of, at the beginning.

However, the production of some incorrect sounds is less likely to make a student difficult to understand than different stress and intonation patterns. If a student has great difficulty with a particular sound it is not worth spending too much time on it. Other aspects of language are more important.

2. Practising stress

a. Word stress

(i) Listening and identifying

Ask the student to listen to and recognise common word stress patterns.

e.g.	teacher	correct	holiday
	student	repeat	hospital
	paper	again	alphabet

Notice the effect strong or weak stress has on sounds, e.g <u>stu</u>dent/<u>dent</u>ist. Make sure you pronounce the words naturally and that you say them in the same way each time you repeat them. It helps to record material for pronunciation practice to ensure a consistent model.

You can help the student hear the stress patterns by beating the rhythm.

(ii) Ask the student to repeat the words. It is useful to record him/her to compare the student's version with the model.

This kind of practice can easily be incorporated into lessons when, for example, introducing new vocabulary.

b. Sentence stress

Getting this right means that the language has the correct rhythm. Again the sequence is listen, identify, repeat.

Start with short sentences or phrases following the same stress pattern and build up to longer ones.

(i) Tell me.
Buy it.
Show her.

(ii) He knows.
It's nice.
I'm hot.

(iii) He's gone to work.
I bought some shoes.

(iv) Tell me.
Tell me about the film.
Tell me about the film you saw yesterday.

(v) See if the student can identify the prominent word and understand the meaning of it by saying the same sentence in different ways.

I want to see the <u>film</u> on BBC 1.

I want to see the film on BBC <u>1</u>.

<u>I</u> want to see the film on BBC 1.

3. Practising intonation
(a) Ask the student to distinguish rising and falling tones using one word examples,

e.g.   No.   Me?   Right.   Who?

Then practise recognition of sentences with falling and rising tones.

(b) Practise saying sentences which use the falling tone.

e.g.   I liked the film.

Who was in it?

I can't remember.

Write it down.

(c) Practise sentences which use the rising tone.

Did you see the film? ↗

Would you like to go to the cinema? ↗

(d) Practise pairs of sentences, one falling and one rising.

(i)   He's not coming to the class today. ↘

       Is he coming to the class today? ↗

(ii)   Finish your work quickly. ↘

       Could you finish your work quickly? ↗

(e) Practise words and sentences where the intonation changes the meaning, e.g.

Sorry. (apology) ↘

Sorry? (question) ↗

They've arrived. (statement) ↘

They've arrived? (question) ↗

4. Practising fluency

(a) Practise contractions. 'I've seen them', rather than 'I have seen them.' Students who have learnt formal English are not used to doing this and it tends to make them sound rather stilted.

It is important, however, that students know what the contraction stands for, especially where there could be confusion.

I'd (had) finished my work by 7.00pm.

I'd (would) finish my work if I had time.

(b) Practise linking the sound at the end of one word with the sound at the beginning of the next.

e.g. He broke an arm and a leg.

Sometimes a slight 'y', 'w' or 'r' sound is put in to help glide from one word to the next, e.g. Theʸ others; goʷ in; on herʳ own.

(c) Long sentences can be difficult to say fluently. Ask the students to identify phrase groups.

e.g. He gets up / at 7 o'clock / and walks / to the station / to catch the train.

Practise building up the sentence phrase by phrase until the whole sentence can be said fluently.

Finally all these elements can be practised together by working on simple dialogues where the language content is familiar to the student. This means s/he can concentrate on good pronunciation.

A. Excuse me/I bought this yesterday/and it's got a mark on it.

B. Oh, I'm sorry./Would you like/to change it/for another one?

A. Yes, please.

B. Oh dear! I'm afraid/there aren't any more/in your size/in the same colour.

Would you like a different colour?

A. No, thanks. I'd rather have my money back.

B. All right. I'll get you a refund.

A. Thank you.

In all pronunciation work the tape recorder is an invaluable aid. Not only can the student listen to the examples over and over again but s/he can record her/himself and compare her/his pronunciation with the examples.

Correcting spoken language

- At all stages in speaking practice you need to give the student feedback about how well s/he has achieved the task and how it could be improved. Be encouraging and do not expect perfection.

- It is important to distinguish mistakes, where the student really knows what is correct, and errors, where the student does not know the correct form. In the first case a quick reminder may be sufficient. It is also a good idea to point out a mistake and see if the student can correct it her/himself. This encourages language awareness. If the student makes an error then you may correct it but should also record it as a language need to be dealt with in the learning programme.

- How much you correct depends a lot on the nature of the task. If the student is repeating and practising new language, you need to give immediate feedback and correct for accuracy. Controlled practice such as a drill or a dialogue also focuses on accuracy. However, if a student has difficulty you have to decide at what point further correction is counter-productive and leave it to another time.

- If, on the other hand, the purpose of the activity is to develop fluency and to practise communication skills, then accuracy is less important than the successful outcome of the task. First give feedback on how well the activity has been carried out before dealing with grammatical errors or pronunciation difficulties.

- It is important not to interrupt the student's flow or train of thought. Wait till at least the end of the sentence in controlled practice or the completion of the task in communicative activities. You can make a note of problems and decide what needs dealing with immediately and what can be incorporated into the programme in future lessons.

Further reading

Baker Ann,1981, *Teaching English Pronunciation: Tree or Three?* (Elementary) 1982, *Ship or Sheep?* (Intermediate), Cambridge University Press.

Barr V, and Fletcher C, 1984, *English for Driving*, National Extension College. Multi-lingual.

Collie Joanne, Slater Stephen, 1995, *True to Life Elementary: English for Adult Learners*, Cambridge University Press.

Doff A. (Series Ed), 1991-92, *Cambridge Skills for Fluency, Speaking*, Books 1-4 Pre-intermediate to Advanced, Cambridge University Press.

Fletcher M, *Flexible Friends Learning Cards*, English Experience.

Flower J, Berman M, 1989, *Build Your Vocabulary*, Language Teaching Publications (Self Study Series).

Hancock Mark, 1995, *Pronunciation Games*, Cambridge University Press.

Headway Pronunciation Series, Elementary to Upper Intermediate, Oxford University Press.

Hewings Martin, 1993, *Pronunciation Tasks*, Cambridge University Press.

LDA Learning Development Aids, Useful sets of picture cards.

Maley A Ed Oxford, *Supplementary Skills, Speaking*, Elementary to Advanced, Oxford University Press.

Naterop and Revell, 1987, *Telephoning in English*, Cambridge University Press (Advanced).

O'Connor J D and Fletcher Clare, 1989, *Sounds English*, Longman.

Rinvolucri M, 1984, *Grammar Games*, Cambridge University Press.

Rinvolucri M and Davis Paul, 1995, *More Grammar Games*, Cambridge University Press.

Seal Bernard, 1988, *Vocabulary Builders 1 & 2*, Longman.

Soars J and Soars L, Eds, *Making Headway: Everyday Listening and Speaking*, Pre-intermediate, 1993, and Intermediate, 1992; *Talking in Pairs*, 1994, Pre-intermediate and Intermediate, Oxford University Press.

Ur P, Wright A, 1992, *Five Minute Activities*, Cambridge University Press.

Wallwork Adrian, 1997, *Discussions A-Z, Intermediate and Advanced*, Resource books of speaking activities, Cambridge University Press.

Watcyn-Jones P, 1997, *Pair Work 1 and Pair Work 2*, Penguin.

Wilkins Meryl and Spiegel Marina, 1993, *Chart Your Course in English*, Wilkins and Spiegel Publications, 31 Washington Road, Caversham, Reading RG4 OAA (an ESOL/EAL specific course book).

There are many EFL materials which, if selected carefully for appropriateness, can be used with EAL students. Only a small selection is included above.

7 | Developing Reading and Writing Skills – 1

Planning

Chapter 2 examined how to start planning a learning programme with a student. The first step was to identify long and short term goals and break these down into the skills needed. This chapter looks at reading and writing skills, approaches to teaching these skills to beginner and elementary students and the kinds of material that can be used.

1. Needs

The five students featured in Chapter 1 exemplify a considerable range of reading and writing goals.

Nazia: reading letters from school, stories to the children, medicine labels, information from the clinic. Writing notes to school, filling in forms.

Abubaka: reading letters and bills, job adverts, computer manuals, on screen instructions, course task sheets. Writing cheques/giro, filling in application and claim forms, writing letters, completing course tasks.

Yasmin: reading newspapers, letters, textbooks, children's books. Writing letters, filling in application forms, writing a CV, making notes, writing essays and assignments.

Omer: reading job adverts, training information, newspapers. Writing CV, application forms, letters and eventually articles.

Ladda: reading signs and labels, letters, cleaning instructions, a menu, safety instructions. Filling in a time-sheet, filling in forms, writing a cheque.

2. What sort of skills are needed to achieve these goals?

Basic reading skills include:

- directing reading from left to right
- knowing the names and the sounds of letters

- knowing sound/spelling relationships
- distinguishing upper and lower case letters
- recognising 'key' words, e.g. this, is, has, the
- recognising where a word or sentence ends
- knowing how to blend sounds together
- understanding as well as working out what a word is (decoding)
- using context.

More advanced reading skills include:
- reading words as groups rather than word by word
- skimming and scanning
- predicting and using context to identify a word (context cueing)
- making analogies
- knowing how texts are structured
- understanding both surface meaning and inferences.

Basic writing skills include:
- holding a pen/pencil correctly
- moving from left to right
- forming letters correctly, both upper and lower case
- spacing words.

More advanced skills include:
- knowing when to use upper and lowercase letters
- punctuation
- spelling
- paragraphing
- layout
- grammar
- appropriate style.

3. Prior learning

The next step is to look at a student's previous learning experience and see which of these skills the student has already acquired in her/his first language and in English.

Some skills may be transferable from the first language to English but other factors may hinder the process of reading and writing in English.

The relevant factors when considering first language literacy are:

- the system and direction of writing in the first language

- the general level of education in the country of origin

- the level of literacy in the first language

- the use of literacy in the first language

- differences between the first language and English, e.g. in sounds and in structure.

An additional factor is whether the student has learnt to speak, read or write any other languages.

Factors connected with the student's experience of English are:

- educational experience in Britain

- length of stay and experience of life in Britain

- oral competence in English

- gap in competence between listening, speaking, reading and writing skills.

For example, **Ladda** and **Yasmin** both use a different script in their first language but **Yasmin** is also highly literate in English. **Ladda** has conceptual skills to transfer to reading English but has had to learn a new script.

Nazia also uses a different script in her first language and one which is read from right to left. Her level of reading is higher in Urdu than in English which she reads quite slowly. She has basic skills to build on but needs to develop faster reading skills and her ability to understand and extract information from a range of texts. Her free writing skills are not strong and she needs to work on grammatical accuracy, spelling and punctuation.

Abubaka and **Omer** are both familiar with the Roman script but have to learn new sound values for the letters. Any difficulties with pronunciation will affect their ability to spell. **Abubaka's** level of first language literacy means that he has few higher level literacy skills to transfer. He can read a range of texts but has difficulty extracting the meaning, using layout clues and understanding the task. **Omer** was a beginner in English in all skills so his lack of knowledge of grammar and vocabulary will be reflected in his literacy skills. However, his experience of learning French, his level of education and his lack of exposure to spoken English could mean that his reading level moves ahead faster than his spoken English.

Students who are not literate in either their first language or English have to learn both the concepts and the basic skills of literacy.

4. Assessing reading and writing skills

In Chapter 2 some suggestions were made on suitable tasks for assessing reading and writing skills in English. For initial assessment of reading it is better to talk through the text you have selected rather than give written exercises. In this way you can adapt your approach to the individual, asking questions to check understanding, asking a student to select bits of information and maybe read some of the text aloud. See if a student can tackle an unfamiliar word or guess at its meaning. In this way you can assess a student's ability in some of the skills identified above. When assessing writing you can observe how s/he holds the pen, forms the letters and how fluently s/he writes, as well as analysing the result in terms of grammar, spelling, punctuation, etc.

5. What materials to use

When learning a language, listening and speaking usually come before or are closely integrated with reading and writing. Reading materials must, therefore, be within a student's spoken competence. This is particularly true in the early stages. Only when a student is a reasonably confident reader should new words be introduced through the written text. However, even at an advanced stage there should not be too high a proportion of unknown words. It is also important that reading is not an isolated activity but is closely related to and integrated with listening and speaking practice.

Reading materials can be –

Texts based on spoken language practice
These could be a written dialogue or a paragraph or some sentences which reflect the structures or functions being taught. These are specially written texts designed to be within the learner's oral competence. You can write them yourself or choose appropriate texts from a course book. They are useful in reinforcing the spoken language. However, if a student's reading competence is far behind her/his spoken competence you will have to select a simple sentence within her/his capabilities. It is not always necessary to be able to read what is spoken and for beginner readers it may be better to concentrate on reading which relates to the spoken context but is at the right level.

For example, reading from a substitution table can reinforce oral practice.

What do you like doing? / What does he/she like doing?		
I *We*	*like*	*cooking* *swimming*
Wendy *My son*	*likes*	*driving* *watching TV*

Texts based on a student's language experience

The tutor writes a text based on a student's own words when talking about experiences and opinions. This ensures that the language is within a student's oral competence and that the subject matter is of interest. This could lead to the development of a personal reading book.

You agree with the student the sentences to be written down bearing in mind the level of competence in reading. It is also important with a language student that any errors in the spoken language are discussed and corrected before the sentences are written down. There is no point in a student reinforcing errors by reading them. (The language experience approach is widely used in basic skills classes).

Graded readers

These are books at different levels written specially for learners. The language at each level is controlled with regard to structure and vocabulary so it can match the competence of a student. There is usually plenty of repetition to help a student remember words. Sometimes the language may be rather stilted and unnatural and sometimes the stories may not be very interesting. However, reading a story can give enjoyment and a sense of achievement. EAL students who are fluent speakers do not need such tight control over structure and vocabulary.

Authentic texts

These are real texts appropriate for the areas selected by a student e.g signs, labels, advertisements, letters, articles, materials and books from a college or training course. It is important to try to select materials at a suitable level or to simplify them to suit the student. Signs and notices, even though short, can use difficult vocabulary and structures.

Teaching reading to beginners

There are a number of approaches used to teach reading to beginners who are native speakers of English. Three of the commonly used ones are:

1. whole word recognition   2. context   3. phonics.

It is useful to consider how effective and appropriate they might be with beginner readers who are speakers of other languages bearing in mind the factors listed at the beginning of this chapter.

1. Whole word recognition

What is it?

This approach aims at meaningful reading by a student learning to recognise a known word as a whole. The word is identified for the student by someone reading it or by a picture. The student looks at the word and says it. By constant repetition the student learns to recognise the word as an entity. It is similar to a Chinese speaker learning to recognise Chinese characters. The skills of visual discrimination and memory are involved in identifying the word. Memory is an essential element in learning to read whatever approach is used.

Its use with EAL students

This approach is useful for EAL students, especially beginners, who are not literate in the first language and do not have transferable skills.

For those who can read in their first language, whatever the script, it provides a useful starting point but they will soon want to develop strategies for reading independently. Students like **Ladda** will want to relate symbols with sounds in the same way as she can in Thai. Students like **Omer**, who already know the Roman script, would be able to have a go at reading English right from the beginning, but would not be sure how to pronounce words. They may find the approach useful as they can listen to the sounds of a word and begin to build up a picture of the sound/spelling relationship in English. They, too, will want to move on rapidly to acquire strategies for independent reading and will be able to transfer some of those strategies from their first language experience.

How to use the whole word method

- Select the words/sentences to be read.

- If you are writing them, write clearly with good spacing. Line breaking can be helpful, e.g.

- Present the words in context, e.g. with background or accompanying pictures, in a sentence, on a form.

- Read aloud to the student pointing to the words.

- Ask the student to read with you.

- Encourage the student to read alone. Help out when there is difficulty.

- Ask the student to pick out individual words. Start with any already known.

- Do not present too many new words at a time.

- In the early stages avoid teaching words that look similar at the same time.

- Remember that a student will need to see the word many times before instant recognition is achieved.

- Check understanding.

- Remember that a student may memorise words in a particular context or on a particular page and not be able to read them in another context.

- You can record the text (individual words to a whole reader) for a student to listen to and follow on her/his own. This is essential in open learning and useful for any student.

2. Using context and predicting

What does this mean?

This approach also aims at identifying whole words. It encourages a student to concentrate on the meaning of a whole sentence or text and to use the context of a word or sentence to predict or guess what a word is. The visual context (illustrations, surroundings) and a student's expectations of what a text is about are also important. At this level context is being used to read a word that is within a student's spoken competence.

Using context with EAL students

This technique can be used to some extent at all levels of reading but is most useful for students with a good command of spoken English. EAL students have more difficulty than first language speakers in using verbal context because their knowledge of structure and vocabulary may not be enough to be able to predict with any accuracy. Providing a visual context is helpful to all students.

However, at beginner and elementary level, a student is only expected to read what s/he can speak. Therefore, if a student reads a text based on spoken language practice, the vocabulary and topic will be familiar and s/he will be able to use this knowledge to predict words not read before. If the text is a well-known story or on a topic a student knows a lot about then again expectation or knowledge of what comes next will help the student read the text.

e.g.   She went to the shop to *buy* some eggs.

   You can pay by *cheque* or credit card.

A student who is unsure about 'buy' or 'cheque' could guess the words from the context, especially if s/he could also recognise the first sound 'b' or 'ch'.

This approach encourages students to use their own knowledge and experience and to become more independent when reading. EAL students, like **Omer,** who can read well in the first language but are beginners in English, will already use this skill and will be able to apply it to English within the limitations of their linguistic competence.

84

How to use context

- Prepare the student for the text before s/he starts to read by introducing it and talking about it.

- Encourage the student to look through the whole text first to get an idea of what it is about.

- Show the student how to use the layout, headlines, illustrations to help understanding.

- If there is a word or phrase a student cannot read encourage her/him to read the whole sentence, to look back at the previous sentence and to look forward to the next sentence.

A useful technique for developing the use of context is gap-filling. It is helpful, especially at beginner and elementary levels, to provide the missing words in random order to choose from or to give a choice of words for each gap of which only one is correct.

It is important to check that a student has predicted a word correctly. Sometimes it is not possible to guess a word from its context and other reading strategies have to be used.

3. Phonics

What are phonics?

A phonic approach to teaching reading is based on the relationship between a letter or a group of letters of the alphabet and a particular sound. A student may be able to sound out the letters in a word, blend them together and read the word, e.g.

s-a-t = sat, ch-a-t = chat.

There are many combinations of vowels and consonants which relate to particular sounds and rules governing the pronunciation of letters in certain combinations, e.g. The two sounds of 'g' in the word 'garage'.

Using phonics with EAL students

Phonics can help a student begin to tackle reading words independently. If a word is known to a student, then one or two phonic clues may be enough to identify the word combined with the use of context. It is usual to begin with the regular letter/sounds which match the phonic alphabet, e.g. consonant sounds at the beginning and end of words, followed by short vowel sounds in the middle of words such as 'man', 'pen'. Then other combinations can be introduced gradually.

Some points to bear in mind are:

- the most commonly used words in English (the 'key' words) are among the most irregular;

- English is not phonetically regular therefore there are a number of variations and exceptions to learn. This can be frustrating for all students whether they are first language speakers or speakers of other languages. EAL students whose first language is phonetically regular (i.e. the same letters always have the same sound) will approach the relationship between spelling and sound on the basis of previous learning and may find the irregularities particularly annoying;

- reading schemes based on phonics often involve reading lists of phonetically similar words which may be unfamiliar to the student and not very useful to know,

  e.g. *moon, hoop, boon, boom.*

  Sentences based on such words can be unnatural and not the sort of language a student needs to learn;

- phonics can lead to single letter analysis which hinders fluency and the use of context. In the effort to work out what a word is, the meaning can be lost. In addition learning a lot of rules creates a big memory load;

- some sounds may not exist in a student's first language. However, this affects listening comprehension and spelling more than reading. A student can see that *'ship'* and *'chip'* are different words and have a different meaning even if s/he cannot pronounce them differently;

- students like **Abubaka** and **Omer** will only need to concentrate on the differences between their first language and English – the letters that have different sound values, letter/sounds that do not exist in the first language, different letter/sound combinations. .

How to use phonics

- Use phonics when a student has built up recognition by the whole word method of a reasonably sized bank of words.

- Make sure a student who is used to a different writing system can discriminate individual letters and can relate upper and lower case letters. This can be done by matching exercises:

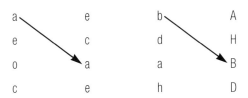

- Make sure a student knows the difference between the names (for spelling) and the sounds of the letters. It can help to make a picture dictionary focusing on the sound at the beginning of the word.

- Practise identifying the letters/letter groups in texts in different writing and print.

- Always use words within a student's spoken vocabulary and preferably ones the student can already read by sight.

- Group these words according to a particular letter or letter group/sound relationship. Group according to first, middle, or final sounds, e.g.

number	man	shop
nationality	hand	fish
name	back	shoe.

- As a student progresses you can introduce common letter groups:

  ee, ea, ou, or, er, ai, st, ing, able, tion, ight, etc.

  This helps a student move from looking at individual letters to the syllable. It is important here to show that the same spelling can have different sounds and group the words accordingly.

  head/bread but *meat/eat*

- Encourage a student to compare a new word with words already known where there are similarities.

- Show a student how to break longer words into syllables - na/tion/al/i/ty.

- Teach some useful rules, e.g. final 'e' lengthens the previous vowel sound – *name, made, ice.*

In conclusion it can be said that none of these approaches is totally satisfactory on its own and in many ways they complement each other. It is best to use a combined approach taking into account a student's preferences and previous learning and experience.

Reading aloud

Reading aloud is necessary with beginners so that you can listen to, check, and help them with their reading. However, it is important to encourage a student towards silent reading as soon as possible. If you feel fairly sure a student can cope with most of a text, it is often better to ask the student to read it to her/himself first. You can then check understanding and the ability to say and pronounce the words in the text by asking oral questions. You can spot check particular words and talk about any words that presented difficulties.

Some students may want to practise reading aloud for a specific purpose such as reading as story to a child. This involves a lot more than being able to decode and understand the text. It means reading clearly with understanding and expression.

Reading aloud can also be used as an assessment tool to identify the sort of reading difficulties a student may have. This process is called miscue analysis.

Using a dictionary

Teach a student from the very early stages to use a dictionary. This could be a bilingual dictionary or an English-English dictionary. There are useful bilingual picture dictionaries and learner's dictionaries at all levels.

Teaching basic writing skills

In the sequence of skills, writing follows reading. Students should only write what they can say, understand and read. Writing can reinforce speaking and reading practice especially if all the skills are approximately at the same level.

However, writing is by far the most difficult skill. Like speaking it is productive but tends to get less practice than speaking. It is less essential, people can manage without it or get someone else to do it.

As we saw at the beginning of the chapter it involves a lot of skills; the mechanics of writing, knowing the language to use (grammar mistakes become much more obvious when written down), spelling and punctuation. There may be a considerable gap between a student's level of speaking and reading and between the level of reading and writing.

1. Teaching handwriting

Students who are not able to read or write in the first language or whose first language uses a different script will need to learn the mechanics of writing.

- A student who has not written before will need to be shown how to sit and how to hold a pen/pencil.

- Writing patterns help a student get used to some of the shapes in the Roman script and the left to right movement.

- Teach a student to form the letters correctly in both upper and lower case using a clear simple print. Many students are familiar with capital letters and yet for reading and most writing tasks lower case letters are more important.

- Teach letters in groups according to the shape rather than alphabetical order, e.g.

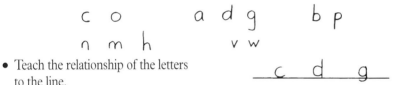

- Teach the relationship of the letters to the line.

- Teach the student how to form numbers.

- Give plenty of practice. Tracing or overwriting is helpful as well as copying.

- There is no need to teach a student to write all the letters at once. You can start with those that s/he needs to write for her/his name, etc.

2. Writing for communication purposes

Students with basic writing skills may have limited goals for writing, such as being able to fill in a simple form or write a note. Writing their name and address, telephone number and date of birth are essential skills for everyday life.

As a student gains confidence with writing or if a student can already use the Roman script you need to give plenty of guided practice in writing. This means that a student is not expected to write freely but follows a model or makes choices thus avoiding grammatical or spelling pitfalls. These techniques help to give a student confidence and reinforce correct language.

As well as developing writing skills for specific goals, written exercises can give useful reinforcement to spoken language practice and reading activities.

It is also useful to show the relationship between the spoken language and the written language. For example:

'Can I see the headteacher about Wendy, please?'

Dear Mrs Brown,

I would like to make an appointment to see you about my daughter, Wendy . . .

3. Guided writing activities

- Copying – name and address, messages and simple letters, sentences giving personal information, sentences written for reading practice, e.g. language experience.

- Selecting and copying sentences from a substitution table or from a model with multiple choice options.

- Writing jumbled words/sentences in the correct order.

- Gap filling – choosing words from a selection in random order.

- Writing a parallel paragraph based on a model substituting different information.

- It can be helpful for some students if instructions for an exercise and maybe some key words can be written in the first language. Others do not want this kind of support and prefer to make their own decisions about what to put into the first language.

- It can also be useful at times for a student to make notes in the first language on what s/he wants to write in English. However, it is better for a student to use language and structures s/he knows in English rather than try to translate language which is far in advance of the level of competence in English.

An example of a substitution table for writing a note.

I He She My son My daughter	can't	come go	to	work school class the meeting	tomorrow tonight on Friday

90

Further reading

Basic Skills Agency, 1995, *Read and Write Together: A Family Literacy Pack*.

Basic Skills Agency, 1991, *The Starter Pack*.

Buckton Chris, *Listening to Children Read*, Basic Skills, Spring 1996.

Byatt Janet and Davies Karen, *Why aren't there any ladies in the gents?* Social Sight vocabulary, Basic Skills, Dec/Jan 96/97.

Collected Writings, 1997, *A Song for Carrying Water and other stories from Somalia*, Gatehouse Books.

Gittins Rose, 1992, *An Introduction to Literacy Teaching*, Basic Skills Agency.

Hartley B, Viney P, *Basic Handwriting in English*, Longman.

Heaton J B, 1986, *Writing Through Pictures*, Longman.

Holt Julia and Phalke Shubra, 1995, *Real Lives Series 2, Asian Superstars*, The Basic Skills Agency.

LDA Learning Development Aids (social sight words in context).

Lindop C, Fisher D, 1988-89, *Something to Read, 1 and 2*, CUP.

Macmillan Folk Tales: a series of collections from 12 countries in South and East Asia.

Newcastle College et al, 1993, *Just the Job: Workshop Materials for Basic English*.

Newslink Readers, PRU, Leeds, 1986,1989.

Oliphant L et al, 1988, *Bilingual Toolkit*, National Extension College.

Our Lives Series, 1988-92, *Readers in English and Community Language*, Croydon English Language Scheme.

Spiegel Marina and Sunderland Helen, 1997, *Friends, Families and Folktales*, LLU.

Spirals, Stanley Thornes, (Basic skills readers).

The main English Language Teaching publishers all have series of graded readers e.g. Oxford Bookworms, Heinemann Guided Readers, Penguin Readers.

Dictionaries

Oxford Elementary Dictionary.

Oxford English Picture Dictionary.

Oxford Picture Dictionary: Dual Language Editions (available in five languages).

Oxford Photo Dictionary.

Longman Photo Dictionary.

8 | Developing Reading and Writing Skills – 2

This chapter looks at developing reading and writing skills at an intermediate to advanced level, identifying and correcting errors, and spelling.

Integrated language work in the four language skills can be done when a student can use all the skills at more or less the same level, even if that level is basic or elementary. When there is a gap, for example, between spoken skills and literacy skills then work can be done on the same topic but not at the same level. They are not fully integrated.

At intermediate level it should be possible to carry out integrated activities, e.g. listening and note-taking, discussing then writing on a topic, phoning about a problem and following up the phone call with a formal letter, etc. It also means that the sequence listening, speaking, reading, writing need not always be followed. Reading an article can be the stimulus for discussion. A story can be read and retold orally. New vocabulary can be learnt from written contexts.

Reading skills

1. Silent reading

At this stage fast silent reading should be encouraged. Reading aloud is necessary with beginners to check accuracy and pronunciation but it leads to slow word by word reading. You only need to read aloud when reading to someone else, like a child. You may find that some students have had little experience of silent reading and tend to mouth the words as they read. Fluency in reading can be improved by showing a student how to read in phrases or word groups, e.g.

Complete the application form/in black ink/and return/to the Personnel Officer/as soon as possible.

2. Understanding

A student who has become proficient at the decoding process may be able to read a text fluently without being able to understand it. It may be that the text is too full of unknown words and is therefore too difficult but it may be that the student finds it difficult to get meaning from the written word and needs guidance in developing understanding.

The purpose of reading

At the beginning of Chapter 7 some of the types of reading students may need to do were identified. What, in more detail, does this entail?

If **Abubaka** has to read a computer manual he has to cope with technical language. He also has to follow precise instructions. Scientific and technical language often uses the passive, e.g.

> The title bar is located at the top of the screen.
> Until your document is saved to a disk it is only in the computer memory.
> The document must be saved to store it permanently.

In reading a newspaper article **Omer** may not need to read everything with such care and may only need to take in the main points. He will have to cope with different styles and with idiomatic and colloquial language. He may have to differentiate fact from opinion.

In reading books for her course **Yasmin** may have to deal with a more formal style, skim to get the gist and select the parts that require more thorough study. Again she will need to distinguish fact from opinion. She will have to select the main points for note-taking and summarising.

Developing understanding

You need to set some tasks to develop a student's reading skills and understanding of a text. Pre-reading questions can give a focus to the reading. Encourage a student to look at layout, illustrations, headings, titles and contents pages to predict what a text or book is about. Suggest the student reads through the whole text before starting on the tasks.

Although a student is encouraged to try using context to work out the meaning of new words it is nevertheless very important for a student to develop good dictionary skills. It is a good idea to practise using an English/English dictionary as well as a bilingual dictionary. A good learner's dictionary gives examples and shows the usage of words. Students can also use dictionaries to find out how a word is pronounced.

There are many techniques for developing understanding such as open and multiple choice questions, true/false statements, matching activities, sequencing, summarising, information transfer, cloze and other gap filling exercises.

Writing skills

1. Handwriting

If a student still uses print you could encourage her/him to develop a cursive (joined up) writing style. This will help the student write more quickly and fluently. On the other hand a student may write quickly but untidily. Handwriting practice in either case is useful.

2. Free writing

In Chapter 7 some ideas for guided writing were presented. At intermediate level a student needs to be able to write independently, but it is a big jump from guided to free writing.

You can help a student with written work by careful preparation. Whether the task is a letter, an assignment for a training or college course or a piece of creative writing, the procedure is the same.

(a) Clarify the purpose of the letter, the meaning of the title of the assignment.

(b) Discuss what should go in it. The student can jot down ideas in English or the first language.

(c) Check the student has got all the necessary information.

(d) Plan the framework, the sequence of ideas.

(e) Discuss the language involved. What functions, grammar, style need to be used? For example: Letter – asking for information, complaining, requesting actions. Assignment – describing, narrating, comparing, discussing issues. Who is the reader? Should the style be formal or informal?

(f) The student writes a draft.

(g) Encourage the student to proof-read looking for grammatical errors, checking spelling and punctuation.

(h) You read it and draw attention to any remaining errors. Discuss layout and paragraphing.

Look at these titles and choose the functions and tenses from the lists that you would use in each piece of writing. You may use more than one for each.		
Title	*Function*	*Tenses*
• The good and bad effects of TV on children.		
• Select and describe a toy suitable for a three year old.		
• How to make a paper lantern.		
• My childhood.		
Functions: describing your experiences, describing an object, giving opinions, comparing and contrasting, giving reasons, giving instructions.		
Tenses: present simple, past simple, used to, imperative, modals (should/ought to/must, etc.).		

(Based on Self Access Worksheets, National Extension College)

(i) The student corrects and writes the final version.

To help a student like **Yasmin** become aware of the functions and tenses required for different types of writing you could do an exercise like the one at the bottom of the previous page.

3. Identifying writing needs

Just as you identified a student's language needs by listening to her/his spoken English so you should identify needs based on a student's writing.

(a) What to look out for?

(i) Overall impression – is the communication successful?

(ii) Organisation – of ideas, of sentences and paragraphs

(iii) Grammar – tenses, articles, plurals, etc.

(iv) Word Order

(v) Punctuation

(vi) Spelling

(vii) Vocabulary

(viii) Style

(ix) Handwriting

Here is an example of a student's writing with some comments.

This student is from East Africa. He speaks and writes Gujerati. He describes his work experience and some of the difficulties he had in getting work in Britain.

Comments

(i) *Overall impression*
Successful – although there are errors there is no real difficulty in understanding the sequence of events described.
Unsuccessful – some re-reading necessary to sort out sentences.

(ii) *Organisation*
Successful – chronological order linking words like 'after that', 'and', 'but', 'so'.
Unsuccessful – sentence division and paragraphs.

(iii) *Grammar*
Successful – plurals mainly correct; prepositions – 'to East Africa', 'to Bradford', one or two correct verb forms.
Unsuccessful – use of past tense – uses present tense 'I start', 'I work' or inserts 'am', e.g. 'I am work'. Some prepositions 'in London' omission of '(at)' 'Nyanza oil mills'.

(iv) *Word order* – mainly correct.

(v) *Punctuation*
Successful – capital letters for names of places.
Unsuccessful – lack of capitals and full-stops to show sentence division. Wrong use of 's'.

(vi) *Spelling* – mainly successful, a few words spelt as pronounced – 'finest', 'operet', 'masin'.

(vii) *Vocabulary* – adequate but a bit repetitive.

(viii) *Style* – not applicable.

(ix) *Handwriting* – neat and legible. 'a', 'o', 'u' not always clearly distinguished. Would flow better if joined.

(b) Follow up exercises

When you have done such an analysis you need to encourage the student by pointing out the successful parts. Then decide with the student what areas are the most important to concentrate on.

In this case the tutor and student decided to work on simple past tense forms and sentence division.

(c) Causes of errors

It is useful to consider why a student makes certain mistakes. They may be caused by first language influence or a partially learnt rule. A student who has acquired the language informally may not have heard certain features such as the 'ed' past tense ending or the 'm' in 'I'm going' and will not be aware of these differences. Sometimes false analogies are made. In the previous example the student may never have heard the past tense ending 'ed'. He may insert 'am' on analogy with 'I am going'.

He has learnt 's for possession and extended the rule to plural – s as well.

He pronounces the 'sh' sound as 's' which affects his spelling.

Gujerati does not have capital letters so making a distinction between the upper and lower case has to be learnt.

(d) Correcting a student's written work

Earlier in this chapter the importance of helping a student become aware of language and of proof-reading written work for mistakes was mentioned. However s/he can only correct things s/he knows about.

There are different opinions about the extent to which written work should be corrected. Should every mistake or only the most important mistakes be corrected? The answer perhaps depends on the level of the student, the number of errors and the purpose of the writing.

If an advanced student makes a few mistakes it would seem sensible to point them all out. On the other hand, if there are a lot of mistakes, it would be disheartening to deal with them all.

Rather than write in corrected forms it is better to underline the errors and see if the student can correct any of the mistakes. Students often can when the mistake is pointed out to them.

You can indicate the kind of error by using a code, e.g. P = punctuation, WO = word order, Sp = spelling, G = grammar, Voc. = vocabulary (you will need to teach a student what you mean by these terms).

If a student cannot correct the mistake give an example or a simple explanation to help.

Ask the student to write down the corrected words or sentences. This reinforces the correct forms and helps the student remember them another time.

Devise some exercises on the priority areas as follow up work.

Opposite is an example of a piece of corrected writing: a student describes his work in Pakistan.

4. Spelling

In spelling a student has to try to relate the sound of a word to a written form. Therefore a student's pronunciation as a result of sound differences between the first language and English may lead to difficulties. In addition unstressed sounds are not easily heard and may be omitted.

Just as with learning to read, students whose first language is written phonetically may find the irregularities and variations of English spelling puzzling and irritating.

Voc Sp   I belong to / from country Pakistan. I got a degree
G   to B.Com from Karachi college(at) Pakistan
              In Pakistan in 89 was working in Pakistan
G steel mill Karachi: My Joba is Instrument
G. Sp. operator. I got and training does in chemical
   Instrument operator.

Check your spelling in a dictionary
Note: I belong to - - - - -
         I come from - - - - -
         I did a course ⎫ for instrument operators,
         got on a course ⎭ in instrument operating.

However, there are some useful rules and an awareness of these and common letter groups can help a student tackle words s/he is not sure of.

It is important that words used for spelling activities, like those used in phonic exercises, should be known to a student. Exercises for native English speakers may use uncommon words because they fit into a particular pattern. EAL students may not have the same difficulties as some native English speakers. For example, the confusion between *where* and *wear*, *here* and *hear* may not occur because the words were learnt according to their meaning and the appropriate spelling associated with them. They are not connected in the student's mind.

There are a variety of strategies for remembering spelling.

(a) Look/cover/write/check. This procedure helps imprint the spelling on the memory.

(b) Memorising a difficult spelling by
   – a saying or a rhyme, e.g. 'i' before 'e' except after 'c'
   – saying a word as it is spelled, e.g. Wed/nes/day.

(c) Find and match helps recognition of what looks right or wrong.

	A	B	C	D
HEIGHT	heigt	height	heigth	hieght

(d) Complete the word. This can focus on particular parts of the word or each letter in turn, e.g. Thursday/Th-rsday/T-ursday.

98

(e) Group words with the same sound and spelling, i.e. station/nation/relation.

(f) See if a student can deduce the rule.

took	week	back	book	sock	clock

(g) Show the range of possible spellings for a sound.

e.g. The long sound i: s<u>ee</u>,   <u>ea</u>t,   thi<u>e</u>f,   th<u>e</u>se.

The 'sh' sound in word endings   sta<u>ti</u>on,   exten<u>si</u>on,   spe<u>ci</u>al.

(h) Word jigsaws   to   ing

morn   noon

after   day

(i) Wordbuilding:

– being aware of prefixes and suffixes;

un-   im-   dis-   -ful   -able   -ment

– related words help especially where there are sound changes

relative/relation   revision/revise.

5. Other writing activities

(a) Dictation
This may seem an old-fashioned exercise but it can give useful practise in relating the sounds and structure of the spoken language to the spelling and punctuation needed for the written. It should be based on language already familiar to a student.

(b) Note-taking
This is an important skill for a student like **Yasmin**. Notes can be taken from a book or a talk or lecture. Listening and note-taking is likely to be the more difficult. As with dictation a student has to relate the spoken language to the written as well as to select and organise the information.

A student may find it helpful to take some notes in the first language even though it means doing an instant translation.

(c) Creative writing

These chapters have concentrated on practical writing needs – the essentials. These will be all many students can cope with or want to do. Some students, however, may enjoy trying their hand at creative writing. Quite often ideas for this may come out of a discussion topic or a reading text. Just as with any other sort of writing, talk about the topic first to get the ideas going. If a student finds it easier to talk than write you could record her/his ideas and then help her/him to write them down.

Some possible themes and starting points are: customs and traditions, memories, people, feelings, TV programmes, a newspaper article, pictures/cartoons, a prompt sheet of opinions, an opening sentence.

6. Word processors and computers

If these are available some students may enjoy and find it useful to develop writing skills using a word processor. This frees students from the mechanics of handwriting, enables them to correct and change what they have written easily and at the same time teaches a new and useful skill. Language activities and spelling games on computer may seem more fun than paper and pencil ones.

See Chapter 10 for more details on using computers and wordprocessors.

7. Dyslexia

In some cases students may have difficulties with reading and writing because they are dyslexic. However, dyslexia needs careful diagnosis as there can be a variety of reasons for a language student's literacy problems. Some useful references are listed in the Further Reading section.

Further reading

Baker Christine, 1996, *Practise your CV Writing*, Avanti.

Buckmaster Erica, 1986, *Self Access Worksheets Books 1 and 2*, Photocopiable, National Extension College.

Doff A, (series Ed.) 1991, *Cambridge Skills for Fluency: Reading*, Books 1-4, Cambridge University Press.

Doff A, (series Ed.) 1991-93, *Cambridge Skills for Fluency: Writing*, Books 1-4, Cambridge University Press.

Grellet F, 1981, *Developing Reading Skills*, Cambridge University Press (for teachers).

Langer Jennifer, 1997, *Intermediate ESOL – Examining the System in Britain*, Jennifer Langer PO Box 15123 London NW11 OWH.

Help Yourself to English, 1989, a self-study series for EAL students with good reading skills who want to improve their grammatical and functional accuracy, Books 1 and 2: Social context – elementary to intermediate, Books 3 and 4: Vocational context – intermediate, Book 5: Academic context – up to pre-GCSE level, Photocopiable, National Extension College.

Leach R, 1989, *Writing a CV,* National Extension College.

Matthews Bob, 1988, *Language Power, Communication skills for a multi-racial society,* National Extension College, Photocopiable.

Redman Stuart, 1997, *English Vocabulary In Use: Pre-intermediate and Intermediate,* Cambridge University Press.

Redman Stuart, Ellis Robert et al, 1997, *A Way with Words, Resource Packs 1 and 2:* Vocabulary Practice Activities (Photocopiable), Cambridge University Press.

Smith Alistair, 1990, *Language Guidelines: Developing reading, writing and oral skills across the curriculum,* Hodder and Stoughton.

Wright Pat, *Miscue Analysis,* Basic Skills June/July 1996.

Grammar

Buckmaster Erica, 1990, *Self Access Grammar,* National Extension College.

Eastwood John, 1992, *Oxford Practice Grammar (with answers),* Oxford University Press.

Jackson A and A, *Grammar Worksheets,* Prentice Hall Europe ELT (Self access).

Murphy R, 1985, *English Grammar in Use (with answers),* Cambridge University Press, (Intermediate).

Murphy R, 1990, *Essential Grammar in Use (with answers),* Cambridge University Press, (Elementary).

Murphy R, 1997, *Essential Grammar in Use: a self study reference and practice book,* Cambridge University Press.

Rinvolucri Mario and Davis Paul, 1995, *More Grammar Games,* Cambridge University Press.

Swan M and Walter C, 1996, *How English Works, A Grammar Practice Book,* Oxford University Press.

Ur Penny, 1988, *Grammar Practice Activities: a practical guide for teachers,* Cambridge University Press.

Walker E, Elsworth S, *Grammar Practice for Elementary Students,* Longman.

Spelling

Abell Sue, 1994, *Helping Adults to Spell,* Basic Skills Agency.

Baker Christine, 1994, *Practice your Spelling,* Avanti.

Basic Skills Agency, 1994, *Spelling Pack.*

Digby C, Myers J, 1993, *Making Sense of Spelling and Pronunciation,* Prentice Hall Europe ELT.

Hulley Jan, 1991, *Self Access Spelling,* Photocopiable, National Extension College.

Pratley Rhiannedd, 1988, *Spelling It Out*, BBC.

Dyslexia

Klein Cynthia, 1993, *Diagnosing Dyslexia*, Basic Skills Agency.

Sunderland Helen, Klein Cynthia, Savinson Rosemary, Partridge Tracy, 1997, *Dyslexia and the Bilingual Learner*, Language and Literacy Unit.

Dictionaries

BBC English Dictionary

Collins Cobuild English Dictionary

Longman Active Study Dictionary

Longman Dictionary of English Language and Culture

Oxford Advanced Learner's Dictionary

Oxford Students Dictionary

English for study and vocational purposes

Barr Vivien and Fletcher Clare, 1984, *English for Driving*, National Extension College.

Coyne Philip, 1996, *Driving for Life: The Complete Course for the Driving Theory Test*, National Extension College.

Heaton Brian and Dunmore Don, 1992, *Learning to Study in English*, Macmillan.

Joint Initiative, 1992, *Food Hygiene Work Pack*, Avanti.

Joint Initiative, 1994, *Health and Safety Work Pack*, Avanti.

Jones-Macziola S, White G, 1993, *Getting Ahead: A Communicative Skills Course for Business English*, Cambridge University Press.

Simpson Ann, Furnborough Peter, 1993, *Angrezi Boal-Chaal, (Bilingual Video and Workbooks)*, Equality at Work, Blackburn College, Feilden St., Blackburn BB2 1LH.

9 | Lesson Planning, Record Keeping and Evaluation

This chapter returns to the point left in Chapter 4 where an outline programme had been planned for a specified number of lessons. This chapter looks at aspects of managing learning, and examines ways of planning an individual lesson, keeping records and evaluating learning.

1. Managing learning

a) The role of the teacher

Whether you are working 1:1 or in a group you will assume different roles at different times according to the learning style and the type of activity.

The emphasis in teaching EAL should be on negotiated learning and a partnership between the teacher and the student. Nevertheless, in planning a programme, planning lessons and activities, you have a major role as an organiser of the student's learning. The student may contribute to a greater or lesser degree to this. Some regularly bring along their own materials to work on. When you are teaching your role can range from being in tight control of the language and the activity to facilitating the activity and leaving the student to carry it out independently.

When you present new language and give controlled practice, the activities are teacher-centred and you are in control of the learning. When you check on a student's learning you are an assessor. If you work with a group and set up pair or small group work where students work together you are more of a facilitator. As you monitor the activities you may also prompt students to help the activity along or become a participant. In a 1:1 situation you have to become a participant to give the student practice in communicative activities such as question and answer, dialogues and role-play. Where students work more independently on individual programmes and in Open Learning the teacher's role is more often that of a facilitator and as a resource to be consulted as necessary.

b) Helping students to work independently

Whatever the style of delivery, it is important to encourage students towards being independent in their learning. Many students will look to you to organise everything and will not be familiar with the idea that they can take control of their own learning. This is an approach to learning that has to be learnt.

There can be a tendency in 1:1 teaching to work alongside the student all the time. This can be very intensive and it is a good idea to plan some activities where you can fade into the background and let the student work by her/himself. You can also suggest activities to do and create materials for the student to use when you are not there.

In groups it is important to include individual and small group activities where students have control of their own learning. This is also a good way of catering for individual needs that are not met by the group programme.

Strategies to promote learner independence

- Materials can be adapted for students to use without a teacher. They need to have clear, simple instructions in English and/or their first language. These can be written or taped. Answers should also be provided for self-checking. Self-access worksheets need to be clearly labelled with the topic, language item and level and to be easily accessible to the student, for instance in browser files or magazine boxes on open shelves.

- Audio tapes can be prepared which explain a particular language item, practise language in a drill or dialogue, develop listening skills or deal with aspects of pronunciation. Tapes can be accompanied by worksheets. Well-prepared material like this allows students to work at their own pace rather than that of the group or teacher, to listen to different accents and to check on their own progress.

- Wherever possible students should be given access to computers which they can use as word processors or use commercially or locally developed programs to work on grammar, vocabulary or spelling. There are more details on using new technology in Chapter 10.

- As well as using the first language for explanations and instructions you can encourage students to use their first language skills in a constructive way. They can compile a personal bilingual dictionary or transcribe English words into the first language writing system as a guide to pronunciation.

- Students should be encouraged to take advantage of, or create, opportunities to use English outside the class. You could begin by role playing situations such as joining the library, or obtaining information from an agency or place of entertainment, and sending students out to undertake specific tasks in pairs or individually. News items discussed in class could be followed up at home using task sheets, or students could undertake projects which require finding out information from a variety of sources and making oral presentations in class.

c) Working with groups

Most EAL teaching takes place in groups. This is to be expected given the communicative nature of learning a language. Therefore, although this book focuses on meeting the needs of the individual student, it is important to consider some strategies for working in groups. You may be a group teacher, or you may work with a group teacher supporting individuals or small groups, or facilitating group activities. Even if you usually work 1:1 it could be beneficial at times to get together with other family members or other students at a centre for communicative activities.

In Chapter 4 we considered planning for a group and in this section we shall look at some approaches to managing a group.

i) Teaching the group as a whole

This approach is used in particular when you are presenting new material, eliciting language and ideas, doing controlled practice and setting up activities. At this stage the students need to listen to a good model and you want to check for accurate reproduction. One way of practising is choral repetition. It can also give confidence to shy students. On the other hand it can be difficult to get everyone speaking together or to hear the individual responses. You could ask students to speak in turn but this can be time consuming and each student will only have a few opportunities to speak. It can also put off a student who lacks confidence. It is important not to overuse any one technique and to check understanding in different ways and at different stages in a session. All the skills can be practised as a whole group especially if the students are at a similar level.

ii) Working in pairs

This approach is ideal for question and answer practice, dialogues and other communicative activities. Reading and writing tasks can also be carried out in pairs. Pairwork enables the students to get plenty of practice at the risk of losing accuracy. It is important to monitor the pairs and make sure everyone knows what to do. You can demonstrate the activity first with one of the students.

Thought needs to be given to how students are paired and their preferences taken into consideration. Women and men may not wish to work together; friends may like to work with each other but it might not be a good idea always to work with the same person. Sometimes it is helpful for individuals who share a language to be paired to give mutual support, but there are advantages in being with someone who speaks a different language as this encourages them to make greater efforts to communicate in English. Similarly a strong and weak student may work together so the one can help the other, but is important that the more advanced student does not feel used. Many students prefer to be paired according to level so that they can work at the same pace. There are no hard and fast rules and you will have to be sensitive to students' needs and wishes.

iii) Small groups of 3-5 students

This is a good approach for roleplay, discussions and task-based activities. It can give a lot of speaking practice and be more varied and less intense than pair work. The factors considered above for forming pairs apply equally to small groups. You also need to be careful about one or two students dominating a group and, in monolingual groups, overuse of the first language. It is helpful to use the first language for explanations, to translate new vocabulary and so on, but not to carry out a task which is meant to give practice in English.

Group work is essential in mixed level classes. It is often possible for students at different levels to work on the same topic and to do some spoken practice as a whole group. The students can then break up into small groups according to level and to do further oral work or reading and writing activities. Listening can also be done in small groups as long as you have headphones and junction boxes for cassette recorders.

Small group work involves a lot of preparation and organisation even if there is more than one teacher with the group. The activities need to be clearly explained and the materials need clear instructions so that students can get on by themselves while you circulate round the other groups.

(iv) Working individually

The emphasis has been on interactive practice but at times students need to work quietly on their own at their own pace, irrespective of whether they are all doing the same exercise or doing different work according to individual needs.

2. Planning a lesson

You will already have an outline of what you plan to do in the learning programme. Now you need to expand this into a detailed session plan. The length of the lesson may vary but, in general, sessions are usually one and a half or two hours.

Your centre may have a lesson planning format, but if not you could use one like the example on page 43 or devise your own. However, the following elements should be included:

a) aims and objectives

b) context

c) content in terms of language and skills

d) methods and activities

e) stages of the lesson

f) timing

g) resources and equipment.

a) Aims and objectives

The aim of the lesson defines in broad terms what you plan to achieve, while the objectives give a more detailed breakdown of what the student will do during the lesson.

You can aim to revise/introduce/teach/practise/develop or assess language. Remember that language learning is accumulative and that you need to build on a student's existing skills. Constant practice and revision is necessary for the language learnt to be retained. In deciding on your aims consider:

- what the student already knows;

- how this lesson links with the previous lesson and fits into the overall plan;

- how much you can reasonably do in the time allowed. This is something that is difficult to gauge at first but gets easier with experience.

The lesson may focus on:

- a particular skill, e.g. listening

- a particular context, e.g. the language and vocabulary needed for using computers

- a grammatical item, e.g. the use of "some" and "any"

- a function, e.g. making comparisons.

Thus the aims and objectives of Session 1 of **Ladda's** programme on page 45 could be –

Aims:	To describe a work routine
	To greet and welcome customers
Objectives:	To practise the present simple tense to describe routines
	To use time phrases correctly
	To greet customers
	To ask for information
	To make polite requests
	To improve pronunciation, especially days of week and numbers 1–12.

Objectives can also be described in terms of outcomes i.e. what the student will have achieved by the end of the lesson. For example, the student will have practised the present simple to describe routines.

b) Context
This is the topic or the situation in which the language is used, such as a restaurant, applying for a job, travel.

c) Content – language and skills
In deciding on your aims and objectives you will already have identified the type of language to work on and the skills to practise. You need to consider these in more detail.

- Is there a sensible ratio of new items to known items? Apart from the first few lessons with a beginner a general rule is not more than 20% new. However, you may not know exactly what is new for the student as you are constantly discovering what a student knows.

- Could the items cause confusion if taught together? e.g. in/on, I worked/I have worked.

- Consider how the language items are really used in the chosen contexts. Make sure your examples are accurate and natural.

- Decide which language skills (i.e. listening, speaking, reading, writing) are needed in the context.

- Decide what proportion of the time will be spent on the different skills.

d) Methods and activities
- Decide on the methods you are going to use.

- Consider the purpose of the activities e.g. accuracy/fluency, listening for gist/detail.

- Consider how to demonstrate or explain the purpose of the activities and how to do them.

- Think about what you are going to do and what the student or students are going to do. Don't talk too much yourself. Provide plenty of opportunity for the student to practise.

- Think about how you are going to organise the activities and which activities the student could do independently.

- Consider whether there is enough variety in the lesson.

e) Stages of the lesson

You need to sequence the activities and think how one can lead into the next. The lesson needs to have shape: a clear introduction, development and a rounding off at the end. A lesson should include some, if not all of the following stages:

- introduction stating aims;

- recap – to link with previous work;

- lead into activities;

- presentation of new items;

- eliciting known language;

- practice;

- development – this can be from controlled practice to freer practice, from the general to the specific or from gist to detail, from spoken to written;

- revision and consolidation;

- assessment – consider how you are going to check understanding and learning;

- evaluation.

f) Timing

- Decide how long you need to spend on each activity. You need to take more time when working on new material but you can move at a faster pace when practising known language.

g) Resources

- Decide on the materials and equipment you are going to use. Make sure the materials are at the right level and appropriate and that you know how to use the equipment.

3. Assessing and evaluating

As the lesson proceeds make a mental note of or jot down the things that cause difficulty and will need more work and the things that were done successfully. Identify any new learning needs that arise during the lesson.

LESSON PLAN		Student: OMER		Tutor:	Date:	Time:

Aim(s): To describe past experiences
To fill in an application form

Objectives: 1) To put events in chronological order
2) To use the past simple accurately
3) To use time phrases and sequence words
4) To give reasons
5) To complete part of an application form.

Time	Context	Language/Skills	Method/Activity	Resources	Evaluation
1) 10 mins	Job applications	Listening, checking understanding	1) Recap on previous work. Introduce and explain tasks.		
2) 15 mins		Listening and sequencing. Dates and time phrases.	2) Play tape of person describing education and work experience. Student puts items in correct order on worksheet and fills in dates.	Cassette player, taped description. Worksheet	
3) 10 mins		Identifying past tenses, regular and irregular. From — to —,	3) S. reads tapescript and underlines past tenses, time phrases and sequence words.	Tapescript. Worksheet	
4) 20 mins		for - years, after, before, then, next. Speaking — using the language.	4) S. prepares oral description of an experience (could record on tape.) Listen and give feedback.	Checklist of irregular past tenses	
5) 10 mins		Writing information.	5) S. fills in appropriate sections on an application form.	Application form.	
6) 15 mins		Giving reasons eg. I left the camning. To get more experience. Speaking and writing.	6) Discuss reasons for leaving jobs and complete form.	Checklist of possible reasons (Topics + Skills Unit 8)	
7) 5 mins		Giving opinions.	7) Evaluate session and fill in record sheet.	Wall record sheet.	

At the end of the lesson allow a little more time to evaluate the lesson with the student:

- what was easy/difficult;

- what needs more practice;

- what was interesting/boring, etc.

After the lesson jot down how you felt about it. Were the aims achieved? What went well/badly? Was the level all right? Was the student interested and motivated? Was progress made? What could have been done to improve the lesson?

4. Some other points to remember

- Correct what is important without over-correcting.

- Adjust your pace to what is necessary for a student. Move faster when the material is familiar, slower when it is new. If a student finds something easy, move on quickly, if difficult, slow up and go over it again and give more practice.

- Don't feel you have to stick exactly to your lesson plan.

- Be flexible. If a student comes along with something s/he needs to do straight away, have an impromptu lesson and leave your planned lesson for another time. An example might be a letter the student has received, does not understand, and has to reply to. Make sure, however, that you do not just do the task for her/him. Make it into a teaching situation.

There is an example of a lesson plan on page 110.

Keeping a record

Although you will have your lesson plans and the student will have a file of work, it is useful to keep a record sheet which summarises the work done in each lesson and which has space for student and tutor comments. These can be part of the process of ongoing assessment and evaluation. Items which need more practice and those which have been satisfactorily carried out can be noted and new learning needs recorded. The record sheet can be filled in by the student and/or yourself. You will be able to see at a glance what a student has achieved.

Reviewing progress

It is important to review progress at regular intervals. This may be after a certain number of hours tuition, for example 40 hours, or half-way through and at the end of a short course.

Reviewing helps a student and tutor to see that progress has been made. Any difficulties a student has with the learning programme can be cleared up. You can plan the next stage of learning or decide on future action.

1. How to review progress

There are a number of ways of reviewing and assessing progress. You would need to choose one that is appropriate for a student and her/his purpose in learning English.

Here are some suggestions:

- observation by the tutor;
- discussion between student and tutor;
- checklist of language practised – student and tutor evaluate progress according to a scale, e.g. a little, quite a lot, a lot;
- list of competences – tick and date when accomplished;
- tasks set for assessment;
- tests.

2. Evidence

A student may feel that s/he is now more confident in using the language needed for a particular context and is able to carry out a task satisfactorily. However, it is not enough just to say so. There must be evidence of achievement. This may take several forms. It could be:

- samples of work in a student's file. These may clearly show progression. For this reason it is important that they are *dated*;
- recordings of spoken language;
- comments by other people on a student's usage of the language;
- instances of a student using the language outside the classroom.

Look back to the checklist on page 18 for the competences a student could work towards that should be identified in assessment.

Accreditation

Many students may want to have their learning accredited by gaining a nationally recognised certificate. In addition, funders of EAL provision require accreditation as a measure of achievement. Quality standards such as the Basic Skills Agency Quality Mark emphasise the importance of measuring the effectiveness of learning programmes and have set targets to be met, e.g. 80% of students to make measurable progress, 75% of students taking accreditation to achieve their qualification. There are a number of possibilities and different ones will suit different students. Therefore you need to be familiar with the range of accreditation available to be able to help a student to select what is most appropriate for him/her.

PROGRESS REVIEW

Name: _____Omer_____ Date: _____

Tutor: _____

GOAL: To practise the English for getting a job				
WHAT I HAVE DONE	TICK ✓	I NEED A LOT MORE PRACTICE	I HAVE MADE SOME PROGRESS BUT I NEED MORE PRACTICE	I CAN DO THIS WELL
Reading job adverts				✓
Phoning/writing for application forms				✓
Writing a CV			✓	
Writing a letter of application			✓	
Filling in an application form			✓	
Practising interviews		✓		

What I want to do next:

Practise more interviews
Learn the English for particular jobs.

These are some of the Certificates offered.

1. ESOL/EAL

The Royal Society of Arts Examining Board offers the Profile Certificate in ESOL. This is based on continuous assessment. Students can enter for one or all of the four language skills and can obtain a certificate for any number of profile sentences achieved. Students cannot enter singly. The course must be approved by the RSA.

Pitman Qualifications offer ESOL examinations in listening, reading and writing skills and separate tests in spoken ESOL at five levels. The levels are related to the English Speaking Union levels. The examinations are functional in approach and flexible to administer. Centres can enter students on demand at three weeks notice. Pitman also offers an examination in English for Business Communications at 3 levels.

The University of London Examinations and Assessment Council (ULEAC) offers a Certificate of Attainment in English in all four language skills at 6 levels.

CENTRA has a test in English Language Skills at basic and intermediate levels suitable for students interested in studying engineering and science and the Northern Examinations and Assessment Board (NEAB) offers the University Entrance Test in English for Speakers of Other Languages which is also more appropriate for those wanting to study the sciences.

Courses can also be accredited through the Open College Federation.

2.EFL

There is a wide range of EFL examinations offered by the Royal Society of Arts (RSA) and The University of Cambridge Local Examinations Syndicate (UCLES) from basic to advanced.

3. Basic Skills

These certificates are not specifically for EAL students.

City and Guilds – Communication Skills (Wordpower) 3793
This is a competence based form of assessment in which a student builds up a portfolio of evidence of her/his skills. This style is consistent with the framework for National Vocational Qualifications (NVQ), which are used for education and training for adults. It is offered at four levels: Entry, Levels l, 2 and 3. It includes reading, writing and oral communication skills. Wordpower assesses communication skills in everyday life situations. To assist a student to achieve the competence you would need to assess his/her strengths and weaknesses in that situation, and devise an appropriate learning programme.

The London Chamber of Commerce and Industry Examinations Board (LCCIEB) also offers Wordpower accreditation.

Open College of the North West – Foundation Accreditation in Maths and English (FAME) This is a competence based Certificate similar to Wordpower. It offers a basic level called Start Up, a Foundation programme at three levels which equate to Level 1 of the National Credit Framework, and a Foundation Programme at Level 4 which equates to Level 2.

Associated Examining Board (AEB) – Achievement Tests in Literacy Levels 1, 2 and 3 Reading and writing skills. Assessment by examination whenever a group of students is ready. No pass or fail.

4. Key Skills

Students studying for General National Vocational Qualifications(GNVQ) have to achieve Key Skills accreditation. Key Skills are offered at five levels in the following areas: Communication, Application of Number, Information Technology, Working with Others and Improving Own Learning and Performance. They are generic skills which are required irrespective of the vocational area. The first three are compulsory for GNVQs and are also often included in NVQ and A Level courses. Key Skills can also be assessed separately. City and Guilds, the London Chamber of Commerce and Industry and the Royal Society of Arts all offer Key Skills NVQ Units. The RSA also offers NVQ (EFL) Units at 3 levels for students who need to use English in a vocational context and whose first language is not English.

It is relevant to take Key Skills into consideration, particularly Communication Key Skills when planning programmes for EAL students who are interested in progressing to vocational training.

You need to consider the following points when assisting a student to select an appropriate form of accreditation.

- Does it address the student's needs and aspirations?

- Can it be used to accredit language competences being developed in different contexts?

- Can it be used to accredit a student's existing competence in English?

- Can the student undertake it at any time of the year?

- Is it suitable for the student's learning situation, e.g. in a group, 1:1 basis with a tutor, flexible drop-in workshop, as part of another course of training.

- Does it provide a route to other qualifications?

- Will it be widely recognised? e.g. a certificate specially designed for EFL or EAL/ESOL may not have the same status as those designed for native speakers.

Further reading

Basic Skills Agency, 1997, *Assessing Progress in Basic Skills: Literacy.*

Basic Skills Agency, 1997, *Initial Assessment: an assessment test for reading, writing and maths.*

Basic Skills Agency, 1992, *Basic Skills Assessment Pack.*

Crofts Sally, 1992, *ESOL Wordpower and Accreditation,* Basic Skills Agency Newsletter No.44, Winter.

English Speaking Union, West R and Walsh G, 1993, English Language Examinations From Britain (A chart showing the examinations offered by members of the Association of British ESOL Examining Boards).

Gladstone Carol and Randall Hillary, 1997, *Key Words,* National Extension College, (Photocopiable materials for Wordpower and Key Skills).

Chanda Noyona and Callachand Bibi, 1997/8, *Accreditation in Literacy/Numeracy/ESOL and Key Skills,* Language and Literacy Unit.

O'Dell F, 1991, *Pitman Examinations ESOL Practice Tests,* Longman.

Pill Liz, 1994, *Using the Basic Skills Standards for ESOL,* Basic Skills Agency.

Scottish Community Education Council, 1992, *Assessment and Evaluation.*

Teacher Training

Gower R and Walter S, 1995, *Teaching Practice Handbook,* Heinemann.

Harmer Jeremy, 1991, *The Practice of English Language Teaching,* Longman.

Harmer Jeremy, 1998, *How to Teach English,* Longman.

Sunderland Helen and Cottington Helen, 1996, *The Teacher's Video: An ESOL Tutor Training Resource,* Language and Literacy Unit.

10 | Resources

This chapter looks at selecting and adapting resources, writing worksheets and using equipment.

The range of materials

The references in previous chapters show that there is a considerable range of resources that can be used by EAL tutors and students. There are, however, very few resources written specifically for EAL learners.

There are some course materials such as *Chart your Course in English* (Wilkins and Spiegel) and *Intermediate English – Examining the System in Britain* (Langer). *Help Yourself to English* (Leach et al, National Extension College) is an open learning course for good speakers who want to improve their literacy skills, grammatical accuracy and study skills. There are also a number of readers at different levels, often based on students' own writing, and sometimes available in both English and community languages e.g. *Asian Superstars* (Basic Skills Agency), *Our Experience* (Gatehouse), *Our Lives* series (Croydon) and *Friends, Families and Folktales* (Language and Literacy Unit).

A few materials are bilingual to some extent e.g. *English for Driving* and the *Bilingual Toolkit* (National Extension College) and *Angrezi Boal-Chaal* (Equality at Work, Blackburn College). Using bilingual materials gives value to a student's language and previous learning. It can make understanding easier and enable a student to work independently. Discuss with a student whether s/he wants to use such materials. S/he may not think it is necessary and some students may find it patronising.

However, EAL teachers can, on the one hand, draw on a very wide range of English Language Teaching (ELT) resources aimed at the EFL market and, on the other hand, the increasing selection of materials for developing basic skills and key skills.

All the main ELT publishers offer general English course books at all levels, skills practice, readers, games, communicative and pair work activities, grammar and vocabulary development. In addition there are materials which teach English for Specific Purposes (ESP) e.g. for business, catering, medicine, the law, study skills. The choice is enormous. These materials can provide a sound basis for language development. However, they tend to be eurocentric and aimed at young adults learning English in their country of origin or on short courses in the UK. Therefore some topics, situations and cultural references are inappropriate for EAL students and care needs to be taken in selecting which materials to use.

Basic skills materials are particularly useful for good speakers who need to develop literacy and study skills. Again, care needs to be taken in the selection and use of such materials as they are devised primarily for first language speakers of English and are not graded in terms of vocabulary and structure. They focus on the spelling and grammatical difficulties of first language speakers which may be different from those faced by the EAL student. However, these materials develop skills needed by EAL students who wish to progress to training, further education or work. Some of the self access materials produced by the National Extension College are suitable for both EAL and Basic Skills learners e.g. Self Access Worksheets, Grammar, Spelling.

Another important resource is the use of real or authentic materials not specially designed for teaching or learning purposes, such as newspapers, magazines, leaflets, letters.

Finally an increasing amount of ELT and Basic Skills materials are produced on CD ROM for use on multimedia computers. These include grammar programs, dictionaries and programs to develop literacy skills.

Selecting materials

When you are looking at materials to choose something for a student it is useful to have a number of criteria in mind. This checklist will help you.

- Is it appropriate for use with adults?

- Does it take into account a learner's previously acquired skills and knowledge? e.g. a student's first language.

- What does a student already have to be able to do to use the materials? e.g. know certain tenses, vocabulary.

- Are the contexts and examples relevant to the needs of an EAL student?

- Does it lead to self-assessment and the development of learning skills?

- Is the level of language and the style suitable for an EAL student?

- How long is it and how much work is covered?

- Is there a focus on the practical use of language?

- Is there any bias or stereotyping, cultural, sexist or racist?

- Is the presentation and layout clear and attractive? – size of print, legibility, amount on a page, illustrations.

- Do illustrations show people from different ethnic backgrounds?

118

- Are there any cultural references which might cause difficulty to an EAL student?

- Is it interesting?

- Is it only for use with a class or can it be used with individuals?

- Can it be used by a student working independently?

- Can it be adapted to suit a particular learner?

If you think that a piece of material would be useful for a student but does not meet all the necessary requirements then you may be able to adapt it.

Adapting materials

1. Some ideas

The suggestions below apply to both spoken and written materials. Some adaptations can be very easy to make.

- If there are just a few words or phrases that are inappropriate or offensive you can blank them out or omit them.

- Instructions can be changed to make them suitable for a one to one situation.

- Instructions can be added to make the exercise self-access. These could be in English, in the first language or on tape.

- Pictures or drawings can be added.

Other adaptations are more time-consuming so you need to consider whether it is worth doing or whether it would be better to look for something else.

- If you are using a piece of authentic material you will have to produce your own exercises.

- If you like the idea of an activity but not the content you could produce your own version.

- If the text is too long you can select from it or summarise it.

- If the text is too difficult you can (a) gloss or explain difficult words and phrases in simple English or in a student's first language, (b) simplify the text.

- If the material is suitable but the activities based on it are not, then you can adapt them. For example, a recording may be at the right level for a student with good understanding but the activity may involve reading or writing which s/he is not able to do. You could help the student by devising activities within the student's competence.

Example

On the tape there is an announcement about a missing child. The instruction is simply, 'What does he look like? Listen to the tape and take notes.'

(a) You could draw three sketches of the child, two of them differing in essential details.

(b) Draw up a chart with multiple choice answers to be ticked.

Age	9 ☐	7 ☐	11 ☐
Coat	Blue ☐	Brown ☐	Black ☐

(c) Use a similar chart but the student fills in the information.

(d) Ask the student to make notes in the first language.

2. Simplifying a text

Assessing the difficulty of a text

There are formulae for measuring the difficulty of texts by looking at sentence length and word length, e.g. the FOGG Index or the SMOG Grading. The level of difficulty is then described in a child-referenced reading age. This kind of measurement may be inappropriate for judging adult reading material. The student's previous experience and present motivation are more important factors in assessing a text. It is quite adequate for you to analyse the text in terms of your knowledge of an individual student.

You have chosen a text because it is relevant for a student's needs, therefore the student should be well motivated to tackle it. You have assessed its general suitability in terms of the criteria described above.

You now need to consider:

- length of text – a very long text can be off-putting;

- length and complexity of sentences – the meaning can become lost in sub-clauses;

- length of words – a large number of words of three syllables or more adds to the difficulty of a text but it may be important to teach these words rather than paraphrase;

- repetition – the more repetition the easier the text;

- style – a straightforward, simple style is easier than an elaborate, flowery style;

- vocabulary – if there is a lot of unknown vocabulary but the words are important for the student, you would be better to introduce these words gradually using simpler texts;

- grammatical structure – does it use tenses and constructions unfamiliar to the student? e.g. conditionals;

- print and layout – how can you improve or add to the text to make it easier to read? e.g. larger print, better spacing, line breaking, illustrations.

Stages of simplifying a text

- If you want to shorten the text select the main points. Do not omit anything that is important for overall meaning.

- Simplify vocabulary where appropriate. Do not remove essential technical words or familiar vocabulary, merely because of their length. Omit idioms or colloquialisms.

- Break long sentences into shorter sentences. Keep to the most commonly used tense forms. Change passive forms to active forms, e.g. *'The bank was robbed by a masked gunman'*, becomes *'A masked gunman robbed the bank'*.

- Reduce the range of vocabulary by repeating words where appropriate. Add illustrations, maps or diagrams which will give clues to the meaning of the text. Write clearly and space the text well. Line break if this will be helpful.

Here is an example.

(i) An extract from *'The Food Hygiene Handbook'* (necessary for food handlers).

Bacteria are microscopic organisms, often referred to as germs, which are found everywhere, including on and in man, on food, in water, soil and air.

Most bacteria are harmless and some are essential, for example, for breaking down decaying matter, or in cheese and yogurt manufacture. However, a small number of bacteria cause food spoilage and some, known as pathogens, are responsible for causing illness.

The number of bacteria present in food may be used to determine whether or not the food has been handled correctly.

A possible simplification.

Bacteria are very small living things. You can only see them with a microscope. They are often called germs.

Bacteria are everywhere. They are on and in people. They are on food, in water, soil and air.

Most bacteria do no harm and some bacteria are very important. For example, bacteria are necessary to make cheese and yogurt.

However, some bacteria make food bad and some make people ill.

A lot of bacteria in the food means you may have done something wrong.

A small number of bacteria means you have handled the food correctly.

(The Food Hygiene Handbook, Richard A. Sprenger, Highfield Publications)

Making your own worksheets

1. Points to consider

- When you make worksheets for a student make sure you are clear about the purpose of the worksheet. Is it to introduce a new skill or topic? Is it for revision or practice? Is it for information?

- What exactly is the language skill, function or grammatical structure you want a student to practise?

- What skills or knowledge does a student need to have to do the worksheet?

- Check the language of instruction. Sometimes the instructions can be more difficult than the language the student is to practise. It may be appropriate to use the first language for the instructions or to put them on to tape. It is useful to teach a student the language of instruction and to some extent of grammatical terminology. Use standardised instructions to make it easier.

- Give examples to demonstrate what to do.

- Don't try to cover too much on each worksheet. It is better to have a series for a student to work through.

- Make sure the layout is clear. Use different sized letters, use upper case and lower case, underline and box items.

- Consider whether a student will do the worksheet under your supervision or whether a student will do it on her/his own. If it is for independent work then it is very important the instructions are easy to understand. You may want to provide answers as well.

2. Layout

Worksheets should have the following elements.

- A title which shows the topic and the skill, function, language items practised. These can be related to an accreditation scheme if appropriate.

- The level – beginner, elementary, intermediate, advanced; or Entry, Level 1, etc., if they are related to a scheme like Wordpower.

- Instructions that are clearly differentiated from the exercises.

- If the worksheet is part of a series it should also have a number.

- It may also be helpful to show what a student should already know, e.g. the past simple tense, and what might be needed to carry out the task, e.g. a dictionary.

- You may also want to provide an answer key.

- If there are other related worksheets refer the student to them.

- If other people may use your worksheets put your name on it so it can be attributed.

Using equipment

1. Cassette recorder

This is an indispensable aid for a language teacher. A number of ways of using a cassette recorder have already been mentioned.

These include:

- for listening comprehension either using published material or making your own recordings;

- to practise grammar and functions;

- for analysing a student's use of language;

- for discriminating elements of pronunciation;

- to allow a student to listen to her/himself and compare the pronunciation with a model;

- to record dialogues for a student to listen to and practise;

- dictation;

- to record a reading text to facilitate reading;

- to record instructions for worksheets (can also be in the first language);

- for assessment.

Try and use a cassette recorder as often as possible and teach the student to use one. It is essential for independent learning. It helps to have one with a rev-counter so you can rewind and fast forward to the exact place you want.

Making your own audio tapes

Although commercial tapes are professionally produced and usually of good quality there can be advantages in making your own:

- they are inexpensive;

- you can copy them freely so students can keep copies;

- you can tailor them to the needs of the student – the right level, amount, context, speed, local accents and so on;

- a resource bank can be built up for teachers to share.

When you make your own recordings make sure you find a quiet room without too much echo. It is best to use an external microphone to avoid buzz. If it is unidirectional you will not pick up surrounding noises. Plan carefully what you want to say, but try and speak naturally and not too quickly. Don't worry if it's not perfect. You are trying to meet an immediate need, not make a professional recording.

2. Video

It may not be feasible to make your own videos but if you have access to a video recorder you can make good use of recordings of educational television programmes as well as commercially produced videos. The added dimension of vision as well as sound helps a student's comprehension. You can turn the sound down and see if the student can guess from the body language what people's attitudes are and what they might be saying. The student can try to predict what might happen next.

3. Computers

The opportunity to develop computer skills in, for example, an open learning centre may attract some students who might not otherwise come for language tuition. Becoming computer literate is often a chance to improve employment prospects.

Language skills can be improved within this context. Whether a student wants to learn basic computer skills or work on vocationally linked programs there is plenty of scope for developing language support work.

There are educational programs aimed at the EFL and Adult Basic Skills market some of which may be suitable for EAL students. The most useful programs are those where you can add in your own texts and exercises. Remember to apply the same criteria to computer programs as to any other resource. Use a student's first language where possible for instructions and information.

Some students find word processing very helpful when working on writing skills. If they have difficulty with the mechanics of handwriting the word processor frees them to concentrate on what they want to say and the finished result looks very professional. They can try out words and phrases, correct, move sentences and paragraphs about until they are satisfied with what they have written and how it is presented. They can use a spell check program if they are uncertain about spelling.

Some wordprocessing programs can produce community languages so you could make bilingual materials and compare English structure with a student's first language. A student could also develop writing in the community language.

The use of an overlay keyboard gives many possibilities to create language programs for a student. This is an A4 or A3 electronic pad connected to the computer. It is divided into squares and when you press a square a word comes up on the screen. You can make overlays with pictures or words on to place on the overlay keyboard and program the computer to display a matching word or sentence when the appropriate square is pressed. (From *Using Computers with Bilingual students*' – see Further reading). If you have access to multimedia computers you can use the increasing number of CD Roms that involve sound as well as visual materials.

Finding out more about resources

If you want to find out more about EAL and other Basic Skills materials the Basic Skills Resource Centre based in the Library at the Institute of Education, University of London, 20 Bedford Way, London, WClH OAL has a comprehensive selection for you to view.

These catalogues will also help you:

- *The Avanti Book Resources Guide*, 8 Parsons Green, Boulton Road, Stevenage, Herts SGI QG;

- *Basic Skills Agency Publications Catalogue*, Admail 524, London, WC1A 1BR;

- *Open Learning Resources for Education and Training*, National Extension College, 18 Brooklands Avenue, Cambridge CB2 2HN;

- Sunderland Helen, 1992, *A Tutor's Guide to ESOL Materials for Adult Learners*, The Language and Literacy Unit.

You can also find many useful materials in the publishers' English Language Teaching catalogues and in guides, such as The English Book Centre Tel: 01865 514770 and The Keltic Guide to ELT Materials, Tel: 01932 820485. Publishers also have websites on the Internet.

Language Development Network
This is a network of language support tutors in further education colleges which has been set up to pool and exchange language support and communication skills materials covering a range of academic and vocational contexts. Member colleges pay a fee and have to contribute materials on a termly basis. The colleges then have access to materials in the database. The materials are not available to non-members. The Language Development Network, Shipley College, Exhibition Road, Shipley, West Yorks.

Further reading

Baker Christine, 1995, *Practise your Word Processing Skills*, Avanti.

Basic Skills Agency, 1996, *The Worksheet Generator*, CD ROM.

Leach R, 1985, *Making, Using and Adapting Materials*, National Extension College.

Making Reading Easier, 1992, Basic Skills Agency.

Multi-What? Progressing on to Multimedia, Basic Skills, Spring 1995.

Sauzier Catherine, *Use of IT*, ESOL News 15, Winter 1997/98.

Smith Glenys, *Using Computers with Bilingual Students*, Basic Skills Agency Newsletter, No.45, Spring 1992.

Tomalin B, 1990, *Video in the English Class*, BBC English.

Words in Action, 1997, CD Rom, IBM.

Wright Andrew, 1994, *1000 Pictures for Teachers to Copy*, Longman.

Teacher Training

Gower R, Walter S, 1995, *Teaching Practice Handbook*, Heinemann.

Harmer Jeremy, 1991, *The Practice of English Language Teaching*, Longman.

Harmer Jeremy, 1998, *How to Teach English*, Longman.

Sunderland Helen and Cottington Helen, 1996, *The Teacher's Video: An ESOL Tutor Training Resource*, Language and Literacy Unit.

Journals and Newsletters

Language Issues, produced twice a year by NATECLA (The National Association for English and Other Community Languages to Adults) – Hall Green College, 520-524 Stratford Road, Birmingham Bl 1 4AI. NATECLA also produces a regular newsletter.

Basic Skills Magazine, published four times a year by the Basic Skills Agency.

National ESOL News, published by Bradford and District TEC, Ed. Joan Uttley, 42 Stockport Road, Mossley, Ashton under Lyne, OL5 0QY Tel: 01457 833346.

Glossary

Accreditation – recognising a person's skills by a qualification.

Active (of verbs) – the form of the verb when the subject does the action, e.g. Jim *cooked the dinner*.

Adjective – a word that describes the person or thing referred to by a noun – a *good* book; it's *interesting*.

Adverb – a word that tells you about a verb, e.g. She speaks *quickly*.

Articles – a(n), the.

Authentic – language which is not specially composed for teaching – real language.

Bilingual – speaking and using two languages.

Cloze – a method of checking comprehension by omitting every 7th to 10th word and asking a student to fill in the gaps, using context and knowledge of structure.

Communicative – an approach to teaching which concentrates on the purposes of using language, i.e. functions.

Competence – a description of a skill or task to measure what a person can do.

Conditional clause – part of a sentence beginning with 'if' or 'unless'.

Consonant cluster – a group of consonant sounds, e.g. str, thr.

Consonants – all the letters of the alphabet except 'a,e,i,o,u'.

Content words – words that have a lot of meaning in themselves, e.g. book, pen, write, clever (i.e. nouns, verbs, adjectives).

Context – the situation in which language is used. The words/sentences that come before and after a word which help to give meaning.

Contraction – when two words are spoken as one – e.g. I will = I'll.

Cursive – joined up writing.

Decoding – working out how to read a word.

Dialogue – a scripted conversation for teaching purposes.

Diphthongs – a sound made up of two vowel sounds, e.g. 'oi' as in 'boy'.

Drill – practising sentences which follow the same pattern.

Dyslexia – problems with reading and spelling because of a brain condition which causes difficulty in seeing the difference between letter shapes.

Functional – language described according to its purpose.

Gist – the main points.

Grammar – the rules for forming words and putting them together into sentences.

Information transfer – taking information from one source and representing it in a different way, e.g. from a text to a diagram.

Intonation – the way the voice goes up and down when speaking.

Key words – the 100 most commonly used words. The most important words to listen or look out for.

Language functions – the purposes for which language is used, e. g. describing, explaining.

Line breaking – writing a sentence so that each word group is on a separate line.

Minimal pairs – two words that sound the same except for one sound, e.g. pen/pan.

Mono-lingual – speaking one language; a class of students who all speak the same language.

Monologue – when one person speaks without interruption.

Multi-lingual – speaking many languages, a class with students who speak different languages.

Noun – a word which names an object, place, person, feeling, e.g. book, Manchester, Jane, happiness.

Objectives – what you plan to achieve in a lesson, at the end of a learning programme.

Outcomes – what you actually do achieve in a lesson or a learning programme.

Passive (of verbs) – the form of the verb when the action is done to the subject, e.g. *The dinner is cooked.*

Performance criteria – the standards by which a task is assessed.

Phonetic – spelling which corresponds closely to sounds.

Prefix – a syllable added to the beginning of a word to change its meaning, e.g. happy/*un*happy.

Preposition – words which show a relationship like time and place and are followed by a noun, pronoun, or the '-ing' form of the verb, e.g. *on* the table, *at* the weekend, *by* working hard.

Prior learning – skills that someone already has.

Productive skills – speaking and writing.

Pronoun – a word that is used instead of a noun, e.g. he, she, it.

Receptive skills – listening and reading.

Rhythm – the beat of the language.

Scan – to look quickly through a text to find a particular bit of information.

Self-access – being able to select materials and carry out learning activities independently with little help from a teacher.

Sentence patterns – sentences grouped together which have the same structure – There is a picture/on the wall. There is a book on the table.

Skim – to read quickly to get the main points.

Social sight words – words commonly seen in the street, etc, on signs and notices.

Stress – the emphasis put on part of a word, or a word in a sentence, e.g. se<u>nt</u>ence; I <u>*saw*</u> him.

Structural words – a small number of frequently used words that give the framework to a sentence e.g. the, a, this, to, some.

Structure – the way language is put together.

Study skills – essay writing, note-taking, using a dictionary, taking part in a discussion.

Substitution table – a chart of sentences which follow the same pattern for reading and writing practice.

Suffix – a syllable added to the end of a word, e.g. care/care*ful*.

Syllable – parts of a word which form a sound group, usually vowel plus consonant/consonant plus vowel, e.g. con/son/ant.

Tense – a form of a verb to show the time of an action, e.g. the present tense – I work.

Transferable skills – skills learnt in one situation/language which can be used in another.

Verb – a word describing an action or state. Every sentence has a verb, e.g. I *wrote* a letter, He *feels* happy, She *gets* up early.

Vowels – the letters 'a,e,i,o,u' .

WAR

Yorkshire and the North East

Stories of adventure and tragedy
told in their own words

Caroline Brannigan

Caroline Brannigan

This book was published in 2014 by

Caroline Brannigan
Memoir Writer
Richmond, North Yorkshire

By carrying out extensive interviews,
Caroline helps clients to tell the story
they have always meant to write.

www.carolinebrannigan.com
01748 821041

ISBN: 978-0-9574415-1-4

Printed in the UK by
Berforts Information Press

I run a business writing people's memoirs for them. Since 2008 I have produced more than 60 books and manuscripts capturing fascinating stories of people who consider themselves ordinary but have lived through extraordinary times. These stories are usually for the enjoyment of family and friends and are a wonderful heirloom for generations to come. Some people sell their books.

Many of my clients were children during the war. I was struck by how little my own children were taught at school about the war in Yorkshire and the North East. It was all about London evacuees.

My clients and other people I have interviewed have very kindly given their permission for me to use their stories to show that it didn't all happen down South. Cities and towns here were bombed and even the countryside was far from safe.

It's a miracle some of these kids survived – messing about with unexploded bombs, playing in ammunition dumps and throwing bullets into bonfires. For those who experienced tragedy first-hand the war was a serious, life-changing event but for the lucky ones it was a fantastic adventure.

You can find out what happened next to many of these children by going to my website to see the books I have written for them.

If you have memories you'd like to add to future editions of this book, please call or email me through my website. I am looking for people who were not evacuated and who have stories particular to them and their area. Looking forward to hearing from you!

Caroline Brannigan
Richmond
North Yorkshire

www.carolinebrannigan.com
01748 821041

This book is dedicated to my parents who married at the age of 21 in 1939. Dad was English, Mum was German, so it must have been love! It certainly wasn't easy. They stayed in love for the next 50 years until dying within a few months of each other. How I wish I had asked them more about their lives!

DOUG BRADBROOK

Doug was born in
1934 and lived in the
village of Wycliffe
near Barnard Castle.

'My friend found an explosive shell which blew up when we tried to break it open with a hammer. I was blown into a muck midden and was unconscious for a while. There was shrapnel coming out of my wrists and knees for years afterwards.'

My father worked as a groom at a big house called Wycliffe Hall. Although our home in the coach house was humble, it was a marvellous area for a young boy to grow up in. All the horses in my father's care were hunters because the work horses were down at the Home Farm. There was a quadrangle with stables, coach houses, a blacksmith's shop and a modern garage for the cars. These were under dust sheets for the duration of the war because there was no petrol for private use and I remember an 8-litre Bentley being taken away to be made into an ambulance.

Meals were tasty and filling and my mother was always baking and there were stews and hot pies and teacakes. I could eat anything. Even before the war there wasn't a huge amount of meat because it was expensive but during rationing there was very little, so we ate a lot of rabbit because we could catch those. My dad kept a few hens so we had eggs and used to get some milk from the big house. We never went really short of food but it was only basic, bread was the main thing, and I can remember bringing 10 loaves back from the shop. It was known as black bread because the government had banned white bread and adults moaned but I'd never known any different, so I liked it.

Getting around meant walking or going on the bikes. Some Sundays my dad used to get me on the crossbar and my mother would have my younger sister June in a carrier on the back and we would go the seven miles to her parents at Staindrop. Sometimes in the summer we'd go over on a Saturday and stay the night so we could go to the cinema.

I wasn't quite five when war broke out on September 3rd 1939. My mum came out of the house to tell us that Britain had declared war on Germany and we were with an Austrian girl who we called Fraulein. She was a nursery maid to the children in the big house, a very nice girl who made tree houses and all sorts of exciting things for them. As soon as she heard what my mother had said, she rushed down the drive, crying in her strong accent, "Mudder, my poor mudder" (meaning mother) and she rushed off and we never saw her again. She was taken away more or less the next day because she was now viewed by the authorities as "an enemy alien" because Austria was on the side of Germany. All people like her were rounded up and put in camps, though most were entirely innocent and some had fled Hitler's persecution. We never saw her again. She ended up in the Isle of Man where many Germans were taken. We tried to tell the authorities that she wasn't a spy at all but of course it was very difficult in those days because everyone thought there would be an invasion and there was a great deal of suspicion of foreigners. Fraulein was released eventually, as were many others, and went to London.

I didn't really understand what the war was all about - what child could really? - but I knew it was something serious. My father always believed we would win and said very firmly, right from the beginning, "We will win, right will prevail" and that was a comfort to me. One of the first big impacts on me was the arrival of evacuees from places like Middlesbrough and Stockton which were at risk from bombing. I'd not long started at St. Mary's Roman Catholic School, Wycliffe, when so many new children arrived that we had to have an extra class. Our school was one long building with a grey slated roof and had three coal fires which were smoky and struggled to keep us warm in the winter. We used to freeze to death in the bad weather because it was so draughty. Normally we had 35 to 40 children but the evacuees swelled numbers to 70 so you can imagine that it was pretty crowded. Luckily they brought a teacher with them. They didn't know anything about the countryside and often had to walk two miles to school from the homes in which they had been billeted, which was a shock for them.

One girl, Nancy Peacock was her name, and a lad called Guy Blacket and a couple of others were upset because some of the lambs in the next field had got away from their mothers, or so they thought. Of course we country children knew they'd find their way back but these evacuees spent ages trying to find the mothers. When they eventually turned up late for school, the teacher caned Guy for being so daft, for not knowing, but the girls got off because they didn't really cane girls. Even though some of the evacuees came from poor families - and there were plenty of them at that time - they didn't stand out particularly because many country homes were very poor too. I remember some farm children coming to school with no socks, just boots on.

My mother always managed to keep myself and June well dressed, even on the little money she had, usually buying our shoes from a pedlar chap who came round with a horse and cart. She was a good manager but I know it was tough for her because there was very little money to go round. People just laugh at it today. Children's clothes were very simple and we didn't have many of them. There was no school uniform. Boys wore short trousers, shirts and jumpers, girls wore frocks and cardigans.

From September 1939 until May 1940 there was what became known as the Phoney War because nothing much happened but suddenly that ended and Hitler's armies swept across mainland Europe. We knew we'd be next on the list. The first I knew of how serious the situation had become was one night when my sister and I were in our bedroom upstairs, supposedly asleep, and my mother came up and knelt by my bed. My father was out because he had volunteered to be an Air-raid Precautions Warden (ARP) and she was on her own and was very scared because she could hear planes droning overhead. I remember her kneeling by my bed in the darkness, praying for everyone to be kept safe. She was terrified. Although we were never an obvious target for bombers, unlike the cities, they used to fly in from the East and navigate by the rivers across to the cities in the West like Liverpool and Manchester. You could never be sure that on the way home they might not jettison a spare bomb to lighten to load. Ironically, the one time a bomb dropped near Wycliffe we were seven miles away at Staindrop visiting my grandparents. Nobody was hurt but a huge crater was blasted into the road.

The Home Guard was formed in 1940 made up from men too young, old or unfit to fight or who were in reserved occupations – vital work such as farming. It really was like Dad's Army. One day my parents and I were on our way to Staindrop on our bikes and the Home Guard had put up barriers across the road. On duty was this chap who worked at Wycliffe and he demanded to see our identity cards even though he knew who we were. We hadn't got them so my dad had to cycle three miles back to our house to get them to show the daft devil who we were.

The next big thing I noticed was the arrival of thousands of Canadians, mainly Air Force pilots, to the many bases which sprang up near us and over towards Teesside. Crashing planes were another hazard. One very brave pilot, William Stuart McMullen, was on a bomber training flight when he realized the plane was going to crash, so he ordered the crew of six to bail out but stayed at the controls to direct the plane away from Darlington so that it crashed into fields. He lost his life to save others. There's a citation to him on a stone. Although it was some distance from us, I remember being told all about his bravery.

At another point in the war an RAF Spitfire crashed into a cliff at Whorlton Bridge about a mile from where we were and the poor chap was killed. We heard the bang and went along to see what had happened and saw the flames. A young lad called Neville who was about 14 was working on the farm on the other side of the river to where the crash happened. He waded across the river, which was quite shallow at that point, and salvaged a lot of explosive shells.

Later he decided to make cigarette lighters out of these shells – people often turned debris from the war into all kinds of things because materials were hard to come by. I was only very young when this happened, about six years old, and Neville, being a bit older, was my hero. One night after the crash we were out at the back of the house and he had one of these things. After hitting the cannon shell twice with a hammer to try to open it, he made me hold the knife while he cut the end off and of course it exploded while I was hanging on to it.

The resulting blast blew all the concrete up from the floor and he was pretty badly injured. I was blown into a muck midden and was unconscious for a while until they got me into the house and went rushing for my mother and doctors and goodness knows what. You can still see the scar on my hand where the knife bounced off and hit me. There was shrapnel coming out of my wrists and knees for years afterwards. They were little bumps under the skin and gradually worked their way out. I was at home recovering for six or seven weeks – I didn't go to hospital, the doctor came to the house, that's what people did in those days.

When I got back to school a policeman was waiting for me and he lifted me up on to the desk to tell the others what happened when you messed with things you shouldn't. He didn't do anything else about it because it was happening all over. Another chap at school, about 13 years old, came in one day with no hair on him and his face was all black. He and his mates had piled up gunpowder in a big heap which they got out of old shells and threw a match at it and of course it went up completely.

Youngsters did some mad things. The lad who got injured when the cannon shell blew up also risked his life just to get a bit of old plywood. There was a battle school nearby where they made images of German soldiers out of painted plywood and used them for target practice. Neville used to creep out even while the firing was going on and steal these wooden figures. There were supposed to be guards all round but Neville managed to get the stuff out somehow and used it to make fretwork designs.

Whorlton Lido, a little swimming area on the Tees now sadly closed, was a battle school then where I think there were some Marines training and they used to climb across the cliff with ropes. Sometimes they'd accidentally drop their rifles in the river and later we kids would fish them out, fasten them to a fence and put a string on them to pull the trigger. At least by then we'd learned a thing or two about not getting blown up. We had the sense to know that if gravel had got in and blocked the barrel, the guns would explode - hence the string so we could stay clear. It was hugely exciting for kids because stuff was lying everywhere just waiting to be played with. As well as things left behind by our own side, people were warned not to pick up pens because German planes were dropping them and when you picked them up they exploded.

At the beginning of the war David Peat (the boy from the big house) and I built our own air-raid shelter by digging a hole and covering it with bits of corrugated iron, just below our house where we lived in the stable yard. There were no proper air-raid shelters because we weren't considered a high-risk area. We had candles in there and apples to eat but there was never a heavy raid in which to use it. The cities and towns had air-raid sirens and we could just hear the ones in Barnard Castle but in the countryside air-raid wardens like my father would blow a whistle which would, with any luck, be heard by the next warden along and so the warning would travel. It was amazing how far it would go. For the all-clear they rang a bell – or maybe it was the other way round. One day as an exercise my father blew the whistle and David and I rushed into the shelter and lit the candle. Unfortunately my father forgot to ring the bell for the all-clear and David and I were in there for ages until finally we were missed and they came looking for us.

People were suffering bereavements all the time during the war but as a child I didn't really understand how they felt. We had one young teacher, Miss Brown, whose brother Ray had been killed when his bomber was shot down over Wilhelmshaven in Germany. She was in a bad way, awfully bitter. At the beginning of the war she had been evacuated with her class from Hull, which was very badly bombed, to Winnipeg in Canada. Thousands of children went to safety in America and Canada during the war. After about 1942, when the bombing wasn't so bad, Miss Brown returned to England to teach at our school and brought a small parcel for each of us containing little luxuries like chocolate. That was amazing.

We knew something was wrong because she was so sad but they never told us about her brother. I only found out later. Despite her bitterness she was a very good teacher and when I met her later she said, "I knew you'd do something with your life". By then she was able to talk about her brother and she was bitter because he'd been sent up in a poorly defended plane which was as slow as a snail and she felt he hadn't had a chance. I also remember the father of one of my sister's friends. He had been badly wounded at Dunkirk and had a metal plate in his head. So although we were in the countryside, the sadness and destruction of the war touched us in many ways. At the back of the school was a longish garden where we had to "Dig for Victory" to provide extra food as so little could be imported. We used to grow cabbages and potatoes and all kinds.

The cities and big towns were protected by barrage balloons which were huge things filled with gas and winched up on thick cables high into the sky to stop enemy planes from dive-bombing. One of these escaped from Teesside and blew on an East wind over us. It came right over our school which was very exciting, dragging the heavy cables behind it. I guess it probably took a few tiles off roofs and chimney pots along the way.

Towards the end of the war my sister started school and she and some of the other little ones got a lift home in a car each day but there wasn't room for me. I was about nine years old. I used to jump up on the back of it and my sister could see me but didn't tell. I'd hang on tight until we were nearly home then roll off on to the grass. That was a favourite trick.

There were very few private cars around, it was mainly military vehicles. Me and a friend had bikes and we'd cycle along the A66, which was very narrow and quiet then, most of the traffic being military. One day a massive convoy appeared and trucks and armoured vehicles rumbled past all day and all night without cease, which I believe were Canadian forces on their way from training grounds in Scotland to southern ports from which they staged the raids on Dieppe in 1942. Thousands of them died on that raid.

1942 was a very bad winter, my dad had pneumonia and we were very short of coal because supplies couldn't get through. He sent me to the stables to fetch a huge lump of timber. I had to get this heavy thing up the stairs to my sick dad in bed and hold the wood while he chopped it up. Because the roads were so bad the doctor came to us on an old horse. When he went he said he'd make up some medicine and arrange for it to be left at Whorlton Bridge a mile away for us to collect. Me and my mum had to go in a snow storm to get this medicine. I was only about seven but she was nervous of going on her own. You didn't get long trousers until you were much older so there I was in short ones with little cold legs and my Wellingtons full of snow.

In that bad weather, me and a friend took our sledges two miles through the snow to Ovington, which was the nearest shop. We crossed a road which had been cleared of snow by soldiers so the tanks could get through to the A66. Drifts at the side were 12ft high, *(4 metres)* so we had to slide down, then get across as quick as we could and scramble up the other side. If we heard a tank coming we were terrified that we wouldn't be able to climb out of the icy valley in time and would get run over because there was no way they were going to stop. Then we'd have to bring the bread home on the sledges.

As 1944 came round we knew that one day soon the Allies would invade mainland Europe. The date was top secret. One of the first things we noticed on the lead-up to what became known as D-Day on June 6th 1944 was the noise in the training camps around us. The din one night in the wood near our house was tremendous, machine guns and thunder flashes and hand grenades. You couldn't sleep for what was going on. Then suddenly everything went very quiet and they were gone. Later we heard on the radio that the long-awaited invasion had begun.

My friend David Peat and I built ourselves a little den in the cliffs overlooking the river and from here David would fire his father's World War I revolver into the trees. He wasn't meant to have it! One night David was in bed at home and had the revolver with him. He pulled the trigger, thinking it wasn't loaded, and the bullet went right through two walls, so he was found out of course because it shattered the bathroom.

Being very active little boys we were permanently hungry. Even when we were fairly young we used to go off and catch waterhens *(moorhens)* and cook them in a pan over an open fire. We were pretty good at cutting off the heads and legs but didn't know about taking the guts out, so we left them in but they still tasted alright with a couple of potatoes from the field. It was good meat and meat rations were very low.

Around that time, at the age of 11, I caught my first trout in the river with a home-made split-cane rod. I shaved the cane down into segments and fitted it together. That was a hell of a patient job. At the end of the fishing line was my own hand-tied fly, so everything was by my own efforts and that first fish tasted good.

On the last day of the war in Europe in May 1945 *(it carried on for several more months in the Far East)* I was in the stable yard at Wycliffe, sitting in a little trap pulled by a donkey. Next to me was David's sister Avie Peat who was about three years older than me. We used to go all over the place in that cart because there were hardly any cars. My mother came out and said, "The war's finished. Mr Churchill's going to come on the news and speak at six o' clock."

She was ever so pleased but Avie and I didn't take too much notice because we were more interested in our donkey and cart, though I remember listening to the broadcast later. I was old enough to understand how tragic the war had been and the

12

pictures which came out of the terrible things which had been done at the concentration camp Belsen made a deep and lasting impression on me.

Doug grew up to develop a successful horticultural business with his brother-in-law in Ravensworth, North Yorkshire and told his life story in his memoir *Seeds of Success*.

JOAN McELVANEY

Joan was born in Middlesbrough in 1931 where her father was a steelworker. At the age of eight the family moved a few miles away to Grangetown to a new housing estate completed just before war put an end to all house building.

'I know a lot of children suffered during the war, especially in other countries, but for many of us in Middlesbrough our memories are of a very exciting time.'

Not long after we had moved into our new home war broke out. I was eight. I was sitting in the living room with my mother, sister Audrey and my cousin Mary who were all shouting at me to be quiet because they were trying to hear the radio, the wireless as we called it. My mum was crying, Mary was crying, then my sister started though I don't think she really knew what she was crying about, being only 10. The Prime Minister had announced that we were at war with Germany. When I asked why they were all sobbing I was told to shut up so they could listen. My dad and one of my brothers dug a hole in our back garden ready for the corrugated iron which was delivered to all houses which had enough space out the back. The iron was shaped to make the roof and sides of what was known as an Anderson shelter then it was all covered by soil. Dark and damp they may have been but many lives were saved as they could withstand most things other than a direct hit by a bomb. Dad added a door and a couple of bunk beds. We'd all been warned to expect mass bombing immediately but nothing happened for months and, as flowers and grass took hold across the top of our shelter, it just looked like another corner of our beautiful garden.

We had to traipse down to a hall in Grangetown to be fitted for gas masks in case of poison attack, though this never happened. Masks had to be carried everywhere in their little brown cardboard boxes slung on string over your shoulder. You were in trouble if you were caught without it but people soon got bored with the extra burden.

Though the gas masks and the shelter were a bit frightening, the war seemed exciting to small children. A combination of rationing and shortages made some things hard to get like soap and chocolate but by this time my older brothers had been called up into the Army and Navy and came home on leave with their pockets stuffed with goodies they had saved for us.

All my older brothers went to war except Ken who was very put out because by then he was a farm worker in Stokesley which was a reserved occupation. He was ordered to stay in his job and was very disappointed but the country desperately needed people like him to stay where they were as many of our imports were being sent to the bottom of the sea by German U-Boat submarines. However he was delighted later to be able to serve in the Royal Navy for many years. Nothing happened on the home front for a long time but on May 25th 1940 Middlesbrough became the first big town and industrial target of the war to be bombed. Houses in South Bank where we had once lived were badly damaged as the lone bomber tried to hit the nearby steelworks. As in many other towns and cities, it was the poorer homes near the industry and docks which suffered most in air-raids. Our new home was about half a mile from the main target so we weren't badly affected. We went down to see the damage and saw rooms blown open to the sky, wallpaper hanging down and furniture in splinters. That was frightening and I thought, "I don't want that to happen to us."

After that we slept in our air-raid shelter whether the siren had gone or not. After an early supper we were bathed and put into our pyjamas. We had to put out our clothes ready for school the next day then about 8 o'clock we pulled on our coats to go outside to the Anderson. All windows were covered with blackout material at night and you weren't allowed to show a light outside. As autumn began to draw in, it was a very dark walk out to our underground bunk beds.

With the steelworks and other industries so important to fighting the war, our town suffered many raids. In our shelter we would hear the siren go and at first tried to distract ourselves by playing guessing games and things like that. Then the sound of the bombers would come and everyone would go quiet and that was very frightening, wondering if a bomb would drop on us. My dad rarely came into the shelter and stayed in the house but from time to time he would come out to see if we were alright. One night a week my mum had to act as a firewatcher at our school looking out for incendiary bombs which, though small, had to be put out quickly to avoid a blaze, and that was when Dad would come into the shelter with us.

At the age of 11 I moved to the senior school, Sir William Worsley. Here discipline was much more strict than at the juniors with boys being hit with a cane for disobedience. If the siren went we had to line up and go into the long brick shelters in the playground, sitting on the forms along each side until the all-clear sounded. Small lamps sent out a little light into the darkness. Because we were all together it didn't feel as frightening as being in our Anderson shelter at home and there didn't seem to be as many raids in the daytime.

My mother bought Audrey and me little Air Force blue coats with matching Glengarry hats. She was very pleased with the sight of us but we hated them and felt stupid. One day, dressed in these outfits, we were walking home from Sunday school when we heard an aeroplane above us making an awful noise then watched it spiral down and explode on Eston Hills. We could see it was a German plane from the markings. Being more afraid of our mum than the Germans, we ran home as fast as we could to change into old clothes so we could go up to the crash site. Children and adults alike were speeding up to where a plume of smoke was erupting from the hillside. On reaching the site a terrible smell filled our nostrils which I now realize must have been from the burning bodies. Sometimes I wonder, did I really see that? But sadly I believe I did, it is still so vivid. Children were picking up bits of jagged metal to add to their shrapnel collections. Back at school all kinds of tall tales were told about the crash. Boys would make a hole in an oblong tobacco tin, push their thumb through into a patch of red-stained cloth then open the box to claim it was a German finger they'd picked up.

It was a good way to make the girls scream. With no TV and no computers, going to the cinema was a big treat. One day I was enthralled by *The Hunchback of Notre Dame* when the sign came up on the screen, as it so often did, "The air-raid warning has sounded, please file out quietly and go to the nearest shelter." My brother and sister got up straightaway but my mother had to haul me out of my seat because I wanted to stay and watch the end of the film. In the areas where houses had no gardens and couldn't have an Anderson like us, every street had a communal brick-built shelter and if caught in a raid away from home you had to use them. They smelled horrible of cats and dogs but we had to squeeze in there on the hard benches along the walls until the all-clear sounded. Being out in the blackout was almost as dangerous as being bombed because it was so dark you couldn't see where you were going. On our coats were sewn luminous discs to stop others from bumping into us.

The area being so much less built up at that time, our home was close to fields and here an Army camp had been established. We were forbidden to go there but would sneak off to chat over the barricades in the hope of being thrown a sweet by the soldiers. We got into a lot of trouble if our dad caught us. Many of the soldiers were billeted in homes around us but we had no room. The camp operated the huge searchlights which shone into the sky during a raid trying to pick out enemy planes for the anti-aircraft guns to fire at and for a small child that was a wonderful sight. Each evening gas-filled barrage balloons were floated above the town. Seeing these great grey shapes rise up into the sky was a thrill.

I was so young that the horrors of it weren't particularly real though I do remember that a girl who went to my school was killed in a raid. I am surprised they didn't evacuate more youngsters into the countryside than they did but perhaps their parents didn't want them to go to strangers. I know a lot of children suffered during World War II, especially in other countries, but for many of us in Middlesbrough our memories are of a very exciting time. Yet fear was in my subconscious. After seeing a newsreel at the cinema about a mine at sea I had a recurring nightmare throughout the rest of the war about bobbing among the waves with all my family and calling out to them to hold on to the spikes of the mine so we would be saved. Ironically it would have blown up but not in my dream.

Easter eggs were no longer made so my mother mixed up semolina with almond essence and shaped it into eggs, moulding them with two dessert spoons and using a tiny drop of chocolate for decoration. She was a very good cook, an excellent manager and very imaginative so despite the rationing and shortages we were never hungry. Sundays always meant a proper roast dinner but with Yorkshire pudding often served first to fill you up and even afterwards with jam as a dessert. My mother had many talents but knitting wasn't one of them and when she made pixie hats for me and my sister, which were all the rage in the 1940s, we had to fold back the edges to stop them covering our eyes.

During the war my mother worked as a weigh driver at the Dorman Long steelworks sitting in a little cabin beside the weighbridge on which lorries were weighed to check they had the right load. Now that she was earning good money, as a treat my mother would get all dressed up and take me and my sister to Spark's cafe. Downstairs it was quite ordinary but upstairs it was silver service, nice cloths, shining cutlery and a waitress and this was where we went. The idea was to teach us good manners. When I was about 11 my dad took Audrey and me to King's

Lynn in Norfolk to see where he had come from. He must have saved for ever to pay the rail fares and we travelled overnight, presumably because it was cheaper, the first time we had ever been on a train apart from short trips to the sea at Redcar. Arriving exhausted about six o'clock in the morning we emerged from the station and went to find his relations only to find my dad's old familiar streets a pile of rubble from the bombing. I don't think he can have told anyone we were coming, nor had he had much contact with his family since leaving so many years before. He said, "We'll go and find my auntie." Her house was intact and it was my dad's cousin Alice who opened the door to us. This poor woman answered an early morning knock at her door to be confronted by a man she didn't recognize and two children she had never seen before. "Who are you?" she asked warily.

"Who do you think I am?" said my dad and as soon as he spoke she knew who it was. She put us up in her tiny cottage for a week.

In June 1944 came D-Day when the Allies invaded Northern France in the long-awaited fight back. Hearing the dramatic announcement on the radio, my little brother and his friends immediately ran off to the village of Normanby and stopped a woman to ask, "Where are the Germans?" She told them to stop being silly but they insisted, "No! It said on the radio that we're fighting the Germans in Normanby!"

"Get home, you silly beggars," she replied. "It's Normandy, not Normanby."

Joan wrote a moving memoir called *The House on The Hill* in which she described caring for her husband Ron who suffered lung disease. He became one of the first lung transplant patients.

PETER PYBUS

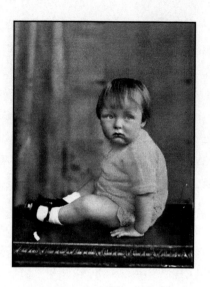

Peter was born in
1936 in Hendon,
a deprived area of
Sunderland which
suffered heavy
bombing.

*'One morning after a bad raid we emerged to the news
that two of my school pals had been killed. They had been
in a shelter which received a direct hit from a bomb and
their family of 15 was wiped out. Up until then you're
just a kid, then you suddenly go to school and your mates
aren't there, they're dead. After that you're different.'*

Hendon contained a lot of heavy industry and from the
end of our street you could see the huge cranes of the
shipyards towering above. Our cobbled streets housed
a very close knit community with many relatives living nearby
and I was always very well looked after. There were plenty of
doors, usually unlocked, through which I could go and be sure
of a warm welcome.

Home was a small terraced house with two bedrooms, a scullery and kitchen, living room, a backyard and no bathroom. Bath time was in a tin bath in front of the fire. The toilet was outside and you didn't spend long there at night, especially in winter. The house was typical of thousands thrown up in Victorian times to provide the cheapest housing possible to workers flooding in from the countryside to what they hoped would be a better life in industries such as shipbuilding. My father worked as labourer and had been able to buy the house and this provided a home for us and my mother's parents.

In 1939 when I was only three everything changed for my family. War was looming and my father was in the Territorial Army, a part-time force to which he belonged in addition to his civilian job. This meant he was among the first to be called up, quite some time before war broke out in September. At first he was in the Royal Artillery, then the RASC (Royal Army Service Corps) and for the first few years of the war was based in Britain, later taking part in the invasion of Italy.

But far worse than my father being sent away from us was the death that same year of my mother from appendicitis. I don't remember her at all as I was so young and have only photos to show me what she looked like. The first person I really remember was my Gran, who was my mother's mother and called Ethel.

With my father away in the Army and my mother gone, suddenly there was nobody to look after me so Ethel and my granddad Peter stepped in, closely supported by my mother's brother Uncle Bob and his wife Auntie Bella, who lived nearby. I had no brothers and sisters. Gran did a wonderful job bringing me up for she had rheumatoid arthritis and used a stick to get about and must have been in considerable pain.

Auntie Bella was a qualified confectioner and made wedding

cakes and iced them. If there was any icing left over, she used to write our names in it then hand it to us to eat. I used to complain that I always got the least because my cousins had longer names. Sweets were rationed so the icing names were a real treat and even icing sugar became scarce.

Childhood injustices stay sharply in the memory and I also remember that later on, when American soldiers arrived in Britain to prepare for the invasion of Europe, they sent sweets to our school for children whose fathers were serving in the Forces overseas. Well, my father was still in the UK so I didn't get any. I felt that deeply.

People today are mad on home improvements but the only addition ever made to our house at 5 Lawton Street was a brick air-raid shelter in the back yard. I grew up not knowing a world without war. In 1940 and 1941 when I was about five and the Germans were bombing Wearside's heavy industry, there was hardly a night that Gran and I weren't in the shelter. Our street was within about 200 yards *(180 metres)* of a petroleum storage station and only half a mile from the shipyards and the gasworks so we were a prime target.

Granddad was an ARP warden who had to go out as soon as the siren sounded and off he went to patrol the streets and help find survivors in bombed buildings. Gran and I were straight off to the shelter where, huddling in her arms, I could hear the bombs whistling down. There was a small gap into the adjoining shelter next-door and I remember Gran talking to our neighbours Mr and Mrs Pell, putting the world to rights as we were bombarded from the skies. Behind us was the Hendon cricket field which was filled with anti-aircraft guns, one we nick-named Big Bertha and when it went off you knew it because it used to shake everything.

People know a lot about the London Blitz but far less about the pounding of northern towns and cities. Bombers came over as regular as clockwork. Like millions of others in Britain we loved the radio show ITMA - It's That Man Again - a comedy starring Tommy Handley, and you could guarantee that as soon as that started the siren would go. There were no transistor radios then so we missed it.

During the winter of 1940 and 1941 they were over nearly every night and stayed for three or four hours. That was the worst time but raids continued on and off until around 1944 as the Germans were pushed back from their bases so for me it was a normal part of life. Everywhere we went we were supposed to take our gas masks. Leaving for school in the morning I'd dash off with this horrible thing in a cardboard box hung by a string across my shoulder and my bait bag containing lunch. The pupils were trained to run out of the classrooms to the playground shelters as fast as possible if the siren went though I remember raids only at night.

Quite a few of my friends had been evacuated to the safety of the countryside but I wasn't. One night my school, Valley Road Infants, was bombed and the big bakery at the end of our street was also hit. When we emerged from our shelter after the all-clear siren had sounded there wasn't a door or a window left on any of the houses and the streets were deep with still-hot shrapnel, jagged pieces of metal which were bits of anti-aircraft shells fallen to the ground after exploding.

We were very lucky to survive that night but me and my pals soon forgot the danger and were out collecting shrapnel to add to our collections, for there was a lot of competition for the biggest and most interesting bits. After the school was bombed the teachers set up classes in the Cairo Street Methodist Chapel. Education was disrupted hugely by the war. Many teachers were in the Forces, others were hauled out of retirement to take over and not all were any good. There was one I remember in particular called Miss Walton who was really nasty.

Despite being so young it soon came home to me that war was not a game. One morning after a bad raid we emerged to the news that two of my school pals had been killed. They had been in a shelter which received a direct hit from a bomb and their family of 15 was wiped out. The shelters offered protection from blast and flying debris but if a bomb dropped right on top, that was it. It was a very sad day. That was when you realized that the job was serious. Up till then you're just a kid, then you suddenly go to school and your mates aren't there, they're dead. After that you're different.

Granddad taught me how to recognize enemy aircraft. Standing outside our front door, him in his warden's uniform and tin hat, me standing half afraid half excited beside him, he'd say, "Now this is a British plane coming" and I'd listen to its engine humming. "And now this is a German one" he'd say and I'd hear the distinctly different notes. If they came right overhead it would be straight into the shelter for me. You had to know what to listen for because often they'd be over before the siren went so if you heard enemy planes approaching you'd take cover.

While these dramatic events went on around us we children carried on doing the things children always do. Because many factories had to switch over to making things for the war, toys were few and far between but one glorious day my father appeared with a tin wagon about a foot long with a trailer on the back. Where he got it goodness only knows. I thought the world of that wagon. I used to walk a mile and a half to Sunday school every week to the High Street Methodist Church. Once a year we'd board a big, black Sunderland and District bus and trundle off on the Sunday school outing, lumbering out of the city into the countryside as far as Middleton-in-Teesdale on one occasion which is 48 miles. For a child whose life took place almost entirely within a few miles radius of home this was a huge event.

Here was my first taste of farm life, walking past farm buildings with cats galore, there must have been 40 of them, which to me was heaven, though I could never manage to catch one to stroke.

A weekly highlight back in Sunderland was a Saturday morning children's club at the Havelock cinema where they'd put on films with Roy Rogers, the cowboy with his famous horse Trigger, and you were living in a land of make believe for a few precious hours.

Before TV, cinema was the big thing and there were several in the city. We'd stand for ages in queues for the big hits like *The Wizard of Oz* and you often went in as seats came free, no matter what stage the film was at. You just watched it round, and all the supporting features, until it got to the bit where you'd come in and then you'd go home. Queuing was a regular part of wartime life. Many things were rationed, including meat, butter, eggs and sugar, and you bought what you were entitled to. Unrationed food was often in short supply and I'd be sent by Gran or Auntie to join a queue. We'd queue for bread or for fruit and many times you'd get to the front and they'd be sold out. Oranges and bananas were very few and far between. If you were very, very lucky you might get an orange in your Christmas stocking. They were a luxury.

One evening when I was only about six or seven I sneaked

up to some allotments, crawled under the wire and pinched four sticks of rhubarb, which I thought would be marvellous. But as I crawled out again who should be stood there but a policeman. I can see him now, towering over me, Bobby Jordan whose son was one of my pals at school. He just clipped me round the ear'ole and said, "Don't let me see you pinching anymore!" And that's my first and last criminal event. He let me keep the rhubarb. "Now you've got it you take it but don't you dare come back!" he said. Gran wanted to know where I'd got the rhubarb and I told her I'd been given it.

How Gran managed to cope with all this I don't know. She was well into her sixties which in those days was getting on but I was always well fed, clothed and warm. Every night she pulled a fine comb through my hair to keep it free from the dreaded nits which were considered a mark of deprivation and poverty.

There wasn't much meat available but plenty of vegetables especially potatoes and I remember rice puddings. My auntie did the baking and the mending. I felt loved and well cared for and think I was quite a good little boy overall. I remember standing in line for soup which was being given out at the local Methodist church hall probably after a heavy raid. Gas, electric and water supplies were often cut off by bomb damage and soup kitchens or mobile canteens would fill the gap.

Nothing was wasted and food scraps, peelings etc were taken up to Mr Stuart's who kept a few pigs. He'd give me a couple of boiled sweets and I thought I'd got the world! If there weren't many scraps, you only got one sweet.

As if we didn't have enough to contend with, in 1942 at the age of six I got diphtheria and was carted off to the isolation hospital. Instead of walls inside, there was a long line of large windows. I was alone in my room and could see the other patients and our visitors but we couldn't hear each other.

They sent for my father who was still based in Britain at that point and he was granted three days' compassionate leave. He could only wave through the windows. I can remember him standing there in his Army uniform, not being able to hear anything he was saying.

To me it was all very strange but quite interesting and not particularly frightening. I don't even remember feeling very ill but disliked the daily injections in my thigh with what looked like knitting needles. Six weeks later they let me out.

That same year Granddad died and Gran and I were left on our own. Until he was posted abroad my father would come to us on leave occasionally, I'm not sure where from. Then he was sent to a billet between the villages of Aldbrough St. John and Melsonby near Richmond in North Yorkshire and this brought me another taste of country life as he would take me over there during the school holidays. At home, my experience of open spaces was restricted to Tunstall Hill in Sunderland where in winter we'd go snowballing and sledging, and Backhouse Park, a favourite place for trainspotting where the steam locomotives emerged in a cloud of smoke from a very long tunnel. I'd be there with my pal Nigel Minkovitch, who was Jewish. At that time I had no idea of the terrible things Hitler was doing to the Jews but Nigel's family must have lived in even more fear of invasion than mine did.

Today a car makes short work of the 37 miles from Sunderland to Aldbrough St. John but in the mid-1940s our journey was by bus to Darlington which took two hours then service No.29 from Darlington to Melsonby, which is still running today, and took another hour. At first my father came to fetch me but after I'd done the journey a time or two I went on my own. Tired and dishevelled I'd jump out of the bus into the fresh air and open spaces of the countryside for, despite being a city-born lad, that is where I am happiest.

By this time my father had met the woman who was to become his second wife, a lovely person called Bella who was always kind to me. Her brother rented High Langdale Farm near Melsonby and from their fields on a hill I could look east to where the industrial towns and cities on the coast were getting a pounding. In the distance searchlights criss-crossed the sky and the bright orange of explosions burst below. I hoped Gran and Auntie and Uncle were alright in their shelters but thought, "At least I'm safe here tonight."

May 1945 saw the end of the war in Europe, though fighting continued in the Far East until August, and Sunderland rang to the sound of street parties and big feasts. Where the food came from I just don't know. Tables and chairs were out in the road and people were dancing.

My father had been sent to Italy when the invasion took place. I'm not sure when he was demobbed - demobilised - but I remember him coming home looking quite smart in the de-mob suit issued to all ex-servicemen who had spent so many years in uniform that they had nothing else.

Jobs were scarce as so many men were returning from the Forces but peacetime industries hadn't got going again properly. However he found a job as a bus conductor and I got a free ride or two as a result.

As a child I had known nothing but war and I didn't really understand what peace would mean but I was very glad that my dad was home again and that there wouldn't be any more bombs falling on me!

When Peter grew up he became an agricultural seedsman, setting up his own business. His memoir is called *The Dancing Seedsman*.

JANET SNOWDEN

Janet was born in Helmsley, a small market town in North Yorkshire, in 1939. As a baby she moved with her mother, two brothers and sister to York where her father had joined the city police. They later returned to Helmsley again.

'At the top of Helmsley High Street was the mortuary where a drawn net curtain meant a body was in there. As kids we were very curious and peeped through the window to see who it was. Sometimes a soldier would be lying on the slab, still in uniform, after one of the accidents which happened during service training. That was just normal life for us, people were getting killed all the time and we accepted it.'

In York in a raid we had to go under the stairs. The rest of the family had gas masks but babies like me were put into something like an enclosed carry cot with a pump for air. My older sister had instructions from my dad that she was to pump the air "if Mum goes to sleep". He didn't want to frighten her by saying "if Mum dies". How successful that would have been I don't know and luckily we didn't have the chance to find out.

When I was only 10 months old we returned to Helmsley after my father died. He had a muscle disease which paralysed him completely. My earliest memories are of a town full of soldiers and tanks for several regiments were stationed at Duncombe Park nearby. Nissen huts were hidden beneath trees so they couldn't be seen from the air. When the tanks rumbled through town there was a tremendous noise, so different from the horses and carts we were used to. Hardly anyone had a car in Helmsley. To ride out in a car for pleasure was unheard of and we hardly went anywhere outside our little town. I didn't have a holiday until I was about 14. When I went to my aunt's near Selby after the war I thought I was going to the ends of the earth.

Most of the soldiers were in their late teens. My mother did some work with the Women's Voluntary Service *(now the WRVS)* and the Royal British Legion taking soldiers into their homes now and again to give them a meal and play cards and chat. They were just boys a long way from home.

Treats were in short supply, even apples. One day we were told to take a jar to school into which was spooned some precious cocoa powder. I don't know where that came from but we were all given a small portion and that was a real treat. As a little girl it was my job on a Saturday morning to go to the grocer's and draper's shop run by my grandparents to get the weekly rations for our family of five and was able to bring them back in one small shopping basket, so you can tell how meagre they were.

War was just an everyday thing for me. I knew that I'd got to hate the Germans but when I met a real one, well half a one, I couldn't hate him. Klaus was a local boy whose father was English and his mother German. He had a very hard time but I was always one for the underdog and decided to make a great friend of him. He couldn't help his mother being German. Later his name was changed to Claude which was more acceptable.

Enormous concrete barricades stretched across the roads into Helmsley – the remains of one are still there – which were supposed to stop an invasion but how good they would have been I don't know. We used to sit on top of them and wave to the soldiers going past.

Duncombe Park had a garrison theatre which showed films to locals and in the pitch darkness of the blackout we would walk the mile up there and back again. I fell into the grass many a time.

At the top of the High Street was the mortuary in the old workhouse where a drawn net curtain meant a body was in there. As kids we were very curious and peeped through the window to see who it was. Sometimes a soldier would be lying on the slab, still in uniform, after one of the accidents which happened during service training. That was just normal life for us, people were getting killed all the time and we accepted it.

One night an enemy plane strafed the area, hitting a train and killing the guard I believe. During that same attack my future husband Ernest, who was only a little boy at the time, nearly lost his life. Growing up on his parents' farm in Helmsley he became friendly with June the Land Girl who worked for them. This particular summer's evening he went down to her caravan for a chat and was lying on her bunk as she knelt beside him with a picture book. Usually he would have been sitting up. Suddenly the plane roared over and fired at the caravan, bullets hitting the top of the bunk. Had he been sitting up, Ernest would have been killed. There's no doubt about it. Had June been standing she would also have been killed. He told me later, "I don't remember her ever showing me a book before" so it was a very lucky escape.

With no swimming pools we learned to swim in the River Rye where unexploded incendiary bombs would be nestling in the mud. We used to pick them up and throw them at each other, not seeing the danger. I think the river would shine on a moonlit night and attract the bombers. In the 1990s some local children found one and took it into the police station where all the officers immediately ducked for cover. The Army used one of my husband's fields to blow it up and made quite a mess.

When Janet grew up she married Ernest and they ran a farm in Helmsley.

MARY HALL

Mary was born in Hull in 1938.

'Our dog was always first down the shelter.'

My father was a foreman lighterman on the River Humber. Lightermen used barges to ferry goods between ships and warehouses on the quay. During the war he directed ammunition up and down the Humber under great secrecy. When the air-raids started my father sent us to stay with relations in the village of North Newbald to be safe. From there my mother stood on the hill watching the bombing of Hull and said, "That's it, we're going back to your Dad." And so after only two nights we went home again.

Our house wasn't hit but all the windows and doors blew in from a blast nearby. We were in our shelter in the garden at the time but our dog was in the house and afterwards he was always the first down the shelter when a raid started. As children we just accepted the war as normal life and I don't remember being scared. As soon as the siren went I'd run into Mum and Dad's room and sit on their bed while they got ready quickly. Outside I could see the bright lights of flares which the Germans dropped to show up their targets and to a small child that was exciting. Watching the searchlights criss-cross the sky my only thought was, 'Oooh, have they got a plane?' I never thought about the person in the plane.

When Mary grew up she became a hairdresser and ran her own business.

EDWARD BROWN

Edward was born in 1937 in the small Yorkshire Dales village of Low Row near Richmond where he lived with his parents and sister.

'There was a lot of Army activity, soldiers on exercise and tanks. At night time if you were out it wasn't unusual to come across a figure hiding in a tree with a gun.'

Before war broke out we were all fitted with gas masks. Because I was so small my first mask was a Mickey Mouse one – they made them look a bit like him to be less frightening for small children to wear. But I was quite pleased when I was allowed an adult one later because it made me feel grown up. Every community, no matter how small, had to have an ARP warden though we were not expected to be a target for enemy bombers. He had a loft over a stable, often called a 'chamber' round here, and he had the gas masks up there so we all trooped along to be fitted out. We had demonstrations to show us different types of bombs, small incendiaries mainly, so that we would know not to touch it if we found an unexploded one. There never were any bombs dropped on the village. The nearest we got was when someone at the top of Arkengarthdale a few miles away thought they were far enough out in the country not to bother with the blackout. A German plane returning from a raid somewhere else dropped a leftover bomb there. Luckily no-one was hurt but my father was called out to repair the damage to the farm buildings and he brought some shrapnel back to show us.

You sometimes heard the bombers droning overhead because they would come up the east side of the country and use the river shining in the moonlight to navigate across. My parents would always listen to see if it was one of ours or the enemy because the German bombers had a very distinctive sound and I think obviously they were nervous but I don't ever remember feeling frightened.

I'd never known anything different. What struck us most as children was the shortage of everything. We were told how nice it was to eat bananas but there were no bananas to be had, how nice it would be to have sweets but there were very few. It was all about shortages and ration books and generally being deprived of everything you might have if there wasn't a war. I can remember repeating regularly, "I wish the war was over" even though I didn't know much beyond that.

We used to listen to the radio including Lord Haw-Haw who broadcast in English from Germany telling us how badly we were doing. Everyone used to listen to him just to have a laugh. They hanged him as a traitor at the end.

We weren't too badly off for food because we were producing

our own eggs, milk, bacon and of course everyone was gardening. My father had gardens all over the place, even a bit of pasture way up the hill for potatoes and he'd go trudging off there. There were gooseberry bushes, currant bushes and plum trees and much of this was bottled to preserve it for the winter months.

There was a lot of Army activity, soldiers on exercise and tanks. At night time if you were out it wasn't unusual to come across a figure hiding in a tree with a gun. We'd never known anything else, it was part of our life. At the end there were great celebrations, Union Jack flags everywhere but it took a long time for things to get back to normal and rationing went on for years. As a lad one of the big changes I noticed was that suddenly there were a lot more young men around the village, those who had been in the Services and were lucky enough to have survived.

Gradually the shops in Low Row began to have a few more things in them to buy than they had had before. There was the post office run by the Gill family where old man Gill, who had been a draper, sold material because a lot of people made their own clothes, and also some groceries. There was the dairy which sold milk and butter and cream. Later there was another grocery shop and a hardware store and when petrol became available for private cars again, a petrol pump was installed.

As the war came to an end the world outside Low Row began to open up to us more. In 1945 my father got a van for his business and we'd go places in it with us kids bumping around in the back, sat on boxes or an old rug. If we went the few miles to Askrigg on a Saturday afternoon we thought we were going to the end of the world. Sometimes we'd do a swap with the local minister who had an Austin Ruby saloon car so we were able to travel in comfort on our outings and he'd potter round Low Row in

38

our van for a while. Gradually travel got easier and people were allowed back on the beaches, many of which had been closed because of the threat of invasion, and suddenly I was able to go to the seaside.

Edward Brown grew up to run a successful building business in Low Row where he still lives. He tells his life story in *Building a Life in Swaledale*.

DENISE McCOOL

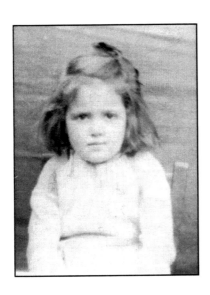

Denise was
born in 1941
in Leeds just
before the city's
worst air-raid.

*'My mother told me that when the air-raid siren went
the nurses carried the babies down to the cellar and all
mothers who could manage the stairs followed. Those
too ill to be moved were placed under the beds to protect
them from falling debris.'*

One, two three! I squeezed my eyes shut and opened them
quickly but nothing had changed. I repeated the chant
over and over again in my head but the chant did not
work. Mum had told me that in three days' time my father would
be home from the war. I was only three and did not understand
how long three days would be but could count and thought
that counting up to three would secure Dad's return. Alas, I was
disappointed.

Three days later as I sat on our back doorstep overlooking the ginnel I watched a very handsome soldier with a kitbag on his shoulder walking towards me. I couldn't take my eyes off him. He made a striking figure, very upright and, to my three-year-old mind, appeared as a hero. Heroes were tall, handsome men who fought enemies for you. Yes, a hero was walking down our ginnel and - here was the surprise - he was opening our gate! This is the first memory I have of my lovely dad. The year was 1945 and he was returning after being away for years during World War II.

Dad must have saved up all his sweet coupons for in his kitbag were chocolates, sweets and toffees which we had never tasted in our short wartime lives. My sister Barbara and I were surrounded by excitable, happy neighbourhood children, arms outstretched to get a share of this wonderful feast. Nothing could compare to that time. I had a dad, not only that but he could distribute golden hoards of sublime sweets. My sister and I bathed in the afterglow and our status grew amongst our friends.

I was born in a nursing home, Hyde Terrace in Leeds, an industrial city in West Yorkshire. It was 1941 and I arrived in a world of war. As I slept peacefully in my cot, just a few days old, about 40 German aircraft were heading for us. First incendiaries were dropped to start fires and mark the way for the heavy bombers which followed. About 65 people were killed and 100 homes destroyed in the worst raid Leeds experienced. Thousands of fire fighters, wardens and ambulance crews struggled to cope. My mother told me that when the air-raid siren went the nurses carried the babies down to the cellar and all mothers who could manage the stairs followed. Those too ill to be moved were placed under the beds to protect them from falling debris. She praised a Welsh nurse who refused to go into the basement and stayed with the patients upstairs, some who were in labour or had just given birth. I think my mother was able to come down with me to safety. I don't think the nursing home was hit but, even so, what horrific times those women lived through!

The city was not usually a target but you never knew when a raid might come and I was told that my sister Barbara, who had been born five years before, was never undressed fully for bed but stayed in some of her clothes in case she had to be taken to the shelter at the bottom of our garden. After I came along I was scooped up into the washing basket when the siren went and whisked along there as well.

I had never known a world without war. Many things were rationed and I could never work out why I could go into a shop with a penny but couldn't buy sweets without a coupon. I didn't understand what it was all about. I remember pointing at what I wanted and being told by the shopkeeper, "Go away, you haven't got a coupon!" Even if you had a coupon there were very few sweets on sale because sugar was in short supply.

After the war ended in 1945 and dad came home it was lovely to be a complete family again because I'd never known that.

When Denise grew up she trained as a nurse. Later she became one of Leeds' first female postal delivery workers after equality laws were brought in. She told her story in *Speaking for Myself*.

BRIAN KENT

Brian was born in 1936 in the mining town of Castleford, West Yorkshire. His father was a miner who developed TB silicosis, spending years in and out of hospital.

'For me, watching the searchlights criss-cross the skies in search of planes to shoot at were a fantastic light show just for us kids.'

Being only three when war broke out I didn't really know what peace meant. Air-raids and rationing were normal to me. All our windows had to be covered with blackout blinds at night. In our home was a stirrup pump which could spray water from a bucket in case of fire though I don't remember it being used. Everyone was given a gas mask. Me and the other boys would put ours on for fun and pretend to be aliens.

Anderson air-raid shelters were built in our back yards. When the sirens went we had to run to the shelter and crouch on little wooden stools in the light of an oil lamp with another family who shared it until the all-clear sounded. Sometimes that meant all night. Often planes were only passing overhead on their way to bigger targets but some bombs did fall on our town. Every time planes were overhead our big guns would open up with a huge booming sound which was quite a thrill for a small boy.

Once their shells had exploded high in the sky the cases burst into jagged fragments which fell to earth and could take your head off if you weren't under cover. Next morning little boys and girls scoured the streets to add to their shrapnel collections. I don't remember being frightened, just a bit startled if there was a big bang but the adults would say, "Don't worry, you'll be alright" though now I realize they must have been much more scared than I was. They knew that a direct hit by a bomb would mean we certainly wouldn't be alright, even in the Anderson, or we might come out to find no house. To keep our spirits up we'd sing or recite nursery rhymes or just chat. The family we shared with had two boys a bit younger than me so they were company. Sometimes my mother got fed up and stayed in the house, saying she'd get under our stone stairs if things got bad but I always had to go to the shelter where the wardens wanted us to be, coming round from time to time to count us.

I wasn't scared like the grown-ups because I didn't really know what it was all about. For me, watching the searchlights criss-cross the skies in search of planes to shoot at were a fantastic light show just for us kids. "That looks nice!" I thought. Enemy planes dropped flares to light up the town so the bombers could see their targets and that was even prettier.

During the early years of the war when the bombing was at its worst, my father was living at home and well enough to be an air-raid warden. This meant he might be out in a raid with only his tin hat for protection. In Castleford an RAF Spitfire crashed in fields not far from us and just missed the home of my friend.

The pilot, 22-year-old Bruce Smeaton, stayed with his damaged aircraft to steer it away from the houses instead of baling out. In my school we had a plaque commemorating his bravery and when the building was demolished this was saved and given to his relatives.

Castleford began to ring with the sounds of unfamiliar accents as refugees from countries over-run by war came to Britain and went to work in the mines. Poles and all sorts arrived. From all over Britain came the Bevin Boys, young men told to work in the mines instead of going into the armed forces. Quite a few remained after the war and married local girls. Around the streets marched soldiers in uniform who I now realize were probably members of the Home Guard.

At the height of the bombing in 1941 I started at Cutsyke School where lessons were interrupted occasionally by the siren and we'd have to head down into the long, T-shaped shelter dug into the playground. Covered in corrugated iron and soil, it was a dark tunnel which scared me far more than any bombs. In the distance was the faint glimmer of an oil lamp. Sitting on wooden benches against the walls we waited for the all-clear as the teachers did their best to reassure us.

The war in Europe ended in May 1945 and all us kids were invited to a street party. Everyone was so excited. "Everything's going to be great now, we'll do this, we'll do that!" they said, not knowing how many tough years lay ahead as all the chaos left behind after the war had to be sorted out. Many of the dads, being miners, had remained at work but some of my mates were excited because their fathers were coming back from the Army but I had no idea when I'd see mine again *(his father was by then in a sanatorium many miles away)*. In August two atom bombs ended the war with Japan and finally the fighting was over completely. There were more parties but I couldn't feel the same sense of rejoicing as the others because my dad was still ill and not a lot had changed for us.

I had no idea how bad he was. A few months later in October 1945 my Uncle Ben broke the news to me that my father had died. "He's gone to a better place," he said, trying to comfort me, but I couldn't understand why my father would leave us when I'd hardly ever seen him.

War and our empty purses had restricted travel and I hardly ever set foot outside Castleford. My life was very local and I was 10 before I saw the sea. Filled with excitement, we headed off in a coach on an outing arranged by the Working Men's Club. "Wow!" was my first reaction when I saw all that water and the waves. No films at the cinema or pictures in books had prepared me for how big it was and, unlike in the cinema, it was blue instead of black and white!

When the war was over a few little luxuries began to reappear. One day the news went round that someone had bought a bottle of the fizzy drink Tizer and that was a huge excitement. If you were lucky enough to get one you made it last a very long time.

When Brian grew up he emigrated to Australia under the Government-sponsored scheme offering a £10 boat ticket. Several years later he returned to England and became a postman. He told his story in *26,000-Mile Round Trip to Castleford.*

ROBIN BUTLER

Robin was born in 1930 and spent his childhood in the small market town of Kirkbymoorside on the North York Moors where he lived with his mother, grandmother and younger brother Roy. Robin's father had been killed in a motorbike accident when Robin was a baby. He is pictured left as a choirboy.

'We had two evacuees. They were nice little boys but had come from a very poor family. When bedtime came my mother lent these two little waifs some pyjamas to wear which they put on over their clothes.'

The last week in August 1939 was hot and sunny. The grown-ups in my family were scanning the papers and listening to the radio as events pushed ever further towards war. But for my brother Roy and me it was a time of fun and excitement for we went on holiday for a week to Redcar, a resort on the East Coast within sight of Teesside's heavy industry. In those days there was a railway station at Kirkbymoorside, sadly long since closed, and from here we travelled down to York and then up again to Darlington and on to Redcar. Money was usually too tight to afford a holiday but my granny had been left some by a relative and took us all off for the week. Already there were signs of war with sandbags around buildings and defences going up on the beach. Us children took no notice. My cousin Michael was with us and he sculpted a speedboat out of the sand complete with seat for us to sit on and in our imaginations we sped across the waves.

On Saturday September 2nd we came home and on the Sunday war was declared. Suddenly there was a lot of activity as my mother and granny scrabbled around for black material to cover the windows at night.

Our school numbers were swelled greatly by the arrival of evacuees from the towns and cities where bombing was expected to be heaviest but nowhere was completely safe. Even little Kirkbymoorside was a target for nearby was a factory making gliders which had grown up during peace time and now had been taken over by the military but we didn't get the pounding the larger places did, like Hull, Teesside and Tyneside.

The evacuees arrived by train and were marched up to the memorial hall where people were waiting to take them into their homes. My mother couldn't take any because she went out to work and my granny had enough on her plate already. These poor children were more or less picked over, a girl who would be able to help in the house or a strong boy to do heavier work. Little boys, especially ones from poor homes, were the least popular and last to be chosen.

At the end these two little lads were left and I'm not going to say they were dirty but they were certainly scruffy. About teatime that Friday there was a knock on the door and it was the vicar with the two boys standing beside him who looked tired, fed up and rather tearful. Nobody wanted them. My mother explained her circumstances but the vicar persisted. "Please, Mrs Butler, could you at least take them for the weekend?"

So she replied, "Alright, Vicar, but it must be just for the weekend because then I'll be out to work." And in they came.

Their names were Brian and Raymond and they had been sent out of Hartlepool, carrying very little beyond the clothes they were wearing. Roy and I showed them where to wash their hands then we all sat down for a boiled eggs and soldiers tea. The brothers stared uncomfortably at the eggs. It turned out they hadn't had a boiled egg before so my mother took the tops off for them and they copied us, dipping the toast into the yoke. Spread out across the table were jam tarts, cake and buns to eat after the eggs but they helped themselves to the tarts immediately and ate them with the eggs.

They were nice little boys but had come from a very poor family. We were hard up but things had obviously been much tougher for them. At the beginning of the war there was still a lot of unemployment and no welfare state to help, just a very limited and cruelly administered dole, so maybe that was the reason. On the other hand, my mother and granny were very clever at making a little go a long way and that made a big difference to us. When bedtime came my mother lent these two little waifs some pyjamas to wear which they put on over their clothes until she put things right. They had only one set of clothes which they wore day and night. The soles of their feet were like leather and we guessed that most of the time they ran about barefoot, being put into socks and boots only for their journey to Kirkbymoorside.

In the end they stayed until the following Wednesday when someone else was finally persuaded to take them. I can only hope they were well treated. Not all evacuees were, though for many it was a happy introduction to country ways leaving a lifelong impression. Despite the overcrowding at school we soon accepted the evacuees and I became good friends with one, Gordon Jackson, who sat next to me.

Gas mask drill at school was carried out by a visiting inspector who sat us and the teachers in the classroom wearing our gas masks then let off some painful but ultimately harmless tear gas, ordering us to lift the corner of our masks. When the gas got in your eyes it stung like nettles then we were allowed outside. Perhaps he wanted us to know how awful gas could be as we were all pretty unmoved by the many lectures we'd endured. All the windows were criss-crossed with paper tape to lessen the impact of flying glass during an attack but there were no air-raid shelters either at school or at home as we weren't considered a high risk area. Our instructions were that if the siren went we were to get under our desks but I don't remember any raids happening during school time.

For two small boys like Roy and me the war brought a few irritations such as the sudden disappearance of sweets but then there had rarely been much spare money for those anyway. For us the war was mainly one big adventure.

In 1941 a large lorry rumbled into town and the townspeople watched fascinated as pieces of a German plane, a Messerschmitt 109 which had been shot down and salvaged, were hauled out and reassembled. The propellers were all bent and there were bits missing. It was touring the area as a morale booster. Children were allowed to sit in the cockpit and I scrambled up, settling awkwardly into the metal, bucket-shaped seat, imagining myself as an air ace and wondering how the pilot could sit for hours in such an uncomfortable seat. Later I realized he would have been sitting on his parachute.

Despite being a rural area, Kirkbymoorside was bombed as the Nazis tried to hit the glider factory. On August Bank Holiday Monday in either 1942 or 1943, the siren went and instead of taking cover under the stairs as I should have done I peered out of the back door to see what was happening. The roar of a plane filled the air and I saw its great black shape from which bombs were dropping. However, no explosions came, just clouds of dust, so I thought perhaps they were dropping great bags of soot.

We had a lodger staying with us at the time who was sitting on the outside toilet and I heard his voice screaming out at me from behind the wooden door to get inside. "They're gunning on us! They're gunning on us!" he cried. It makes me laugh to think of it now but it was only by a miracle that I didn't lose my mother in that raid. The bombs dropped near the railway station, one near the bridge and the other on the joiner's shop of Russells and another on Mill Field. Most failed to explode. Hitler used so much slave labour that bombs were sometimes sabotaged and failed to go off. Another dropped on the laundry where my mother usually worked but again was a dud. Luckily the laundry was closed, being a Bank Holiday. Had these bombs gone off there would have been devastation.

The plane veered off and started strafing anything that moved including someone working in the graveyard where bullets hit the church. The man who was later to become my father-in-law was walking in Tinley Garth and was showered with masonry as bullets struck a building. The main street was packed with people waiting to go into the pet show but none was hit.

As the pilot headed back out over open countryside he took

pot-shots at the local huntsman who was in what we called the Kennel Field. Some friends of ours were camping and the husband leapt under a hedge into a bed of nettles as the bullets whistled round the tent in which his wife was cowering. After just a few minutes it was all over leaving Kirkbymoorside shocked but grateful for its narrow escape. For me it had been a hugely exciting adventure. As far as I know nobody in Kirkbymoorside was killed or seriously injured during the raids but that was by pure luck.

There were other raids. Sometimes I'd be woken by my mother during the night to the rising and falling notes of the wailing siren and the crump of bombs exploding in the distance. With no proper shelter we had to take cover in the passageway between the kitchen and lounge.

Half asleep, we stumbled down the stairs. My mother and granny sat on chairs, hugging us to them as we shivered under the blankets in which we had been wrapped. Outside we could hear the roar of the planes, the explosions of the bombs and the sharp crack of our anti-aircraft guns.

At this point the war seemed less exciting and much more frightening, wondering if we were going to get hit, for our passageway would have provided precious little protection. The raids were always short-lived, involving only one or two planes, and after about 20 minutes the single continuous note of the siren would sound the all-clear and we'd be back to bed. In daylight our fears abated and we'd be out on our bikes with our mates hunting for bomb craters and picking up shrapnel. My best piece was the size of my hand and an inch thick.

Wandering across the fields we'd keep our eyes open for incendiary bombs, some of which hadn't yet exploded but we knew not to touch these and reported them to the local ARP wardens. I was very jealous of my friend who found one which had gone off but remained almost intact. He kept it as an ornament in the fireplace.

I never remember my mother or granny, who was in her seventies, showing their fears but the war must have been a tough time for them, struggling to make ends meet, coping with raids and rationing. I remember only one time hearing them weep and that was the day in 1942 that the dreaded telegram arrived from the War Office. My cousin John who had been living with us was in the Navy and the telegram brought the stark news that he had been wounded. News began to filter out of a disastrous attack on Dieppe and that's where John had been hurt. Shrapnel had lodged in his brain and surgery was too risky. He recovered, carrying that metal with him to the grave when he died from cancer aged only 52.

Not being classed a high risk area, civil defence measures were rather haphazard. Our first siren was made out of a converted cream separator on Pump Hill. Later an electric one was mounted on the memorial hall, the shelf for which is still there. The local ARP wardens were based in what was called the dug-out, a dark and damp cellar under the hall which had once been a prison.

Enemy action was one way of being killed and injured in the war, our own forces were another danger. Accidents involving military vehicles were common and Roy was knocked down by an Army motorcycle despatch rider but was unhurt.

Ordinary life continued as best it could. Aged about 11, I joined the Scouts. Easter was camp time in a field not far from home, no matter what the weather was like, and we survived rain, hail and snow. Occasionally the sun shone. A beck ran through the field in which there was a great deal of larking about, whatever the weather, and was more enticing than the portable shower block which our Scout leaders had thoughtfully supplied. Water was pumped to them from a nearby farm and was stone cold, so we rarely risked it and returned home smelling strongly of wood smoke.

Because of the war my Scout group changed its name to Air Scouts and instead of the hat with the big brim we were allowed to wear berets, grey shirts and black or navy trousers. We were taught to recognize different aircraft so that we'd know whether to take cover or not.

Clothes and material were in short supply and one day when I was about 13 my mother heard on the grapevine that our local tailor, Ernie Sherwood, was selling off old Army uniforms which could be bought without using any of the precious coupons which customers usually had to present, so she nipped down with me as soon as she could. Ernie slapped a huge bale of uniforms on the counter, snipped the string and, looking me up and down, picked one out that wasn't quite as huge as the others for, despite being quite tall, I was on the skinny side.

Back home, out came the sewing machine and soon there was my own little uniform of which I was extremely proud. I didn't even mind when I discovered that my mother had found two bullet holes in the uniform before cutting it up. That became my main outfit and lasted for years for I even wore it later in my first job.

A huge anti-aircraft gun had been set up in a field to protect the town and Roy and I would take cans of tea and a few cakes to cheer up the soldiers. In return they'd let us listen in to radio exchanges between units which made no sense to us but sounded exciting. Generally the soldiers stationed around Kirkbymoorside were very tolerant of the small boys and girls who liked to tag along. One winter's day the snow lay thickly enough for some grand sledging down a steep hill at the bottom of which stood an open gate. If they hadn't gritted the road you could shoot through and far beyond but this carried the risk of hitting the gatepost.

Roy took a sickening crack on the head as he missed his target and a platoon drilling nearby sent two men over to help. Luckily Roy was ok, if a bit dazed, and I had to haul him home on the sledge, which I wasn't best pleased about as I wanted to get back in the snow.

Robin remained in Kirkbymoorside and grew up to be a blacksmith, also playing a big part in setting up the Ryedale Folk Museum on the North York Moors. His story is told in *A Will to Win*.

BERNARD SHANNON

Bernard was born in 1928 and grew up in Scarborough. One of a family of nine children, he had several older brothers as well as his father away in the war.

'After the raid we went to look at the smoking ruins of Dennis's the print works and couldn't believe it had happened. The works made holiday postcards and they were scattered all over the place, half burned. It was a real mess. The damage was astonishing.'

I was one of the oldest still at home and felt quite a lot of responsibility. I was the man of the house. We brought each other up. My father had been gassed twice while in the Army during World War I. Later he worked as an upholsterer and when the next war broke out his business was ruined because he couldn't get any material. He had to join up again just to earn a living, this time into the RAF, and passed the medical but wasn't A1 because of his earlier injuries. After becoming a barrage balloon operator he was sent to help protect London during the Battle of Britain in 1940 then moved around the country, ending up back in Scarborough billeted in the Grand Hotel and working as a batman.

Our home was near the railway station. The first change for us was the arrival of evacuees, mainly from Hull, which made our school so overcrowded that sometimes classes spilled over into church halls or we'd have to go out for nature walks. Some of the evacuees became good friends of mine and stayed in Scarborough after the war. Our town was safer than Hull but we had quite a bit of bombing, being a port and a training centre for RAF aircrew.

One very bad night we called The Blitz we got a real hammering. One family with five or six children was wiped out when their home about a quarter of a mile from us took a direct hit and Dennis's the printing works just down the road went up in flames. We were in a Morrison shelter, a heavy steel table which you could use by day and shelter under by night, the sides covered with wire mesh to keep out flying debris. Five of us would snuggle inside wrapped in blankets and try to sleep but you couldn't, feeling a mixture of excitement and fright. There was no room for Mother who sat under the stairs. We were too young to appreciate the danger we were in and annoyed at being dragged out of bed, the siren droning outside, and made to come downstairs. You could hear the planes above and the crash of bombs and certainly didn't put your nose outside.

Next morning we tried to find out what had been hit but had to go to school. Lots of other children failed to turn up after having no sleep at all. That afternoon the teacher said, "You'd all better get under your desks and try to get a couple of hours sleep." But we didn't and just played about. It seemed a bit of a lark. Even when we found out about the children who had been killed it seemed unreal because they had been at a different school.

We got as close as we could to the smoking ruins of Dennis's and couldn't believe it had happened. The works made holiday postcards and they were scattered all over the place, half burned. It was a real mess. The damage was astonishing.

A small Lysander plane crashed on the allotments near our playing field – the pilot survived - and we all went up to get souvenirs when the guard wasn't there. I got a lever off the dashboard which was a real treasure. We all had collections of bits and pieces of planes, shells and bombs and would swap them.

From our top bedroom you could look out to sea and watch the ships passing far away on their way to join convoys, protected by barrage balloons which rose from their decks. Towards the end of the war we saw some of the thousand bomber raids leaving for Germany and that was quite exciting.

At 14 I left school and got a job as an apprentice in machine woodworking making ammunition boxes and aircraft engine casings, among other things for the war. Even as a teenager I had to take my turn fire watching, sleeping on the premises in case there was a raid. What I would have done if all that wood in the timber yard had gone up I don't know but we got an extra half crown for that *(12½p)* which a fortune to us then.

All Bernard's brothers survived the war but his cousin Sidney, who was 19 and in the Merchant Navy, died when his ship was torpedoed by a German U-Boat. Just after the war finished Bernard himself joined the Merchant Navy and received danger money because mines remained a menace at sea. After three years he returned to his work as a wood machinist.

PAMELA McMASTER-MORGAN

Pamela was born in 1930 near Stockton. Her family ran Fewster's, a well-known market gardening business, and she lived near the nursery with her parents and brother. There were 25 huge greenhouses.

'Running out of our house, we saw the greenhouses sitting amid piles of glass shattered by the bomb blast. We all stood in shock, with the sound of tinkling glass puncturing the silence as more pieces fell to the ground, wrecking anything growing beneath.'

After war broke out life continued much as usual until the day when I had to queue up at school to be fitted with a gas mask. Putting it on was ghastly, one of the worst bits of the war. Despite being in a semi-rural area, our home was near the railway line which was considered a target and we were only a few miles from Middlesbrough, an important industrial area which got a pounding. I spent most of the war either at home or at boarding school not far away but was evacuated briefly.

I'm not sure if I left Stockton at the outbreak of war or if I went in 1940/41 when the raids got really bad. Nothing much happened to civilians until the summer of 1940. However, at some point I was sent to Wales in what was, I think, a private arrangement between my parents and someone they knew. Many other children were sent by the trainload from cities to the countryside as part of a Government organized operation and parents had no idea where their children would end up. But others like myself were luckier and went as individuals. I assume my brother, who would have been about 16 by then, was finishing school. Anyway, he didn't come with me. Later he was an articled clerk to an accountant.

I found myself in Borth-y-gest near Porthmadog on the Gwynedd coast in a terraced house just across from a lovely beach. There were beautiful blue butterflies everywhere. When I went to school it was all in Welsh and I wasn't there long enough to learn more than a few words. Despite the sudden upheaval in my world, I don't remember being unhappy except when I asked for some toothpaste and my hostess said, "You don't need that, just use soot," which was an old-fashioned way of rubbing the dirt off your teeth. I decided to wait until my mother could send me a tube of toothpaste.

Much to my joy there was a piano at the house and I wrote home asking for some of my favourite music to be sent but when it arrived it was with a parcel of Ragworth Beauty tomatoes, a speciality of our nursery, which had got squashed and somewhere I still have the music covered in tomato stains. From then on whenever I was away from home for whatever reason, I was always getting parcels of tomatoes which were lovely, assuming they survived intact. During my exile in Wales I don't remember being particularly homesick, as many evacuees were, and looking back I am amazed at how I coped with it all.

I don't remember being frightened and perhaps I wasn't there for very long. Eventually I was home again where my father was forced to plough up many of his precious flower fields to grow more vegetables as part of the war effort. Only a few flowers were grown, I suppose for funeral wreaths and weddings. Petrol was strictly rationed because oil had to be brought by sea and after a while, there was none at all for private cars which were stored on piles of bricks so the tyres wouldn't rot. Occasionally my father drove up to see our friends at the farm in the nursery van and took a few goods in the back so that if the police stopped us we could say we were making a business delivery.

At the front and back of our house were reasonable sized gardens which my mother took care of. When the war came my father built a very elaborate brick shelter in the back garden. Steps led down into a room rather like a bedroom equipped with bunks and somewhere to make tea.

He planted a bramble over the top to make it less conspicuous. Safely stored on the steps inside was a large earthenware pot containing preserved eggs covered in a liquid called isinglass. Eggs were in short supply in those days and to have lost them in a raid would have been a disaster. Games in the garden with my lovely dog Spot would be interrupted by the hum of distant planes and I'd hold my breath, waiting to see if I should wave because it was one of ours or run for cover from a German bomber. If I detected the distinctive droning of an enemy raider, Spot and I would run to hide under the kitchen table, always preferable to the dark shelter. Sometimes when things got very bad we'd sleep in the shelter but I wasn't very keen on that.

Living at the nursery and keeping some of our own livestock meant we had a better choice of food than some people during the war. Another advantage for my father and I, who were both keen riders, was that he was able to continue to keep our hunters because feed was available for the nursery's cart horses. There was our lovely Jersey cow in a field behind our house, which I used to try to milk but never succeeded, and chickens and pigs. One night there was a great kerfuffle outside and we rushed out to discover that a fox had taken the heads off all our chickens which was terrible. When you keep animals like that there will inevitably be rats which we'd dig out from their nests and good old Spot would get them and kill them, just like that!

My mother was very upset that you couldn't buy white, refined flour any more, only flour that was a muddy white which the Government had ordered because it was more nutritious and less wasteful than white and needed less time and energy to produce. I believe it also contained barley as wheat was in short supply. We got extra butter because my father was entitled to it instead of sugar, which as a diabetic he didn't need.

We were all issued with ration books which we had to register with various suppliers, such as the butcher and baker, who were sent enough supplies to cover that number of customers. Meat was rationed from March 1940 and was done by cost, so you could have one shilling and tenpence worth a week *(about 9p)*. Children got an extra allowance. Cafes and restaurants were exempt but there was a cap on what they could charge, so you couldn't just walk in and order a huge meal. I went with my mother to the cinema in Middlesbrough and then to a café where we were offered stewed heart which I couldn't face. Rissoles were another frequent menu item as cooks could mince up whatever meat they had, no matter how poor in quality.

During the war our neighbours also kept pigs and we'd take

turns in killing them. You weren't allowed to do it without a licence. When the time came to kill the pig you had to smother its screams. Afterwards my mother was terribly busy in the kitchen, jointing the meat which we'd share with the neighbours, then we'd get some meat back when they killed theirs.

A big bucket full of blood would come into the kitchen for my mother to make black pudding and after seeing that, I've never been able to touch the stuff but she made the most wonderful brawn. My father had the tricky job of salting the hams which had to be right or the precious meat would go off. My mother was always moaning and groaning that he wasn't doing it right. Afterwards the sides of bacon were hung up in the loft so that if an inspector came he wouldn't see them.

So we were lucky and had nice bacon and eggs in the wartime, which a lot of people didn't, and were able to produce quite a lot of food ourselves. My mother was very good at managing things and we never really lacked for anything.

Sweets were another matter. When we went on holiday to Scarborough we sent my father out early in the morning to queue outside a shop where we had heard they would be selling rock. It was a huge treat and he was such a kind man that he would do that sort of thing for us.

Scarborough or Whitby were the places for holidays now and, with no petrol for the car, we had to go by train. There was a lovely swimming pool at Scarborough and a miniature train to go on but I don't remember much about the beach, perhaps part of it was cordoned off because of invasion worries or mines. Despite the grim times, there were delightful seaside shows staged and I loved them.

Reading was a great passion of mine but my mother thought

buying books was a waste of money and encouraged me to cycle every Saturday to Stockton Library. At night I'd be under the sheets reading a book by torchlight when I should have been asleep. Then one wonderful day she bought me a *Mary Poppins* book which I treasured and still have. It was the first book I was allowed to own and I read it over and over again. Inscribed inside is: *"1942. My very first book".*

During the war clothes and fabric were rationed but my mother was very clever at what we used to call "Make Do and Mend". My poor father's pyjamas were so patched you couldn't tell which was the original. If a jumper got too small the wool had to be unpicked and wound up again into a ball, then made into something bigger, even if that meant mixing in a slightly different colour from another garment. When sheets wore out in the centre they were cut in half then re-stitched sides-to-middle so the stronger sides were at the centre, though that wasn't as comfortable to sleep on. Leather patches went on worn-out elbows and knees of jackets and trousers.

One day my mother got hold of some parachute silk which was much prized among dressmakers and made nighties and underwear. The silk was beautiful but bright yellow. Ration coupons went mainly on new things for me but, despite getting older, I was allowed no choice in what they were.

We had sticky tape crossed over the windows and blackout curtains which made it stifling on a summer night. If you wanted to open the window for some air you had to sit in the dark. The few vehicles on the road had headlamp covers so only a tiny beam showed. All direction signs were taken down to confuse any enemy who landed but since hardly anyone had a car it wasn't too much of an inconvenience. Most of the bombing happened in bigger towns and cities and if there was a raid over Middlesbrough my mother would take me upstairs into the bedroom and, being careful to turn off the lights before raising the blackout curtains, would show me the searchlights and tracer trails from the anti-aircraft guns flashing across the sky. "Oh look, it's just like fireworks!" she'd say, but it wasn't, it was all these guns firing at the bombers. I think she did it to make it seem less frightening for me.

She took me to look at bomb damage and I can still see it now. Down by Middlesbrough Station a hotel had been hit and you could see all the rooms gaping open and the beds hanging out and half the building down. My mother seemed to take a fascinated delight in taking me to see these things but I thought it was pretty horrific.

My most terrible experience of the war came on August 15th 1941 whilst we were having supper. Suddenly there was a terrific crash and bang. There had been no air-raid warning but an enemy plane had come over and aimed for the railway line close by our home or perhaps it was going for the anti-aircraft guns and barrage balloons. Whatever it intended to do, it missed and the bomb fell nearby.

Running out of our house we saw the greenhouses near our house surrounded by piles of glass shattered by the bomb blast. We all stood in shock, with the sound of tinkling glass puncturing the silence as more pieces fell to the ground, wrecking anything growing beneath. Thankfully, nobody at the nursery had been injured but it was a different story at the site where the bomb had actually fallen.

The next day we walked just for a couple of minutes to see what had happened and on the other side of the railway bridge a row of houses had been completely demolished. In one of the houses lived a young man who worked for my father. On the day of the bombing he had gone out to the pictures, as we called the cinema then, and returned to find no house and no family. They had all been killed. That was the sort of horrible thing that happened and was the worst thing I saw. Some children saw the war as an adventure but I thought it was all horrible.

In 1941 when I turned 11 my parents decided to send me to Ayton School, a Quaker establishment in Great Ayton 16 miles away, because it was safe from all the bombing. I managed to get a scholarship so my parents had to pay only for my accommodation. With my hair in long, fair plaits, I set off in my new uniform of a navy blue tunic, long thick cotton stockings and jumper. There were different coloured jumpers for different houses with a matching colour sash. Mine was Pendle House, which was red. In summer we wore checked summer frocks and could change into them as soon as the big tulip tree outside the Friends Meeting Room bloomed.

You could see across to Middlesbrough and watch the flashes of the guns and the fires caused by bombs but at Great Ayton itself there was nothing. There were air-raid drills where we had to rush for the cellars but there never was a real one. The school felt very remote from the conflict, partly because of the location and partly because, being Quakers, they didn't believe in fighting. Whether you agreed with their pacifist stance or not, their regime taught you not to be aggressive towards people and treat your neighbour as your equal, it didn't matter if they were black or Asian or what. That didn't stop the pupils carrying out awful initiation ceremonies on new pupils, like pushing their heads under a basin of water or making apple pie beds with sheets and blankets folded so you couldn't get in. I couldn't get home in term time but my parents often cycled over to see me, dragging my brother with them much to his resentment. It was a very long way. Of course they came with lots of tomatoes, some for me and some for matron.

Downstairs was a room full of lockers containing tuck - all the snacks and treats brought from home. Some pupils shared lockers but no-one could share with me because mine was always full of the stuff sent by my mother - cakes and of course Ragworth Beauty tomatoes. You couldn't eat when you liked and the keys to the lockers were brought out only for about a quarter of an hour at 11 o'clock in the morning when a huge plate of bread and butter was provided by the school and you spread on any jam you might have of your own. Being wartime the food was nothing fantastic but mostly it was good, plain cooking.

Totally against the rules were dormitory feasts but of course we loved them, saving bread from our meals and then adding in whatever had been sent from home. Being wartime we had completely different ideas about what was a treat compared to today. One night one girl stuffed herself with so much of the cucumber and tomatoes sent by my parents that she was sick, so we were caught and well and truly told off. But it didn't stop us, it was great fun, though there wasn't much you could get, maybe a bit of treacle or jam or the odd cake. It was the excitement that mattered.

When I was at home there always seemed to be an awful lot of shopping to be done and we also saw dozens of films. Norton had two picture houses, one across the road from the other, and we'd walk the couple of miles to see them because there was no petrol for the car. There was always a queue and we'd see whichever film had the shortest queue. Winter evenings were spent playing cards beside the fire. Baking, knitting and embroidery also passed the time.

The war seeemd to drag on and on, though we were sheltered from much of the horror. I was lucky that neither my father nor brother were in the Forces. My brother wanted to join the Navy but when the time came we were both suffering from yellow jaundice and he was not considered fit enough, which he was very disappointed about. Peace came in 1945 when I was 15 but there were no great celebrations because our Quaker school believed neither in fighting nor flamboyant celebrations of peace. Rationing went on for years after the war as our weary country tried to pick itself up again and, since I had been shielded from most of the bombing and had not lost anyone close in the fighting, life in peacetime didn't seem so very different to life in wartime. Yet the scenes of devastation I had witnessed in Middlesbrough and near our home had made a deep impression on me and I know I must have been glad that it was at an end.

When Pamela grew up she became a dentist. Her story is told in *A Life Well Lived*.

CHILDHOOD MEMORIES OF A BOMBER TRAINING BASE

In 1943 a bomber training base was built across fields near the village of Wombleton on the North York Moors. Most of the 2,000 servicemen and women stationed there were Canadian. Here are the memories of several children whose lives were affected, often dramatically.

'Every time we spotted a Canadian we'd shout out, Any gum, chum?'

Roy Simpson grew up on Sunley Hill Farm near Wombleton where his father was the tenant. As a young boy, Roy saw his family life turned upside down by the war. Sunley Hill stretched across 220 peaceful acres with a mix of sheep, cows and crops but then came the news that most of the farm would be taken away from them. Roy remembered, "We couldn't do anything about it, you just had to accept it. I think my father received rent and also a shilling an acre *(5p)* compensation. The next thing we knew was the arrival of coaches filled with workers from a building company in Middlesbrough."

His parents, Ernest and Alice Simpson, had to remove all their animals and equipment and retreat to their remaining 60 to 80 acres as tons of concrete covered their land. The perimeter track came to within 100 yards *(about 100 metres)* of their house, with the main runway only 150 yards away. Other farms also lost land but such was the need to produce food that parts of the base remained under cultivation by a handful of labourers. Roy added, "We weren't allowed back on our land at all until after the war. Every now and again contractors would cut the grass and bring it to us but, being wet, it lasted only a short time. Today it would be cut for silage but in those days we were used to making hay. I'm not sure what my parents thought about it all. It was war and you just had to accept it but for a young boy of nine it was an exciting experience."

Moorfields Farm suffered a worse fate. It was almost in the middle of the new airfield, home to George and Grace Clark who remained there while the base was being built but left soon after the first aircraft arrived. The farm house and outbuildings were demolished.

The arrival of the air base had a huge impact on the rural hills and vales around it. Robin Wright was a boy living in Harome during the war, just a mile from the end of the main runway. In an article for the Malton Gazette and Herald newspaper he recalled, "I remember the first plane to land. As I was making my way back to school after lunch, a big bomber came from the West which I knew to be a Halifax. It did a circle of the aerodrome.

"With two pals we ran as fast as we could to climb on a gate near Gale Lane to get a good look. Another twice round, even lower, then next time it did a 'taxi' on the ground and a final round before it came to a standstill. Afterwards, as we were returning to school, it took off and returned to the West, whence it had come. In no time at all, the Canadians were in residence and flying began in October with Halifax bombers. These were later joined by Lancasters. The planes came over our garden, very low, and one thing I shall never forget is the vibration of the glass in our windows. Yet not one pane broke or fell out. My best friend's father worked on the aerodrome as chief boilerman or engineer and also had a smallholding where he kept Jersey cows and pigs. He fed the pigs on swill *(waste food)* which was collected at the aerodrome. I used to go with my friend on Saturdays to help collect the swill with a horse and rulley *(flat-bed cart)*. Many times I received what I really went for, a mug of coffee and a slab of rich fruitcake, which was a luxury in wartime.

"I must admit there were a few occasions when I got up to mischief. I had a catapult and, as the planes were very low, tried to 'shoot' one down with small stones. Try as hard as I could, the stones never seemed to go anywhere near. I think it had something to do with air pressure coming off the bombers. One day we entered a wood called Harome Whin where, in low shelters covered with earth, bombs were stored and boxes and boxes of what I can only describe as machinegun ammunition, something like .303 size. As no-one was about, I filled two pockets full and off we went to have some fun. We wedged one in a crack in the top of a field gatepost and tried to fire it by using a stone to hit a nail on to the end. We were lucky to escape with just some sore finger ends. We hid the rest in a rabbit hole and a few days later recovered the ammunition and took it down to the river where we lit a fire under a tree. Climbing the tree, we dropped the bullets in the fire. Explosions, hisses and thuds in the riverbank soon followed. As a young boy, I never thought I was in any danger.

"At Christmas 1944 children were invited to a party on the 'Drome'. Following a ride in a blacked-out bus, we were taken to a hut where there was food on long tables, followed by Father Christmas. I received a brightly-painted wooden handmade train, a bag of sweets and an orange. Not having seen an orange for a long time, I was surprised. Afterwards we had a singsong round the piano.

"Of the many incidents, two stick in my mind. At 7pm one February night the lights went out and, as candles were scarce, it was off to bed. Next day my father told us what had happened. A bomber was taking off so low that his rear wheel caught an electric supply wire. The plane took off with three pole-lengths of wire trailing behind and, after a circuit or two, landed safely. The crew had quite a shock because they hadn't realized anything had happened.

"One Saturday night a large column of thick, black smoke rose at the far end of the village and I ran to see what had happened. In a field near Harome Whin lay the remains of a bomber. The flames had been put out by the fire crew. The bomber had been taking off on the shortest runway and, passing the wood, his right wing sliced off the top of two trees and he crashed in the field. Next morning I went for a closer look but everything had gone except a small panel from the cockpit which I took home as a souvenir. Five crew were injured but it was a lucky escape.

"When the war finally ended in Europe, they celebrated on VE Night with a very large bonfire on the main runway. Furniture seemed to be the main victim plus a couple of dozen bike tyres – anything that would burn. The aeroplanes and Canadian airmen left just as quickly as they had come. It was not until after the war that I realized Wombleton had been a training aerodrome where nearly 2,000 airmen *(and women)* of all ranks had been stationed."

Robin Butler was a boy in Kirkbymoorside during the war *(see his other memories earlier in this book)*. He remembered, "As a lad I'd lie on the hills with my pals watching the base with our binoculars. It's a wonder we weren't arrested for spying. When the planes took off, a great thunderous roaring filled the air. I also remember the tankers trundling down the lanes to pump fuel into the pipes which went across the base. It was a huge place and had a big impact on the surrounding villages and towns. There was excitement when scouts from Kirkbymoorside, including me, were invited to fly in a Halifax bomber. Our parents had to write a letter of consent and off we went to the base. On arrival, we could see a plane sitting forlornly on the grass where it had careered off the runway and become bogged down in the base's famous mud. To our great disappointment we were told our flight was off but instead we were taken on a tour of the base. We saw the WAAFs packing the parachutes, carefully folding the great waves of silk in the correct way to ensure they would open properly. Considering the accident record at Wombleton, maybe it was a good thing we didn't get to fly that day.

"As far as I can remember, the WAAF quarters were down Gale Lane in huts. After the war, when there was a housing shortage, they were used by the council as temporary accommodation for returning servicemen and their families."

Robin's future wife Edith was a girl of 12 living in Wombleton when the base opened. Her mother took in RAF men as occasional paying guests so that they could bring their wives to visit for a weekend or a week's holiday. "A bus would pick us up and take us to the cinema on the base," she remembered. "Every time we spotted a Canadian we'd shout out, 'Any gum, chum?'"

For Rob Biggins, who was a small boy in Wombleton at the time, the arrival of the base was a big adventure. "My brother

Jim, who was much older than me, sat me on the handlebars of his bike to take me to see the new aerodrome. We stood at the end of the runway and an aircraft came in just over our heads. I was really thrilled. Later one belly-flopped into a field near the church in Nunnington. My father was a farm worker who was contracted to keep the runways swept clean of any stones or debris that could cause punctures. He'd take me down there on a Fordson tractor pulling a big thing on a trailer and up and down the runways we'd go. That was great for a small boy. In one corner called Fox Cover was the bomb store and I'd watch them bringing the bombs up the ramps to be loaded on to carriers.

"I remember seeing the Canadians falling out of the pubs well intoxicated. Bikes would be strewn all over the place and the following morning a truck would turn up to collect them all."

Born in 1936, Alan Smith grew up not knowing what peace felt like. He lived in Normanby, a few miles East. "There was a bombing range below our village," he remembered, "and we used to see them dropping flash bombs on it which, for a small boy, was very interesting. Sometimes the aircraft were so low you could see the crew clearly and I have a vivid picture in my memory of one waving at me with a handkerchief."

Roy Simpson, the boy living in the farmhouse at the end of the runway, remembered, "Many of the young Canadians who found themselves at Wombleton came from a farming background and, homesick for their peacetime lives, rattled over in a truck to our farm at Sunley Hill to help out when off duty." In return, his mother Alice Simpson gave them hefty farmhouse teas. For Roy, these young men in uniform brought excitement with their tales of home and of air force life. "They were marvellous because they always had sweets!" he added. "One name that stays with me is Jimmy Thompson from Saskatchewan. After the war, some kept in touch with us for the remainder of their lives. They were grand lads."

Despite being close to the end of the runway, the base was so widely spread out that it was a two-mile journey for Roy when he was invited for meals in the Naafi. After being thrown together hurriedly, extra comforts were gradually added to the base. A club which could also be used as a cinema and theatre was completed and the base was visited from time to time by ENSA, the Entertainments National Service Association, also known as Every Night Something Awful. Local people were invited to the film shows and, for many, 6pm on a Saturday was a regular visit.

More stories of Wombleton, both of those who served there and those who lived nearby, can be read in *Wombleton-In-The Mud* available through Ryedale Folk Museum www.ryedalefolkmuseum.co.uk

DAVID SHERRY

David was born
in York in 1937
where he lived
with his parents
and sisters.

'I was watching a fleet of our bombers taking off for a raid on Germany, fully laden with bombs and fuel, when suddenly one fell out of the sky. I will never forget the feeling of the blast. The bombs exploded and all the crew were killed.'

L ike most mothers at the time, mine put on a brave face for her children but she must have been having a very tough time coping with wartime restrictions and air-raids. I wasn't aware at the time how hard things were for her because she was a strong, good-humoured person. Only by reading her own short memoir have I come to realize how difficult things were. She worried constantly about her three young children for

York was bombed and her own childhood home was practically destroyed.

She wrote in her own memoir: *The war years were horrific. We built an air-raid shelter in the garden, deep underground with 6ft (2m) of concrete on top. We had beds down there and other useful things. I made siren suits for each of the children, one-piece affairs with a zip up the front, for getting into quickly. We ran to the shelter every time the air-raid siren went off, if we were at home.*

"I well remember one daylight raid when the siren went off and I had three children to get down the steep steps to the shelter. Over in Heslington about two miles away there was an anti-aircraft gun. My parents were staying with us as they had been bombed out of their house in Poppleton Road, York, my childhood home. The roof had been completely blown off. Mother was behind me at the shelter waiting to go down the steps. The gun started firing and the bombs were dropping and she said, "Hurry up, I'm in the line of fire!" I had to stop and laugh even though it was serious really.

My mother stopped going out in the evenings because she couldn't bear the thought of us being without her if the siren went, even though we had been left in good care. I'm sure she must have been scared but she didn't show it. I remember the shelter as being cold and dank, with the crump, crump of the bombs going off in the distance and the heavy drone of the aircraft passing overhead. They were aiming mainly for the station because it was an important rail centre.

There wasn't always a warning, sometimes things happened too fast. One day I was sitting on the toilet looking out of the open window and heard this tremendous noise followed by a plane flying so close that I could see the Nazi swastikas on its side. Our fighters were after it and they shot it down. Very sadly it landed on a farmhouse not far away and the farmer and some of his family were killed.

My parents must have worried intensely about what was best for their children. These fears prompted my father to rent a farm at Huggate near Driffield which was much further out into the countryside on the Yorkshire Wolds and would have been less of a target than the city of York. He decided it could make a safe retreat for his family but in the end we rarely went there. The place was indeed safe but that was because it was so remote. One night early in the war we were at Huggate when I found myself in severe pain from an ear infection. My mother couldn't get me to a doctor easily because the nearest one was miles and miles away down dark, winding lanes. After that we made only short visits, bombs or no bombs.

Several air bases had been set up near our home in York so even when there wasn't a raid on you usually heard the roar of our own bombers taking off to attack German targets. One day I was with my father in the car when we came close to Pocklington airfield. The road was so close to the base that when the aircraft were taking off or landing, barriers were closed and you had to wait. We were sitting there watching a fleet of huge bombers taking off for a raid, fully laden with bombs and fuel, when suddenly something went wrong with one of them and it fell out of the sky some distance from us. I will never forget the feeling of the blast as it hit the canvas roof of the car. It wasn't like a wind but as if every bit of air had suddenly rushed past you. The bombs exploded and all the crew were killed. As a small boy I just accepted this as yet another interesting event but no doubt my father was affected by the tragedy. Many of the bases were Canadian and we often invited the crews to our house for lunch to give them a taste of home when they were so far from their own. As time went on, some of the familiar faces were missing and we knew we would not see them again.

My father had been too young to serve in World War I and was now too old to be called up to the Forces, so in a way he was lucky. Instead he joined the Home Guard. He had a mortar gun and stood it up beside me to show that it would reach the top of my head. It fired shells the size of my hand which he said were to use against tanks.

As a small boy I had no real idea what it would mean for us if Nazi tanks came rumbling down the road but for my parents the threat of invasion was chillingly real for the first few years of the war. One of my father's jobs was to search the fields for small butterfly bombs which were dropped by aircraft but did not go off until hit by a plough or other equipment and were aimed at killing farmers and slowing food production. As children we were told forcefully never to touch anything we found lying in the earth.

Toys, like so many nice things, were in short supply. The war was mirrored in the games boys and girls played who could remember nothing but conflict. Games with my friends usually involved running around with sticks for guns, shooting at each other. I had some Dinky toys, model cars and wagons which today would be collectors' items. I liked to stage bombing raids on them and pound them with pebbles. I also had a Hornby model train which suffered the same fate.

Thanks to my parents' outer calm my childhood felt quite settled to me but looking back I can see that the war was a tough time for my father, who was a builder, because most building work except on aerodromes or armaments factories had come to a stop. He survived by taking what work was going including repairs to bombed buildings and by keeping animals on the field attached to our home. Anyone with a bit of land was encouraged to keep a pig and he kept quite a few.

A licence was needed even to kill your own pig but most people bent the rules. My father would get a licence to kill one pig and get in touch with the pig killer who would then kill six or seven. Afterwards the carcass was cut up by someone who knew about butchering.

My parents kept some of the meat for us, our relations and friends and used the rest for bartering. My father knew a man running one of the many small chocolate factories which were in York at that time, besides the big names of Rowntree and Terry's, and would swap a side of bacon for a barrel of sugar, which was also rationed and very precious.

Despite the fact that everyone was doing it, my mother was worried about getting caught. I heard her say to my father before one of his secret deliveries, "Don't go that way tonight, there might be a policeman there."

One day a policeman turned up at the home of a man we knew and asked if he had been killing pigs. "No, no," he said, "I haven't been killing pigs." The policeman looked sceptical. "Are you sure? Your cat's on the lawn eating a pig's tail!" So he was fined. Then it was our turn. One night after an illicit pig killing, my mother and father were sitting at the kitchen table, the curtains firmly closed, cutting up the leaves, which are layers of fat from inside the pig. These were fried into what were called scraps and were delicious. As they worked away at this greasy job, there was a sharp knock at the door and before they could clear anything away, a policeman had walked in. He must have had his suspicions or been given a tip-off. Anyway, I think he walked away with a nice bit of pig's liver and that was the last we heard of that.

Shortage of food was normal to me and I used to wonder what life had been like in the golden time I was always being told about when sweets, roast dinners, cream and butter were taken for granted by those who could afford them.

I had never seen a banana but I'd heard about them. In 1942 when I was five I caught scarlet fever, a serious and highly infectious illness which you hardly ever hear of today. I was sent to an isolation hospital and wasn't allowed any visitors. Our neighbour's son came home on leave from the Navy, bringing with him some of these strange yellow things called bananas, one of which was sent into the hospital for me. My mother had to give it to the nurse as she wasn't allowed in and, to my dismay, the nurse mashed it up and each child got one spoonful.

August 1945 brought an end to the war. Raids had stopped much earlier and so for me the peace didn't make a huge amount of difference. Sweets were still rationed! The end of the blackout was exciting though, for I had never seen the streets of York lit up at night. That was a magical sight for a small boy who had grown up in world where everything was pitch black at night except for the searchlights and flames from bombed buildings.

David grew up and became a farmer, later developing his land to become the Monks Cross shopping centre near York. His story is told in *Cat Among the Pigeons*.

GRANVILLE DOBSON

**Granville was born in 1937 and lived in the village
of Wyke near Bradford, West Yorkshire.**

*'I was about eight before I tasted chocolate and that was
drinking chocolate powder sent over from Canada. Tubs
were delivered to our school and we were each allowed a
little to dip our fingers in. I thought that was marvellous.'*

As a very small boy I remember my father taking me
outside one night where a huge red glow spread across
the distant sky. He said, "Sheffield's getting a real pasting
tonight." Bright white flashes erupted against the red but I didn't
know what they were. In fact it was a bit of a novelty for me.
Because of the blackout, everything was usually pitch dark.

Fortunately for us there was nothing to bomb in our village but
the air-raid siren sounded when enemy planes passed overhead
on their way to bomb the cities. That happened frequently. We
had to go out to the shelter which had been built in our garden.
It was fitted out with bunks so you could sleep down there if you
wanted but it was always damp so we just ended up sitting on the
edge of them.

You had to go down because you never knew what was going
to happen. There was always the risk a bomber pilot might get
lost and think he was somewhere else or he might ditch a spare
bomb on the way home.

My father had been in the 1914-1918 war, a sailor in convoys going to Murmansk in Russia which must have been terrible and I could never get him to talk about it. Being too old to serve in the next war, he joined the Home Guard and even then, well before the TV series Dad's Army, we kids used to laugh at them.

Petrol was in short supply and the buses towed a tank of gas behind to power them instead. There wasn't much traffic on the road but as small children we'd often go down to the Huddersfield Road when an Army convoy was passing through, dozens and dozens of lorries full of soldiers cheering and waving. Word got round very quickly when one was on its way and hordes of children would come running across the fields to watch.

Near Queensbury, not far away from us, was a huge prisoner-of-war camp filled with Italians. They were taken to work under guard in the woods by day and our parents told us not to go there. So of course we did, hiding behind trees when we saw the prisoners in their uniforms marked with a big diamond to identify them.

About 14 children from Coventry and Birmingham were evacuated to our village and joined the school. I fell in love with one of the evacuees, Eunice Richards, who was very pretty with blond hair in ringlets. I think I managed to kiss her twice. At the end of the war she went back to Coventry saying, "I will write to you and I will remember you all my life." But she didn't.

The evacuees all seemed to be suffering from ringworm, which is a highly infectious skin problem, and they were going round with purple patches on them where they were painted with a treatment called Blue Unction. The feeling among Yorkshire parents was that these weren't clean kids but, like anywhere, some came from dirty families and some were respectable. Eunice was very clean! A crowd of evacuee children came to live at the vicarage for a few months who were considered an odd lot because they came from London and we were told to keep away from them!

I was about eight before I tasted chocolate and that was drinking chocolate powder sent over from Canada. Tubs were delivered to our school and we were each allowed a little to dip our fingers in. I thought that was marvellous.

Grown-ups were always going on about the things you could get before the war. When it was over, the first bananas started arriving again and I thought they looked marvellous. Unpeeling one was so easy, just like it had a zip, but I thought it tasted like soap. I'd rather have had an apple any day. They were rationed to about one a month and there were queues a quarter of a mile long when a greengrocer got any and they soon ran out. I couldn't see what all the fuss was about.

The chap next-door was called up into the Army, sent abroad to fight, got shot and was nearly killed. Arthur Patchett, he was called. After leaving hospital he came home and was quite happy to show off his wounds to any kids who were interested, which of course we all were. He had been shot in the chest, the bullet hit his ribs at the back then bounced up and out, taking off a chunk of his ear on the way. "Let's have a look at your wound, Arthur!" we'd say and he'd pull up his shirt and show where it went in and then the great wedge missing from the back of his ear. That was a novelty for us. Kids like the macabre and don't think about how awful it would be if it happened to them.

Towards the end of the war my parents were very excited because Paris had been liberated. I had no idea where Paris was or what liberated was. Only later did I discover that our armies were fighting their way through Europe and driving the Nazis out. They were always talking about Montgomery, who was our most successful general, and I thought he must be some kind of god.

When the lights went on again it was amazing. What surprised me were all the different patterns and colours on people's curtains which you could never see before because of the blackout blinds. I'd walk along the streets looking at them, fascinated.

Granville grew up to become one of the last firemen on steam locomotives, later transferring to railway management. His memoir is called *Old Flames*.

JOHN PAUL

John was born in
the 1930s
and grew up in a
suburb of York.

*'Stained glass had been blown out of a bombed church
into the road and the heat melted it into the Tarmac,
creating a colourful mosaic.'*

As children growing up in the middle of a global conflict
our games mirrored the war. When the news was full
of the fighting in Burma and Malaya, we built camps
on islands in the ponds of Challenor's Winn and fought jungle
wars with Brian Horner's gang from the other side of the railway
bridge. Our weapons were home-made, including Tommy guns
made from fence timber and practice bombs discarded by the
Home Guard. We made surprisingly powerful bows from briers
with arrows of bulrush stems weighted by nails.

Real danger came on April 29th 1942 during the blitz on York.
I was eight years old. After the siren sounded I went to the shelter

with my mother, aunt and cousin and spent the night listening to the sound of aircraft and falling bombs. Wrapped in blankets I was snug in my bunk but condensation ran down the corrugated iron walls. A blanket soaked in water hung across the door to protect us from any poison gas and our masks were handy. Mum had to pump water from the sump in the corner every now and again to prevent the shelter from flooding because the water table was very high where we lived. A hurricane lamp gave us light and Thermos flasks of tea offered some comfort. Our mothers tried to distract us from the sound of the anti-aircraft guns and the thump, thump of our city under attack.

Mum was worried about Dad who worked in a factory close to the city centre. At the sound of the air-raid warning he had to go there to fire watch on the roof. We were all very relieved when he arrived home safely after the all clear sounded just before dawn.

He carried me up to our front bedroom, still wrapped in my blankets. The window overlooked York and I could see fires burning across the horizon and smoke rising into the first light of the spring dawn. Over breakfast he told us the story of his night as the bombs fell about him.

Fire bucket and stirrup pump in hand, he and a fellow worker watched the many bombs falling on the railway station, across the marshalling yards and in the streets around. Several bombers droned overhead. Suddenly there was a loud whine and a huge crash very close by. They stared at a hole 18 inches wide in the lead covered flat roof beside them. With trepidation they descended five floors to the basement where they found the tail fin of a substantial bomb embedded in an enormous pile of blankets stored for the use of citizens made homeless by such a night as this. The blankets had softened the impact and the bomb had not gone off. Later it was defused by bomb disposal experts. If it had exploded we might never have seen my dad again.

Next day we went into the centre to see the damage. Stained glass had been blown out of a bombed church into the road and the heat melted it into the Tarmac, creating a colourful mosaic. We saw the burned out shell of the ancient Guild Hall and the distorted steel arches and damaged trains at the station. In Holgate we stood on the edge of a deep crater caused by a land mine or large bomb. All the houses nearby had lost their windows, doors and often their roof tiles. School children were allowed time off while the city returned to normal. Poppleton Road School was badly damaged and not repaired until after the war.

When John grew up he did many different things including running an architectural design and building business and working as a yachting instructor. In the 1980s he and his family bought a yacht and sailed 8,000 miles from Yorkshire to the Red Sea and back. His story is told in *A Yorkshire Family Afloat*.

COLIN KIRKPATRICK

Colin was born in 1930 and grew up in the village of Moorends near Doncaster where his father worked in the local mine. He had seven brothers and sisters.

'At school I joined the Air Training Corps. The highlight was a flight in a Halifax bomber to Land's End and back to learn navigation.'

We didn't have our own radio but instead paid to have a speaker and wire connected to our house from the local radio shop which relayed the signal. It was through this speaker that we heard the Prime Minister announce we were at war. We thought the Germans were going to come over straight away with aircraft and ships and blow us to bits.

With no sirens, unlike the cities, our air-raid wardens were issued with football rattles. One was over keen and would sound his rattle at the slightest sign of anything in the sky, even a bird we decided. Later the loud buzzer at the pit, which could be heard for miles, was used as an air-raid siren. If you heard it go off out of the usual sequence, that meant trouble. Official announcements about things like air-raid precautions were made in the traditional way by a man ringing a hand bell and shouting out the latest orders. That's how communication was made in Moorends and the little town of Thorne which was next-door.

Gradually all our usual treats disappeared from the shops and only one baker displayed jam tarts in his window. I wish my driveway today was made of his pastry because it was as hard as stone. Goodness knows what he had put in it. You couldn't get your teeth into them. Sometimes the jam was beetroot.

Before the war the only things I had ever seen in the sky was an old Tiger Moth bi-plane and, on one memorable day, the dramatic bulk of the ill-fated Hindenburg airship. Now we had to get used to the drone of enemy bombers as they passed over on their way to their targets and the sight of our own as they took off from the many bases in Yorkshire, circling like vultures until their formations were complete. If I was up early in the morning I would see them returning, some coming in low with half a tail missing or a hole in the side. One day on my way to Doncaster I saw three piles of smouldering wreckage in fields along the way where planes had tried to land but crashed, killing the crews. One night a British bomber crashed on an allotment behind our village and the crew were burned to death. All the village rushed to help, some still in their pyjamas, but there was nothing we could do. It was an inferno, terrible to see.

Hull was about 35 miles away but on clear nights we could see the glow in the sky as the city burned. I wondered if it would be our turn next, if they were out to destroy everyone.

At first our only refuge was under the table but no bombs were dropped on us, thank goodness. Later blast shelters made from brick with concrete roofs were built in our gardens but they wouldn't have been any use in a direct hit. At school the rugby field was dug up to build a large Anderson shelter, dank and dark.

From time to time soldiers were billeted in empty shops in Thorne. Miss Jackson, who took us for rugby because all the young male teachers had been called up, persuaded a Cameron Highlanders PE instructor to help out. Any boy who had been playing up in class would be reported by Miss Jackson to our Cameron Highlander who would pick out the boy for boxing training then promptly floor him.

One of our bombers crash-landed in a field about a mile away so all of us got on our bikes and looked at it in amazement because we had never seen an aircraft on the ground before. Stuck firmly in the mud and still intact, it seemed huge but was an old crate compared to what came later. The crew had survived and been taken back to base. A policeman stood guard to ward off souvenir hunters.

At the age of 11 I went to Thorne Grammar School where I joined the Air Training Corps. Going for regular training at RAF Driffield, the highlight was a flight in a Halifax bomber to Land's End and back to learn navigation. It took hours, was cold and draughty but exciting, taking turns to sit with the pilot, navigator, rear gunner and wireless operator.

Clothes rationing meant people had to follow government advice and 'make do and mend'. Mothers sat up till late at night darning socks or sewing patches on school trousers which had been worn to paper thinness, on the behind mainly. I have also known the fitting of a piece of cardboard inside a shoe where a hole had been worn in the sole. These were hard times where nothing could be discarded that might be given a few more weeks of wear through improvisation. When I was 13 we heard that some American Flying Fortress bombers had landed at Lindholme RAF station so we took excitedly to our bikes and quickly did the five mile journey to have a look at the giant planes. Their being American was doubly exciting us for we had never seen an American either except at the pictures and they were our heroes, mainly in the form of cowboys. Sure enough, two Fortresses were parked by the road. To reach the runway they needed to taxi across the road from their parking spaces and - how lucky we were - they were about to do just that. We stood almost speechless gazing up at these well adorned giants. I remember to this day catching sight of one of the pilots manoeuvring his aircraft whilst smoking a cigar in the cockpit. What an American flavour it gave to this sighting for we young cinemagoers.

My eldest sister was called on to do her bit for the war effort by working in a munitions factory in Doncaster about 10 miles away. She and many others travelled by bus each day throughout the war. My youngest sister served in the Women's Auxiliary Air Force (WAAF) as a wireless operator. Three of my older brothers were in the Forces and it was very tough to see them leave to fight in the war, especially for my mother. When the war with Germany was over we all expected the fighting to go on for years against the Japanese. My brother Ernest was already in the Far East and I wondered if I would be caught up in it when I turned 18. When we heard the atomic bombs had been dropped it was horrifying but we were glad our family was safe.

Colin grew up to become an engineer, later learning to speak Russian and spending many years working on contracts in Siberia. His story is told in *To Russia for One and Thruppence*.

ROGER DAVY

Roger was born in 1938 and grew up in Ilkley.

'Ilkley was full of soldiers who gave us little ones rides in their Army wagons. No one seemed to mind and we came to no harm.'

I remember my father in uniform as a member of the Ilkley Home Guard. He had been in the Navy during the First World War and volunteered for the Ilkley Company. It wasn't quite Dad's Army but they took their responsibilities very seriously. Dad would go off on a Saturday night with his friend Ken Bradley to do sentry duty high up on Ilkley Moor or Snowden Moor on the other side of the valley. The two of them, amidst those vast areas of open moorland, would have the responsibility of protecting us from possible airborne invasion and the blitzkrieg! On the numerous nights of inactivity Dad would often come home with his tin helmet filled to the brim with freshly picked mushrooms.

Land Girls in their ample green sweaters, khaki trousers, knee socks and sensible brown boots would deliver our milk driving a horse and cart containing a couple of milk churns and a smaller churn to dispense the milk at the houses into jugs left on the back doorsteps using pint and half pint metal ladles.

We had a mother and baby evacuated to us for six months from the bombing in Croydon, Surrey. My mother found it a bit of a strain having them with us and was not too sorry when they went home again. Ilkley was full of soldiers who gave us little ones rides in their Army wagons. No one seemed to mind and we came to no harm. One night a large bomber crashed on the Moor and all the crew were killed. My brother took me up to the edge of the moor and I remember seeing a white tape zig-zagging down through the bracken and heather that had guided the stretcher bearers safely down through the darkness.

During Salute the Soldier Week and Dig For Victory Week the town was dressed over to raise money for war charities and to help to build Spitfires. I remember when all the garden railings were removed for the war effort. There are still scores of little domes of concrete on the wall tops around town where they used to be.

Roger grew up to take his place in the family business in Bradford which recycled textiles. The story of the many fascinating characters he met through his work is told in *Waste Matters*.

GEORGE BARKER

George was born in 1933 and grew up on his parents' small farm near Northallerton.

'Some bombers were so badly damaged they couldn't risk landing with any leftover bombs and jettisoned them into the River Swale. One fell in one of my grandfather's wettest fields where it sank without trace into quicksand and is, as far as I know, still there to this day.'

At home the radio was our link with the wide world. It ran on an accumulator battery which had to be taken to town for re-charging. I remember my parents sitting with grim faces listening to the news of 1938 when everyone thought we were on the brink of war with Germany. Then there was jubilation as the word came through of Prime Minister Chamberlain coming back with his famous piece of paper which promised "peace in our time". But it was a brief respite and by September of the following year they were round the radio again to hear the same Prime Minister announce that we were at war.

I was only six and being so young didn't really understand what it was all about but a lot of things began to happen around me. I heard my mother say, "We'd better get in some big bags of sugar, because that'll be rationed." She meant a couple of eight stone bags *(50kg)*.

By then the agricultural economy had improved a little and so my parents had some cash to spare for stocking up. My mother also added to her poultry stock and ordered a smart new hen house which arrived by lorry. Much was her annoyance when she discovered the heifers giving themselves a good scratching against it, so a barbed wire fence had to be put up quickly.

My mother sat for hours stitching yards and yards of thick blackout material to make our curtains. One night there was a terrific banging on the door and an air-raid warden was there in his tin hat saying angrily, "There's a light showing!" and it was just the tiniest strip down one side of a window. I can't imagine a plane could have spotted that but it was the law and punishable by fines if you didn't put it right.

Children were evacuated from the cities and two arrived at the farm from Sunderland. Our little village school was swamped by a sudden influx of city pupils and their teachers, almost doubling the roll. All we had was a walled yard which was always crowded and if you wanted to go to the toilet there was often a queue. We tried to play football but there were too many feet kicking the ball. So we played 'tigs' instead!

For a long time it was what they called the Phoney War because the battles were mostly out of sight at sea and, with none of the expected air-raids, some evacuees drifted home again. Ours lasted only six weeks, being so homesick. Like everyone else, I was taken down to the Village Institute to be fitted with a gas mask and an identity card, both of which I still have, but nothing seemed real until you heard the air-raid siren for the first time and then you began to believe there really was a war on. It was late afternoon one winter's day as we were sitting round the table eating tea when my father came in and said, "The siren's gone off!" We could hear the one at Leeming Bar. "Come out here and have a look. I think this'll be a German plane!" There was no mention of taking cover. We stood in the yard and suddenly a plane high up swooped into view, the searchlights picking it out in the sky as our defences tried to shoot it down. The 5.20pm train to Northallerton was due along the track which ran alongside my granddad's farm nearby. As the train chuffed its way along, the plane opened up its machine-gun on the carriages but missed, fortunately. Being a small boy, I felt only excitement at the sight.

After that we took air-raids more seriously. In the house was a large cool store with hooks set into the ceiling on which would be hung sides of bacon. A big stone slab which held the lead curing bowls was set on two low walls and when the siren went we'd crouch beneath this for protection. I soon got fed up with that. Concrete blocks were put up by the road by Morton Bridge which could have been moved into place as roadblocks if needed. Pill boxes were built to house guns to protect other important areas.

One evening in 1940 when Hitler seemed poised to invade, my father and Stan went to a meeting at the village hall where they were told what to do if they saw enemy parachutists descending. So now we were ready for them with our pitchforks and the sharp blades of our hedge slashers which would immediately make them surrender. Very early in the war a bomber base was opened at Leeming. Our farm was on the flight path, the house only three quarters of a mile from the end of the runway. Around five or six o' clock most evenings fleets of huge bombers would take off heading for mainland Europe, their big black shapes roaring low over our roof, vibrating through the bricks and filling the air with sound. Fully laden with bombs, these great metal birds had great difficulty gaining enough height to clear our roof. Our neighbours the Hunters at Grimescar Farm were even closer, not much further than a quarter of a mile from the runway. In 1942 a plane was coming in early one morning to land and must have come in too low. It took the roof off their farmhouse and crashed nearby, killing all the crew. Seven people were in the house at the time including the lad I went to school with. By a miracle the family escaped, the ceilings crashing down around them, and the only casualty was the dog. I heard nothing at the time but next morning saw my friends' home with the roof completely ripped off. Sadly, the house eventually had to be demolished.

Sometimes we saw the bombers limping back after their raids, some with gaping holes in the fuselage. Some didn't come back at all. Others were so badly damaged they couldn't risk landing with any leftover bombs and jettisoned them into the River Swale. One missed and landed in one of my grandfather's wettest fields where it sank without trace into quicksand and is, as far as I know, still there to this day.

Severe rationing of petrol saw most private cars disappear from the roads to be replaced by huge convoys of military trucks roaring past at all hours. Some buses were converted to run on gas, hauling great tenders behind them. We got used to the comings and goings of soldiers and airmen. One day a soldier turned up on our doorstep to beg the use of some old clothes and a bike to get to Morton Bridge where he had to lay dummy explosives in an exercise. A radio operator often parked in our farmyard and I used to talk to him and watch him using the Morse code and talking on the wireless. Our sitting room, which was hardly ever used, was let to airmen from the base nearby so they could bring their wives to live with them. One couple were called Foster. Later he was shot down and taken prisoner and his wife asked me if I would write a letter to him to cheer him up. He was in Stalag Luft III and occasionally we were allowed to send him a food parcel. Later came Mr and Mrs Bratley with their three very young children. How they all squeezed into that room I don't know. I don't seem to have minded these regular invasions of other children. Another was called Ward from Staffordshire who had been a builder before his call-up and that worked out grand for my mother. She was rather fed up with the big, old red flagstones which formed the kitchen floor. One had sunk, others had cracked. Our guest re-laid the floor for her. He also replaced the lovely old wrought-iron fireplace in the sitting room, its pretty tiles going up each side and over the heavy wooden sill, with a ghastly modern one, but my mother liked it. His son Reg came to school with me.

Both British and Canadians were based at Leeming and we soon got used to hearing twanging accents alongside our Yorkshire ones. Our paying guests, who were all British air crew, brought their Canadian friends back, especially in summer, and they all wanted to go rabbiting, bringing their 12-bore shotguns. Northallerton was packed with Canadians and the town was full of gossip about what they'd been up to the night before in the pubs. Some had wives in Canada and girlfriends in Yorkshire. Since for some it might be their last night alive, it was understandable, if sad. If they'd had a few too many, they'd often steal a bike to get back to Leeming and the next morning these would be abandoned around the place, closely followed by the angry owners who had to retrieve them.

One day I set off to take out the 10 o' clocks to the workers when I spotted an unusual object. I thought it was a dead calf in the field. I went across the grass to take a closer look and to my astonishment saw that it was no living thing at all but the figure of a lion. Thinking fast, I realized that it was the Golden Lion from the hotel in Northallerton which must be missing its famous statue. Being a haunt of air crew, well-known for their pranks, the finger pointed obviously to RAF lads or Canadians who'd had a few too many the night before. The police later confirmed that a bunch of Canadians had lifted the lion, heaved it precariously on to a bicycle but got fed up with pushing its heavy and unwieldy bulk, so it had been jettisoned. That was the end of their quest for it as a mascot.

Early on in the war the Government had woken up to the parlous state of British agriculture and realized that this, combined with the sinking of ships bringing imports, could starve us into submission. So a huge drive was started to increase production and farmers had to do what they were told. Each area was run by a War Agricultural Executive Committee known as the War Ag, full of men thought to be better farmers than everyone else, so you can imagine how people felt about that! Some of them couldn't farm a clocking hen but they had the right connections. Farmers were made to plough out grassland that had lain undisturbed for centuries.

The fields on our farm were often wet but that didn't matter, you had to do it. At that time it was still all done by horse. We only got a tractor later on. My father fought like mad to save two fields. "You can't plough that out!" he'd tell them. One contained all the hen houses and had to be crossed to reach all our other fields and the pond, which would have been difficult with a standing crop. Another was flooded frequently. Eventually it got through to the War Ag that this was a bad idea but much of our grass went down to the plough to grow wheat whereas before we had grown mainly barley and oats for feed. Now bread was the priority. Being newly ploughed-out land which hadn't seen the light of day for centuries, the crops were magnificent. Whatever the red tape, production on farms around the country soared. To improve efficiency, my father bought a Massey Harris binder from Canada but it was still horse-drawn.

Most people found they had a bit of the spiv in them. Spiv was the name of the kind of wheeler-dealer who could get you anything on the black market. Eggs were supposed to go to the central packing station but a few were sold with a nod and a wink on our doorstep and people were prepared to pay extra for that, for the ration was only one a week, if you were lucky. Farmers were allowed to kill two pigs a year for their own use but it was easy to keep a third surreptitiously and that third pig could get you a lot of clothing coupons, which were needed to buy clothes. Even the local bobby had his eye on a piece of ham. At Christmas a few turkeys, geese and ducks would swap hands in a similar way. Bananas and oranges disappeared completely and I hardly ever had sweets but nobody in the countryside suffered from a lack of food.

Despite the war, many ordinary past-times continued. A lot of my mis-spent youth was passed in the cinema, going at least twice a week and sometimes four times. Roy Rogers and other

Westerns were favourites. A very famous film called *The Way To The Stars* was shot in Northallerton at the end of the war about the RAF and featured The Golden Lion, which was the real-life haunt of bomber crews. So that caused great excitement in the town.

At some point later on in the war, members of the Women's Land Army arrived at our farm. They were based in a hostel at Leeming Bar and when we needed extra help my father would send a message and they would arrive next morning on their bikes clasping packed lunches, to which my mother added the ten o' clocks and pints and pints of tea. Most were from Teesside or Tyneside.

With so little sugar being imported, home-grown production became more important and during the war we used to send our sugar beet to the factory in York by rail and I would go with my father on the cart to Scruton Station. One mischievous day, as my father was busy loading it, I draped a long line of the thick beet leaves on the metal track. Along came a workman's bogie, the kind that moves by being pumped up and down with a handle. Much to my astonishment, when they hit the sugar beet leaves it stopped dead, so I got shouted at.

Towards the end of the war our farm took delivery of our first tractor. Today you'd look at it and wonder what on earth anyone would buy that for, but to us it was a great excitement. I think it cost about £400 which was a huge sum but would pay for itself in efficiency. It was a green Standard Fordson imported from America with spade lugs, great nobbly things sticking out of its metal wheels to give grip. It took some starting. You had to swing the starting handle and, if you didn't get it right, the engine would backfire, sending the handle spinning backwards to thump you on the hand. With it came a Cockshutt two-furrow plough. Being 11 years old, I was keen to learn how to drive it. I was the one to grasp this new technology first and was soon up on the hard, unforgiving seat driving the new machine as my father and the older workers looked on guardedly, especially Stan the horseman who understood better than I what this would mean for the horses. He now had to plough with an iron horse but it wouldn't need to be fed afterwards when he got back to the farmyard. It was about this time that our farm went down from three horses to two but those remained well into the 1950s.

One of the disturbing characteristics of the Fordson was that the clutch and brake were combined. Pushing the pedal down halfway engaged the clutch and fully down was the brake. I soon got used to it. The only machinery which came with it was a plough. Swiftly we converted our carts, binder, grass cutter and other equipment to be hauled by the tractor, which didn't get tired although it did break down occasionally, and it didn't need huge quantities of feed, just fuel.

It was freezing cold sitting still on a tractor in winter ploughing instead of walking behind the horses. Everybody had huge old Army coats to keep them warm and sometimes an old flying helmet. With no power steering, it took all my strength to haul the wheel round at corners. Later my father was able to afford to have the metal wheels replaced with rubber tyres and that made a huge difference, doing the two back ones first and then the front later because it was so expensive. Later we got a larger version called a Fordson Major and some years later I tried to push things on a bit by adding a second tractor, another Fordson, to which I contributed some of my own precious money. In all the time I worked at the farm, even when I was full time, I was paid no more than ten shillings for pocket money, which was often the way on small family farms.

When George grew up he bought his own farm and bred a pedigree dairy herd. His story is told in *Cart Horses to Computers*.

JOAN FOSTER

Joan was born in 1926 and grew up in the large mining village of Horden, County Durham. She is pictured at the age of 15 when she went to work in a munitions factory. At 13 she had been a Land Girl.

'Joining the Women's Land Army looked like a marvellous escape. The fact that I was only 13 and well under age for joining didn't put me off one bit. My identity card said I had been born in 1926 but it was easy to turn the 6 into a 4 because they were hand-written. How proud I was when they handed over my uniform. I thought I was the bee's knees.'

As a child I had no real idea who Hitler was except as some kind of bogeyman who the adults used to threaten the little ones. But as my school days came to an end, I suddenly realized that he was going to have a huge impact on my life and the lives of all those around me.

The prospect of war with Hitler's Nazi Germany was a huge blow to all those who had fought in World War I, which had finished only 21 years before and was supposed to have been the 'war to end all wars'. Wasn't our local park a memorial to those Horden men who'd given their lives? Now here it was happening all over again. By July 1939 I knew something terrible was about to happen. It was the last day of the summer term and Miss Lowden, my favourite teacher, had a very sad look on her face as she stood at her desk. She announced to us that if war came the school wouldn't reopen in September. I was 13 years old and had been meant to stay on until 14 in the following March but after war broke out everything was chaotic and I only remember going back now and again. Miss Lowden was terribly upset. I think her boyfriend had already been called up into the Forces. She must have realized she was unlikely to see me as a pupil again and presented me with a book as a leaving present. It is a birthday book and I still have it, the date July 1939 inscribed neatly in Miss Lowden's hand, and inside I've written, "Miss Lowden was the most dearest, sweetest teacher in the world. This book is my most greatest treasure."

The summer of 1939 seemed unreal. Preparations were going on all around us, with rather nightmarish gas masks being handed out. They were all laid out at the infants school and being fitted for one was frightening because they put it right over your face and it stank of rubber. We all ran out with relief when it was over. We had to buy brown paper and stick it in crosses over the windows. Looking out over the sea, we knew that there was little between us and Germany. Huge defences began to appear along the beaches to keep out landing craft. At the end of our street in Greenside Avenue was a big new drill hall for the Territorial Army and later, when I was older, I went to dances there, which were great fun.

For a long time nothing seemed to happen except a long list of annoying things like the blackout. Once outside you couldn't see a thing for all the street lights were off. You were allowed to shine a little torch downwards but that was all. Buses, cars and lorries had only tiny slits of headlamps so you were more likely to be run over at that point of the war than be blown up by a bomb.

After war broke out and many of the men were called up to serve in the Forces, women took over jobs which had, in those unequal times, been thought of as suitable only for men. Mam became an insurance agent for the Prudential and called door-to-door to collect premiums each week. It can't have been easy for it was very difficult to see where you were going in the dark, let alone pick out the right house.

Rationing didn't make much difference to the poor people in Horden, of which there were many. My mother was a single parent and very hard up. You still had to pay for your food so for many people things didn't change much because they'd never had the money for a lot in the first place. Sweets were rationed but I'd only ever had the odd penny to buy them anyway. There was a lot of queuing for things that weren't rationed but were in short supply, like fish, and that was a big problem for the women who had to stand there. Some families with rations for a lot of children but who were short of actual cash would often be willing to sell half a pound of butter or some sugar and Mam would buy some for us.

War or no war, I had to find myself a job and started work at the age of 13 at Tommy Bailey's corner shop at the bottom of our street but I didn't enjoy it there. Posters were going up calling on women to join the services or go into industry and it got me thinking. In those days women had their own separate branches of the Army, Air Force and Navy and the adverts made it all look so glamorous, showing pretty girls in smart uniforms.

I didn't have anything particular in mind when I started

looking around for an escape from the shop. I walked down to the Labour Exchange where people went when they needed a job. We called it the Dole Office because they generally didn't have many jobs to offer, only the miniscule unemployment pay. They made various suggestions but nothing they came up with sounded interesting. I was much too young for any of the services, they told me sternly.

The Women's Land Army, which had been thrown together in a hurry during World War I, had been resurrected once more and recruitment was swift. A huge operation to control farming centrally was put in motion. Farmers had to take Women's Land Army workers if told to. Some were grateful for the help, others were grumpy and unwelcoming. It was the farmers, not the Government, who paid the wages.

Although Horden was a village, it was a big, industrialised one and farming was well out of my experience but it all looked like a marvellous escape. The fact that I was not even 14 yet and well under age for joining didn't put me off one bit. I think you were supposed to be 16 but I was tall for my age and could get away with it. I lied about my age to get into the Land Army and then told the truth when I wanted to get out again later. My identity card said I had been born in 1926 but it was easy to turn the 6 into a 4 because they were hand-written. At the recruiting centre they accepted me as 16 and I had an interview and medical.

How proud I was when they handed over my uniform, flattering corduroy breeches, a beautiful green jumper, cream shirt and green tie. I thought I was the bee's knees. They gave you big leather shoes and thick woolly socks but Mam had to buy me a pair of wellingtons. A brown coat and very fetching hat completed the uniform. We didn't look so good in the overalls you had to wear for the really dirty jobs. I don't remember seeing any of the posters which have now become so famous. They show glamorous girls in shapely uniforms, forking hay under blue skies and not a speck of mud in sight, their cheeks blooming with health and bulging above permanent smiles. I can tell you, when you're up to your eyes in cow muck it's not glamorous at all.

I never considered what Mam would think about me leaving home. I suppose I was a bit spoilt and had very much my own way. I can't remember her playing hell with me but she probably did. Three of us girls set off together on our big adventure, full of excitement. We were taken in a car to work on farms around Darlington, 20 miles away, which was just about the furthest I had ever travelled in those days when life was generally spent more locally than it is today.

Huts had been put up swiftly to house the Women's Land Army members and it's not so long since they were pulled down. I used to go past them later and remember when I was tucked up in there. I don't think I was particularly homesick though it was a huge change for me to be sharing a hut with four big, hefty girls who were much older than me. They were all Geordies, loud and cheerful, who felt sorry for this bairn far away from home. At night they'd go out drinking but I hardly ever went out. I'd never met anyone like them before and used to be amazed at them laughing and joking and wandering around in their undies. I think they felt a bit protective and motherly towards me. I was always glad to get back to the warmth and companionship of the hostel at the end of the day, even though they were just Nissen huts, a typical wartime temporary building put up quickly and consisting mainly of a huge, arched corrugated iron roof. There wasn't much to do after work and I was exhausted anyway. That first morning we all piled into a truck which lumbered off round the country lanes to drop us off at our various farms. The first one I was sent to was run by an elderly man and his very old mother and I was the only one dropped there. A river flowed through the farm and the truck left me by the river bank and I had to trudge up a steeply sloping field to the farmhouse. The other girls felt sorry for me, setting off on my own, especially since they had already twigged how young I really was. That first early morning, in the spring or early summer of 1940, gazing up at the farmhouse high on the hill, I wondered what was in store for me but held my head up high in the uniform I was so proud of and set off, clutching the pack of sandwiches provided by the hostel for my midday meal.

I was exhausted by the time I got there and I hadn't even started work. At least the people there were kind to me, giving me a good hot meal at midday so I could keep my sandwiches for a snack, which you needed after doing all that manual work. The woman used to wave a white towel out of the window to signal that dinner was ready.

The farmer gave me all sorts of hard jobs to do. The idea had been to train recruits before they went to farms but in the rush to get the first batch of us working many missed out and we had to learn as we went along. First job of the day was milking the half a dozen or so cows. I pulled up a stool and sat down next to this huge animal which I knew next to nothing about and rested my still sleepy head against its warm flank. There's a knack to hand milking, a mix of firmness and gentleness, and I had it and was a very good milker, great squirts of milk ringing against the metal of the bucket. Then it was poured into the churn through a filter to strain out the odd bit of straw and taken to the end of the farm track to await collection. No cooling machines and no pasteurisation, just raw milk which many older people say is the best-tasting. Unfortunately, it could also carry disease and after the war laws came in regulating hygiene. I loved the calves with their big eyes and had to scoop their feed from a big box into their trough.

I stayed only a few weeks because the authorities soon decided that this little farm didn't really need anyone else to work on it and they moved me. At the next farm I was disappointed to find that once again I was the only Land Girl, as we had been nick-named. The farmer's wife was kind but he was a bit odd. By noon I was starving hungry and was invited into the big farm kitchen where the farmer, his wife and their young child were sitting round the old wooden table eating their hot midday dinner. To my surprise, they showed me to a stool in the corner and instructed me to sit there and eat my sandwiches. The smell of their steaming food was torture but I had to make do with what I had brought. Presumably he'd decided that the Government should keep me fed and not a scrap would fall from his table to me.

Back at the hostel I listened jealously to the other girls talking about the huge farmhouse dinners they were given, roast lamb, chops, that sort of thing. It used to upset me, even though we got a good supper in the evening at the hostel because of the heavy, physical work we were doing. They felt sorry for me and in the mornings when I clambered out of the truck they'd shout, "Never mind darlin', once more once less." They were all together on another farm and I longed to be able to go with them.

Land Girls sometimes had to live on their farms and I was grateful that at least I could get away at night. The weekly pay if you were over 18 was just over £1 a week after they'd taken off money for the hostel but I expect I got even less being only 16, which actually I wasn't. We were expected to work 50 hours a week with Saturday afternoons and Sundays off. I worked damned hard and it was tough to sit there every dinnertime and feel like a naughty girl in the corner. At least the farmer's wife didn't rope me into domestic chores, which was against the rules for the Land Army but didn't stop some. On the farm they had one of the early tractors which were just coming in. The farmer taught me how to drive it but would only let me work in the field opposite the house where he could keep an eye on me. I found it quite easy and, like most young people, adapted to the new technology more quickly than older ones.

Horses and people were still usually the main source of power. Cutting the cereal crops took so long in summer that the grain had to be left on the stalks and piled up in ricks until the winter when there was time for threshing, or thrashing. A traction engine would arrive at some point with a threshing machine to beat out the grain which still had to be hauled in heavy sacks by labourers to the grain store. My short time in the Women's Land Army happened at a turning point for farming in Britain when mechanisation was just coming in. But I knew nothing of this except that driving the tractor was good fun and quite easy.

The farmer kept cows and one of my jobs was to clean out the byres which was a filthy job, shovelling the cow dung into a heap and then swilling them down with water and a brush. In my dung-spattered overalls and wellingtons, I didn't look anything like the poster girl in her sun-soaked hay field. Hay making was very hot and dusty work too so I don't suppose even she looked like that by the end of the day. Nor did the posters show huge bulls like the one on this farm and I tried to avoid it as much as possible. It terrified me. But I wasn't afraid of hard work and didn't really mind what I did. Nobody else worked on the farm apart from the farmer and his wife so it was a bit lonely for a young girl. Relief came at potato picking time when I was sent with a gang of other girls round the farms in the area to gather in this crop which was such a vital food source for Britain at that time. That was much more fun and at midday we'd sit down to the most marvellous farmhouse dinners which showed me what I was missing out on.

Picking potatoes was back-breaking work but with all of us chatting and joking away it was a nice change for me. It was a good laugh. We trailed through the mud behind a tractor which was lifting the potatoes out from beneath their leafy green canopy. Then we'd have to pick them up and put them carefully into our baskets and when we had a good heap inside, carry them to the cart behind us, the horse standing patiently until it was time to move forward a few paces to keep up with us.

One morning after potato picking was over and I was back on my own again I woke up feeling ill with a very sore throat but got up and dressed as usual for I wasn't one for not turning up. By the time I'd been at work for a couple of hours I was very poorly but when I told the farmer I couldn't go on he just told me to get back to the hostel under my own steam. It was a very long walk back up the road from the farm and I don't know how I managed it. He wouldn't even give me a lift there. When I got back I just collapsed on my bed, still in my shoes and uniform, and couldn't move. The warden at the hostel was so alarmed that I was sent home to Horden in a car to get better. I heard later that the farm on which I had worked was banned from having any more Land Girls because they hadn't looked after me properly.

Mam was glad to see me back home safely. When I had recovered I confessed to the Land Army how young I was and was released from the service. So that was how I told a lie to get in and the truth to get out.

Joan grew up to become a well-known publican in Peterlee and then Richmond. Her memoir is called *From Land Girl to Landlady*.

JOYCE CLAYTON

**Joyce was born in 1938 and grew up
in the Harehills area of Leeds.**

*'If a bomb fell nearby Mum would say, Good, that's not
us but it is some poor soul.'*

I grew up in a small terraced house and the huge Burton's factory which made uniforms was at the end of our street. I remember that being bombed. When the siren went off we had to go down to our cellar which had been reinforced with steel girders. My uncle next-door was an ARP warden and he'd knock to make sure we'd all taken cover. I had a Mickey Mouse style gas mask but still hated it because it felt so claustrophobic. My brother was a year older and we cowered under a table, holding on to each other. It was really frightening. I thought that if I put my head down I could get away from it.

Dad didn't go in the Army because he was an engineer and he and Mum would sit in the cellar on deckchairs, which looked a bit funny. Mum gave us sweets and biscuits, if she could get them, to try to take our minds off things but it was very frightening listening to the bombers going overhead and the sound of bombs falling. If one fell nearby Mum would say, "Good, that's not us but it is some poor soul."

Things got so bad my parents decided to get us out of the way and we were evacuated to Kilbirnie in Ayrshire to complete strangers who were very kind to us. At the station I was frightened to go, clinging to my mother. My brother said, "Stop being a baby." But I was very happy in Scotland, living near a beach and doing all kinds of nice things we had never experienced before so I had mixed feelings when I had to go home again. I had a good upbringing and my mum and dad were absolute gems so I soon settled down again.

When Joyce grew up she trained as an auxiliary nurse and worked as the manager of a sheltered housing complex.

PETER PARLOUR

Peter was born in 1936 and grew up on his parents' farm in Bedale, North Yorkshire.

'My friend and I took some long cartridges out of an ammunition hut and carried them over to the wood opposite. After taking them to bits we set fire to them. At this point we discovered they were flares as the wood filled with red and blue smoke, sending us running away as fast as possible in the opposite direction.'

I was in the house one day in 1944 and my mother was on the telephone at the time when all of a sudden this great big bang shook the house. "Good God, what was that?" she said. Six or seven miles away at Catterick Bridge Station goods yard an ammunition train being loaded had blown up *(12 people died and 102 were injured)*. When we went down to have a look the big station hotel had been completely demolished.

Later we discovered that my granddad Foster had had a lucky escape. He worked on the railway as a linesman and was waiting on the north platform for a train to Darlington when the train exploded.

Fortunately the blast went southwards so although he saw the great flash he was just left standing there unharmed. He had no idea how bad it was until arriving home. When he heard what had happened he couldn't believe it. The soldiers who had been loading the ammunition were never seen again, blown to smithereens. It was dreadful. I can almost hear that blast today.

The railway line passed within a mile of Leeming air base which the Germans were trying to find. One night we watched the train coming down the line past Bedale as a bomber hovered above. Once the plane got near Leeming the searchlights got it and I think it was shot down. A Messerschmitt enemy fighter which had been shot down somewhere was brought to Bedale and displayed in Bedale Hall. I was rather frightened of it.

On the lead up to the D-Day invasions of 1944 the roads around our farm were full of ammunition stores, semi-circular metal huts camouflaged but not locked. A few patrols were going up and down but not enough to keep away all the curious kids. They were full of boxes of flares, bullets and goodness knows what else.

Naturally we went in to have a look. My friend and I were very inquisitive and brought out two or three things that looked like long cartridges, carrying them over to the wood opposite. After taking them to bits we set fire to them. At this point we discovered they were flares as the wood filled with red and blue smoke, sending us running away as fast as possible in the opposite direction. I've never run as fast in my life. "If anybody sees that there'll be a panic on!" I shouted. But they didn't and we got away with it.

Sunday School was at 2pm but one day just before Christmas my sister and I decided not to go and instead spent the afternoon hiding in one of the ammunition huts. Unfortunately the teacher chose that day to cast the nativity play and rang our mother to ask why we hadn't been at Sunday School.

"Yes they were!" our mother insisted.

"They weren't!"

So we had to confess to spending the time sitting in an

ammunition hut. Somehow my father found the petrol to take us on holiday to Redcar. That must have been earlier on in the war before the private ration was abolished completely later on. When we got there you couldn't get on the beach for rows and rows of barbed wire. It only then that I realized how serious the war was but felt more frustrated than frightened.

Italian prisoners-of-war from camps round Bedale Park came to work on our farm. There were also Ukrainians and one taught me a few words. I can still count up to six in Ukrainian. They were all very good workers, real gentlemen. We had no problems with them whatsoever. I was always sad when the wagon came at five o'clock at night to take them back to camp again.

Bedale High Street was in a dreadful mess during the war because of the tanks which would come roaring down the road, their huge tracks tearing up the Tarmac. My mother once fell off her bike after hitting one of the big ruts and scraped herself quite badly.

Sweet rationing was awful and even if you had a coupon that didn't mean there were any to buy. We would even suck on cough drops if nothing else was available. When they finally came off ration you couldn't get near the shops for the crowds. On a Friday night the ice-cream shop in Bedale would open briefly and I'd join the long queue for Wall's Ice-cream. It stretched all the way down the street just for a tiny ration. She had her allocation and that was it so if the ice-cream ran out before you got to the front that was hard luck.

Uncle Reg was in the Forces in Kenya and sent food parcels from time to time which were a wonderful boost, full of things which were hard or even impossible to get in Britain, even bananas. The first banana I ever tasted was completely black on the outside and so over-ripe inside that you'd put it in the bin today but I thought, "This is alright!"

When Peter grew up he worked at first on the family farm then became a representative specializing in eggs, later setting up his own business and running several shops.

DON BARKER

Don was born in 1936 in Hull.

'We were ordered to take shelter in a school because an unexploded bomb had been found. The bomb went off like a damp squib, which was a disappointment to all the kids, then we were allowed home.'

O ur home was in Hessle Road near the docks in a very close community of dock workers and fishermen. Nearly all my mother's family lived down there. The bomb damage was terrible. I was packed off with two aunts and a large group of cousins to Filey to get away from the bombing and had a great time by the seaside for a few years. For us kids it was all fun really except for Auntie Elsie's porridge which was a grey green colour and you could have eaten it with a knife and fork.

My father was away in the RAF and my mother stayed in Hull with my grandmother who was terminally ill with cancer, though I didn't know that at the time.

Returning on a visit to Hull to see Granddad, a van with speakers ordered everyone to leave their homes and head for the local school because an unexploded bomb had been found in the dock. I remember my uncles and aunts shepherding us down the street. We were all issued with earplugs but that didn't stop us larking about. The bomb went off like a damp squib, which was a disappointment to all the kids, then we were allowed home.

Back in Filey we all helped to 'Dig for Victory' by helping out on a local smallholding. The man who ran it arrived in his pick-up truck and we'd all pile in the back to rattle off to the fields. I learned a lifetime's lesson about work in those fields. Each of us was given a small bucket and trowel and told to work our way up a row of vegetables, pulling out the weeds to fill our buckets. Like all kids we raced each other to see who could get to the end first. I was among the winners and was greeted by the owner, a wry smile on his face, who presented me with a halfpenny. Cousin Freddie was only half way down his row by the time we had finished but on completion he got three pennies for doing the job properly. The lesson was learned.

One day we saw one of our planes flying so low it was terrifying, with smoke bellowing out of the back. To avoid crashing into the town, the pilot fought to keep the aircraft in the air until he could dump it on the sea. All crew members escaped. His bravery became a national newspaper story.

We must have come back to live in Hull towards the end of the war because I can remember going into the Anderson shelter when the siren went. By then we had a much better house on a council estate.

With no shelter of our own we had to share with our neighbours, Mr and Mrs Borril, and it was pretty crowded inside. I can still smell the mustiness and see the grown-ups playing cards as I snuggled up in my blanket. Mr Borril stayed outside, walking round in his tin hat. At the sound of a droning plane he'd pop his head round and say, "It's alright, it's one of ours."

Shelters were so damp and crowded that some took the risk of staying in their homes. A good friend told me later that his grandmother had refused to go to the shelter and his older sister wouldn't leave her. Both were killed.

While we were away nobody told us what terrible things had

gone on in Hull but on our return we saw the devastation. Many once proud buildings were in ruins but for us they made great playgrounds. Our new home stood next to fields and opposite us was a huge bomb crater about 90 feet across *(30 metres)* and very deep, ideal for making dens. We didn't think much about the raid which had created it or all the windows of the houses being blown out.

When Don grew up he set up his own business selling carpets which he ran for 40 years.

JOHN WARD

John was born in Richmond in 1938.

'Land never before considered worth cultivating was forced into production. Up on the moor above Hudswell suddenly potatoes were growing and even as a child of five I was expected to do my bit by helping with the potato harvest.'

My father had been a regular soldier in the Signals but had left to join the Post Office. When war was imminent he was one of the first to be called up and I saw little of him for many years. Just outside Richmond sits the village of Hudswell high on a hill where my mother's parents had a small farm. After my grandfather's death in 1940, it made sense to double up our households and we moved to the farm which was a wonderful experience for me.

The farmhouse, which was not particularly large, seemed always to be overflowing with people. Uncle John Johnson ran the farm and lived there with his wife and three children. Being so close to Catterick Camp, every spare room in the area was in demand from soldiers keen to find somewhere to stay with their wives and someone was always knocking on the door begging to know if we had a room to let or even a bit of one. My grandmother Mary Johnson, who I loved to bits, was a wonderful woman and would never turn anyone away. Consequently I was always having to sleep in corners. There was a constant throughput and some of our lodgers became life-long friends. Adding to the crowds were cousins of my grandmother who came to do war work. One, Uncle Adam, was a tailor who walked into Richmond every day to alter military uniforms.

With this constant turmoil which the war provoked, it was hard for people to keep in touch with each other. Only two telephones existed in the village, one in the Post Office and one in a public call box next-door to our farmhouse. Callers who wanted to contact a person in Hudswell would often ring the phone box in the hope that someone passing would pick it up so I was always running up to my grandmother saying, "The phone's ringing!" Then we'd have to find whoever the caller was after or take a message. The whole village was buzzing with people.

Once a week my mother walked four miles to the camp NAAFI to do the shopping because it was a huge shop where you could find more things, then four miles back again. That kind of journey was nothing then.

A few bombs dropped in fields around Richmond. Wandering for miles with my friends at the age of only five or six we once came across three small incendiary bombs sticking out of the mud beside the River Swale. We had enough sense not to touch them and told my uncle, who was in the Home Guard.

My uncle had two working horses but in a drive for greater efficiency a man called Ted Metcalfe was sent with a tractor to do all the ploughing on the local farms. The Fordson tractor was uncomfortable and tricky to manage but I thought it was fantastic. Sometimes Ted would give me a ride so I could pretend to drive. Land never before considered worth cultivating was forced into production. Up on the moor above Hudswell suddenly potatoes were growing and even as a child of five I was expected to do my bit by helping with the potato harvest. When the war was over my parents, having seen each other for only three months in six years, picked up their married life and we returned to Richmond but I went back to the farm at every possible opportunity. My dad and I had to get to know each other but luckily for me he was a very sensitive man who worked hard to establish a relationship. He would read to me, instalments of books like The Coral Island, and made kites with me which we flew together high up on a hill above the town. It was a wonderful experience.

When he grew up John worked for the National Consumer Council.

JOHN CLARKE

John was born in 1937 in Rotherham.

'Our shelter was shared with neighbours. I'd torment them by chanting, "The bombers are coming! The bombers are coming!" I wasn't very popular.'

My most striking memory of the war is of being in the Anderson shelter listening to the menacing drone of doodlebugs going over. Though London and the South East got it worst, a lot of them made it up North. *(The first V1 flying bombs, nick-named doodlebugs after their sound, were launched in June 1944).* I think they were aimed at Manchester but went off course. Relations who lived out in Derbyshire at Chapel-en-le-Frith told us V1s crashed into hills nearby. As a little boy I knew what an enemy bomber sounded like but this was different, a strange putt-putt-putt noise. Then the adults said, "That must be a doodlebug!"

Rotherham was bombed only once as far as I know when one fell in the local park making a large crater, probably jettisoned by an aircraft going home from a bigger target. Sheffield five miles away had a much worse time and we used to watch the searchlights trying to pick out bombers over the city and hear the sound of bombs falling. Our shelter was shared with neighbours and I wasn't very popular because I'd torment them by chanting, "The bombers are coming! The bombers are coming!"

"Tell him to shut up," they'd say. They knew more than me about the real horrors of war. The man next-door had been gassed in World War I and every now and again, even so many years afterwards, he would be ill with chest trouble. Even my bravado failed when the doodlebugs came over because the adults were much more frightened this time and I picked up on their feelings.

Like many children at the time I was snug in my siren suit made by my mother from thick navy blue wool with a pointed hood – quick and easy to put on when the bombers came over.

One day two of our Lancaster bombers came in side by side very low overhead with a roar that startled us all. Whether they were lost or damaged I don't know but something was wrong. They disappeared into the distance and we hoped they would make it back to base.

My father worked in the steel works which was a reserved occupation, only a few hundred yards away from our home. They had to be very careful when they tapped the furnace to cover up the pig iron as soon as possible because of the fierce glow which could easily escape from the sheds. Slag was the most dangerous thing because that glowed when hot but had to be dumped outside. Hauled in containers up to the tip by a locomotive, workers worked swiftly to drag tarpaulins over the glowing coals so they wouldn't give away the location of the works.

Camps for Italian prisoners-of-war were nearby and one morning there was great excitement when we arrived at school to be told that an escapee had sheltered in the grounds overnight. He had cut the buttons from his uniform to look more like a civilian and flung them away so we were all scurrying around in the bushes to find one of these precious souvenirs. Rumour was that it could even have been an enemy airman! We weren't supposed to talk to prisoners but would go up to the camp and chat to them through the wire. They were alright, no desperados in there. The prisoners were still in the camps during the bad winter of 1947 and were put to work clearing the streets which were thick with ice. By then their uniforms were very tatty but we all looked tatty because rationing and shortages went on for years.

At the end of the war lots of other streets had parties but we didn't. Money had been collected by all the neighbours throughout the war to give to anyone in severe hardship or, when the great day came, to celebrate the end of the war but when it did they couldn't make up their minds. The old ones resented the young ones having fun at their expense and the money stayed in the Yorkshire Penny Bank. I could see the bunting across the other streets but ours was bare.

When he grew up John became an architect.

JOY BRANNIGAN

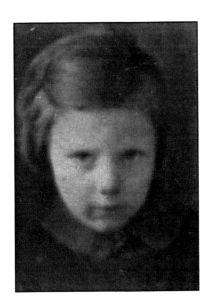

Joy was born in 1937 in Hartlepool where her father was a steelworker.

'One day I was playing in the street when suddenly people started rushing out of their homes and being all jolly. I didn't know what was going on but that must have been when the end of the war was announced. They all seemed happy for a change.'

War was just normal to me growing up, I didn't know any different. When the siren went we had to go into a horrible brick shelter which was built round the back of the houses and shared with other people. Inside it was dank and smelly with a couple of bunk beds at the side. After going in a few times we preferred to take our chances in the cupboard under the stairs or go under the table. Despite disliking the shelter, it made a good playground for me and my friends.

We would gather flowers and pretend the shelter was our house. Being so young I didn't really understand what was happening when the sirens went off, just that everyone had to rush places. I don't think anyone ever explained it to me. It would have been better if they had but I was expected just to get on with it like everyone else. Nothing seemed to faze people. A great survival spirit existed in those days but also an awful lot of rules. One night there was a terrific banging on the door and on the doorstep was the warden who told us off for showing a chink of light through our blackout curtain.

I went to a Catholic school and the big day approached for my First Communion for which my mother had to buy me a white dress. With our precious clothing coupons tucked away in her handbag, we set off on the bus only for the bag to be stolen. Without them we could buy nothing. The bag was returned but the coupons had been torn from our book. It was a horrible thing to do. For my First Communion I had to wear my school clothes among all the other girls in white dresses, feeling absolutely out of it. My old green jersey had holes in the elbows and I kept my arms pinned to my sides as much as possible. It was a real embarrassment. Times were very hard because of rationing, shortages and very high prices. With four children to support in our family, it was very difficult for my mother to make ends meet.

We used to play out in the streets a lot. Our street still had gas lamps, though they hadn't been used since 1939. A favourite game was to tie a rope to the metal bars which stuck out at the top of the lamp-post then swing round and round on it. One day I was outside doing this when suddenly people started rushing out of their homes into the street and being all jolly. I didn't know what was going on but that must have been when the end of the war was announced. They all seemed happy for a change. At our street party there wasn't much in the way of cakes but everyone contributed what they could spare. It was a really jolly time and there weren't many of those. I didn't really know what it all meant but it was good to see people enjoying themselves because the war years had been so dreary.

I grew up in a town of empty shop windows. One day at the end of the war I saw something on display which I had never seen before and ran home to tell my mother. I didn't even know what it was but knew it was special. Dragging her along to the shop to see, I remember her telling me it was Dairylea cheese triangles. That was something nice to relieve the tedium.

When Joy grew up she went into advertising, later working as an artist.

CATHERINE HAMMAL

Catherine was born in 1936 in Sunderland.

'Living near the docks you might wonder why we weren't evacuated. I can remember Mum saying, If anything happens, we will all go together.'

My father tried to join the Army and the RAF but failed the medicals. Instead he took on the highly dangerous job of Senior Fireman in the Auxiliary Fire Service as well as his regular work as a coal teamer down at the docks, sorting coal into wagons. Sometimes he and his crew had to go all the way over to Liverpool and Manchester where the fires were so huge that every available tender was called in.

From our house in Robinson Terrace we could look down to the sea at the bottom of our street and watch the convoys heading off across the North Sea. Being so close to the docks and its massive petrol tanks, the bombing we endured was terrible.

We lived opposite Grandma's house and shared the brick-built shelter in her back yard, along with another family. Grandad went off on patrol as an ARP warden. When the siren went Mum gathered up my little brother Robert into her arms and hurried us across the street, me in my little red dressing gown with the white rabbit on the corner. Robert looked up into the sky which was bright with flares dropped to show the bombers exactly where we were and said, "Look at all the bonny lights!"

If things weren't too bad we'd all try to sleep in the shelter. One night the bombers were right overhead and we could hear explosions all around us. Grandma and Mum pushed me and my brother onto the concrete floor and lay on top of us. My mother always said that if you could hear the whistle of the bomb you were alright, it wasn't going to hit us.

We had a very narrow escape. A bomb blew up Scott's bakery on the corner opposite our home. Down at the docks my father got the message that our house had been hit and rushed to find us, but it hadn't. Grandad in his warden's tin helmet had to climb over rubble piled up round the door of our shelter to see if we were alright.

Emerging after the all-clear we watched all the next day as the bakery's gas main blazed uncontrollably. The thing I remember most was a burst barrel of black treacle which was running all over the place.

Mum's cousin, Auntie Alice we used to call her, had a much worse experience. I remember her walking to us from her house in Robinson Street carrying a bundle of clothes over her arm. She had been in a shelter when a bomb hit and everyone inside was killed except her and one other. A whole family had been killed. Even babies sitting on their mother's knees had died from the blast.

One day I went to visit relations in Castletown just outside Sunderland where things hadn't been so bad. The siren went and they couldn't understand why I was so terrified but they hadn't had the bombing we had. Some people today don't really know what the word means. I heard the other day that children were 'terrified' if they couldn't find their mobile phone. They haven't a clue.

My school, Valley Road, was at the top of our back lane and that was bombed one night. For some reason we were still at home. My mother was in the kitchen with the door open into the yard and she was hurled by the blast through the passageway and into the living room where the rest of us were. I was blown underneath the table. The blackout frame fell from the window on top of Grandma who was sitting with Robert on her knee.

Dad had some terrible memories of the war but rarely talked about them to us. A plane crashed on some houses and he had to help get people out, the living and the dead.

Living near the docks you might wonder why we weren't evacuated. I can remember Mum saying, "If anything happens, we will all go together." Despite the raids I didn't want to leave my home and family. By a miracle we all came through it. I was over at Grandma's when the wonderful news came that peace had been declared and went running through the passageway shouting, "The war's over, the war's over!" My home survived the bombing but was demolished later to make way for the new Valley Road School.

We had no counselling in those days but my experiences didn't affect me in the long term. It was a very different world. Everybody seemed to know everybody in our small community. There was always someone to help if you needed it. The fact that we were all in it together helped.

When Catherine grew up she worked for 40 years for Thomas Cook the travel agent and travelled the world.

TERRY BAKER

Terry Baker was born
in 1936 in one of
the poorest parts of
Scarborough, near
the harbour, where he
lived with his parents,
grandmother and two
brothers.

*'Suddenly there was a massive bang as a parachute
mine exploded over our house and blew the roof right
off. Debris crashed down on us and the air was full of
choking dust. My head was bleeding from a cut.'*

Being only three when World War II broke out in 1939, I
have hazy memories of that time. My dad was called up
into the Army and at first was able to visit us sometimes
but after he was sent abroad to fight we didn't see him for years.

Because we were a seaside resort, children were evacuated
from the cities to Scarborough in 1939 but it turned out we
were a target for bombers after all. Scarborough suffered terrible
bombing considering its size. There were 21 raids in all, 33
people were killed, 57 injured and 3,100 buildings damaged or
destroyed – including our house! During the war the town was

a training base for RAF air crew so as well as being a port that made us vulnerable. Stripped of their holiday visitors, hotels became home for these young men.

When I was growing up many Scarborians could still remember the deeply shocking day in 1914 not long after World War I had started when a German ship shelled the town. It was the first time British civilians had been killed on their own doorsteps and made people realize this was a new and terrifying type of warfare. There were 19 deaths. I suppose we should have guessed we were in for another pounding.

Our favourite place to play was the land in front of the castle called the Castle Dykes where among the bushes and rocks we'd catch butterflies in a net, for this was in the days before I'd discovered nature conservation. One day we were caught out in the open when the siren sounded and my older brother Dennis grabbed me and dragged me home.

There was a shelter down the street but it was dark, damp and smelly so at home we usually got under the stairs or the table. I don't remember feeling frightened. It was just normal life for me.

One night when I was about four bombers droned over our town as I slept in the attic room with Dennis. Our younger brother Brian, being only one, was probably in his cot with my mother on the floor below. There had been no siren to warn us for, though Scarborough had a warning system, sometimes it would sound as late as an hour after a raid had started, if at all.

Suddenly there was a massive bang as a parachute mine exploded over our house and blew the roof right off. Debris crashed down on us and the air was full of choking dust. My head was bleeding from a cut. My mother rushed in and grabbed us from our beds, dragging us downstairs and outside. My grandma, also bleeding from cuts, helped my mother to get us up the steps to the next street. A shop on the corner had all its windows and doors blown out and our feet crunched over broken glass. We made our way to an emergency centre at a chapel nearby where our injuries were cleaned and bandaged.

Along with dozens of others who had been driven from their homes that night, we had to find somewhere to stay and went round to my Auntie Jane's house in High Mill Drive where they took us all in for a while. My Uncle Joe was away in the RAF. Auntie Jane was a lovely person but her heart must have sunk at the thought of me sharing her home. She thought I was too cheeky and I thought she was too bossy.

Auntie Jane had been in domestic service as a teenager in a big house where she had been trained to do everything precisely. If it was one o'clock for a meal, it had to be one o'clock and not five past. It was on the table. I found that kind of constraint puzzling. After a few weeks everyone breathed a sigh of relief when we moved to a house in Seamer Moor Road, a new council estate. This was a huge improvement in comfort and must have made life a great deal easier for my grandma and mother.

There was a front and back garden, an indoor bathroom and the toilet, if not completely inside, was just by the back door. Grandma walked into our new home and turned to my mother saying, "Oh Flo, isn't this great!" Rents at the new council houses were higher than we were used to and life was a struggle for my mother who had three different jobs to make ends meet. My father was away and a soldier's pay wasn't much. In 1941 I started at Hinderwell Infants School, which was quite a new building, and later moved into the juniors. At first my mother took us then we'd set off in a gang to walk there. If the air-raid siren went we had to go into the shelter until the all-clear sounded where the teachers would try to continue with lessons.

If the siren sounded at home we were a bit more daring, despite our last home being bombed, and I can remember standing in the back porch one night watching German planes flying over which were aiming for the gas works. We could see bombs dropping out of them but they missed their target and fell in The Mere, a lake just to the South West of the town. Three others fell in fields at the back of the estate. I didn't feel frightened because I didn't really know what was going on, despite knowing how devastating an explosion could be. My mother would say, "Come and have a look this!" so it all seemed a bit exciting.

If the planes got a bit too close the local Home Guard would be shouting at us to take cover and we'd dart indoors and go under the stairs or the table. There was a shelter in the street but my mother thought we were safer at home.

The following day Dennis, me and our friend Georgie Scotter went down to the Mere to see what had happened and another German plane swooped down, firing its guns. As bullets sent splashes high above the water, Georgie shouted, "Let's get out of it!" and shoved me and Dennis into some bushes. All I can remember is being flat on my face with the undergrowth sticking up my nose. Then the plane droned away. Picking ourselves out of the bushes, we were excited rather than frightened by our adventure but got home a bit smartish and didn't tell our mother.

Before television was widely available, our only source of live news was the radio. My mother got fed up with it, telling my father when he was home on leave, "Switch it off! It's nothing but propaganda and rubbish." But he wouldn't. "No, you're wrong, Flo, we've got to know what's going on," he'd say. I was more interested in getting outside to play football and cricket. I was used to food being rationed but my mother and grandma were very good managers and we never went hungry. They had ration cards which were registered at Hopwood's shop in Queen Street and at Lipton's so she did most of her shopping there. Oats were plentiful because Britain was good at growing those and were scooped out of rough hessian sacks by the shop assistants. When you ate your porridge you had to pick out the hessian strands from your bowl. Grandma did most of the sewing and she and my mother shared the baking and cooking. Yorkshire puddings were a staple in our diet to fill us up, served both savoury and sweet. Semolina pudding was another dessert. Chocolate was a rare treat because even if it was available, we couldn't usually afford it, so we just stopped thinking about it.

When the war was almost over Dennis and me and our gang of Vic Buck, Pete Hunter and Johnnie Scott would take a rope and walk over to Cayton Cliffs to go seagull egging. Seagulls' eggs are much bigger than hens' eggs and made good eating. You hardly got any fresh eggs on the ration so it was worth the risk, or we thought so anyway. With the rope tied around his waist, Dennis would scramble over the edge and down the cliff face.

John and Vic held on tightly at the top with me as anchor and Pete acting as signal man telling us when to lower or heave up. Trying to avoid looking at the waves 300ft below *(100 metres)*, Dennis would bounce from nest to nest placing eggs in his home-made pouch which we would share out. That was a treat!

In May 1945 VE Day was held to celebrate victory in Europe. All across Scarborough the streets were filled with tables laden with food for huge parties. There was singing and dancing under fluttering bunting and banners. People had been through so

much and wanted to let their hair down. There was more food
than I'd ever seen in my life and all kinds of treats that people
must have been hoarding away. It was a fantastic feeling although
I was too young to understand what had gone on and what the
end of it all meant. Us kids were more interested in the party
than the reason for it.

At home there was no further need of the blackout curtains
which were necessary to stop enemy aircraft seeing towns and
cities at night. The rules had been so strict that when the war
ended I'd say to my mother, "It's time for the blinds!" worried
that she hadn't put them up, and she'd explain they weren't
needed any more. I couldn't really understand why.

My sister Pam had been born in 1942 and hadn't seen my father
since he had gone abroad with the Army. When he arrived back
she couldn't get over this strange man who had suddenly come to
live with us. "Mummy, who's that man laid on the settee?" she'd
say and my mother would tell her it was her dad. She'd watch
him curiously as he ate his breakfast. When he returned from
work in the evening she'd say to our mother, "That man's here
again. What's he doing here?" It was difficult for her to take it in.

Some lads found it difficult to suddenly have a father bossing
them around at home but for me my father's homecoming
brought me a lot of happiness. He thought the world of us all.

When Terry grew up he joined the Army, serving in
Kenya and Malaya, and went on to set up his own
steel construction business with projects including
developments in the Falkland Islands after the war
there. His story is told in *A Merry Dance.*